1.45

THEODORE

AND

WOODROW

Also by Andrew P. Napolitano

Constitutional Chaos: What Happens When Government Breaks Its Own Laws

*The Constitution in Exile: How the Federal Government Has
Seized Power by Rewriting the Supreme Law of the Land*

A Nation of Sheep

Dred Scott's Revenge: A Legal History of Race and Freedom in America

Lies the Government Told You: Myth, Power, and Deception in American History

*It Is Dangerous to Be Right When the Government Is Wrong:
The Case for Personal Freedom*

THEODORE

AND

WOODROW

HOW TWO AMERICAN PRESIDENTS
DESTROYED CONSTITUTIONAL FREEDOM

ANDREW P. NAPOLITANO

THOMAS NELSON
Since 1798

NASHVILLE   DALLAS   MEXICO CITY   RIO DE JANEIRO

Published in Nashville, Tennessee, by Thomas Nelson. Thomas Nelson is a registered trademark of Thomas Nelson, Inc.

Thomas Nelson, Inc., titles may be purchased in bulk for educational, business, fund-raising, or sales promotional use. For information, please e-mail SpecialMarkets@ThomasNelson.com.

Library of Congress Cataloging-in-Publication Data

Napolitano, Andrew P.
  Theodore and Woodrow : how a Republican and a Democrat destroyed constitutionally protected freedoms / Andrew P. Napolitano.
    p. cm.
  Includes bibliographical references and index.
  ISBN 978-1-59555-351-5 (alk. paper)
  1. Liberty--History. 2. Federal government--United States--History. 3. Constitutional history--United States. 4. Roosevelt, Theodore, 1858-1919. 5. United States--Politics and government--1901-1909. 6. Wilson, Woodrow, 1856-1924. 7. United States--Politics and government--1913-1921. I. Title.
  JC599.U5N265 2012
  323.0973--dc23

                                                                2012015462

Printed in the United States of America

12 13 14 15 QGF 6 5 4 3 2 1

This book is dedicated to
Congressman Ron Paul,
Whose intellect, industry, heart, and head
Have educated millions on the
Loss of liberty because of big government;
And whose personal courage and fearless determination
Have made him a hero
To lovers of Freedom everywhere on the planet,
And a profound personal inspiration to me.

"The makers of our Constitution undertook to secure conditions favorable to the pursuit of happiness. . . . They sought to protect Americans in their beliefs, their thoughts, their emotions and their sensations. They conferred, as against the government, the right to be let alone—the most comprehensive of rights and the right most valued by civilized men."

—Justice Louis D. Brandeis

"Government is not the solution to our problem, government is the problem."

—President Ronald Reagan

"To tamper with man's freedom is not only to injure him, to degrade him; it is to change his nature, to render him, in so far as such oppression is exercised, incapable of improvement; it is to strip him of his resemblance to the Creator, to stifle within him the noble breath of life with which he was endowed at his creation."

—Frederic Bastiat

"Personal property . . . is subject to the general right of the community to regulate its use to whatever degree the public welfare may require it."

—Theodore Roosevelt

"[W]e are not bound to adhere to the doctrines held by the signers of the Declaration of Independence. . . . Government does now whatever experience permits or the times demand."

—Woodrow Wilson

Contents

Author's Note

My first exposure to Woodrow Wilson was an example of three degrees of separation. As an undergraduate at Princeton University in the late 1960s and early 1970s, a university at which Wilson once taught and over which he once presided as the school's president, I was steeped in the campus lore that he was a great man who saved America from the evil rich who would have kept us all in bondage. I even studied under a professor who studied under a professor who learned from Professor Woodrow Wilson himself.

My intellectual introduction to Wilson was courtesy of Professor Arthur S. Link, who was then and, though now deceased, still is today the academically recognized foremost scholar of Woodrow Wilson. Professor Link, who edited the massive *Papers of Woodrow Wilson*, spent his entire professional career studying, writing, and lecturing on Wilson. Professor Link, a charming, crew-cut, pipe-smoking, tweed-wearing liberal, loved his subject. And he taught his students to do the same.

I have always challenged authority; just ask my parents, brothers, teachers, professors, and even the appellate judges who reviewed my work when I was on the bench. So the good Professor Link, who admitted me as an undergraduate to his graduate student courses, usually reserved for those intending to become professional historians, did not succeed with me.

I believed as a student, studying in the same majestic halls where Woodrow Wilson taught and administered, that Wilson sapped personal liberties, brought America into a useless and highly destructive war, trampled the sovereignty of the states, and institutionalized central economic planning mechanisms in ways that have diminished personal freedoms, reduced opportunities for prosperity, and created a large class of human beings dependent on the government. Though Professor Link never told us, Wilson as president was an old, stiff, cold academic who really believed he was smarter than anyone else in government. He was prepared to bend any rule, avoid any constitutional principle, and crush any individual liberty for what he believed was the common good.

Theodore Roosevelt was not much different, except that he could hardly be called stiff and cold. He was the life of any party he attended, joined, or created. But he also thought that the Constitution was just a guideline, rather than the Supreme Law of the Land as it declares itself to be. I had no youthful romantic familiarity with or adolescent revulsion of Theodore Roosevelt, as I did with Woodrow Wilson. On the contrary, his robust manliness, love of athletics, and nominal Republican roots were appealing to those who influenced my youth.

Interestingly for me, my studies of Wilson under Professor Link exposed me to Wilson's counterpart in the sport of assaulting the Constitution in the name of Progressivism. At a young age, I remember asking, "What is with these Roosevelts? They just wanted to control human life and plan it out for us from the White House."

Theodore's distant cousin, Franklin, is, in my view, second only to Lincoln in the degree of presidentially caused harm to constitutional government and personal freedoms in America; but it was Theodore who paved the way for Franklin to do what he did. It was Theodore Roosevelt who—in moments that today would be compared to Nixon going to China—was a traitor to the values of those who selected and elected him. It was Theodore Roosevelt who first made it acceptable for Republicans to desert their small-government roots, to trample federalism, and to fight wars of imperialism. It was also Theodore Roosevelt who fervently believed that there was no problem too small, no wish too unrealistic, no principle of law too well-grounded or restrictive to prevent him from using the federal government to address whatever he wished, on his own, from the White House.

You can see where we are going in this book. This is not a biography of either Wilson or Roosevelt. It does not purport to present them fairly. This is, quite simply, a case against them. A case you have not seen if you were educated in America's public schools; a case you will appreciate if you think the federal government today is too big and too rich and too controlling, and if you want to understand how it got that way; a case that would have scandalized the amiable Professor Link.

Introduction

The Lives of Theodore Roosevelt and Woodrow Wilson

The idea that a Harvard-trained dude could make a career in the rough-and-tumble of politics appeared ludicrous, and it seemed equally unlikely that such a plunge could be taken by a middle-aged professor with no practical experience in government. Yet such was the force of each man's personality and such was the force of his vision that each somehow made men and events serve his purpose, and the dude and the professor became respectively the twenty-sixth and twenty-eighth Presidents of the United States.

—HENRY W. BRAGDON[1]

Theodore Roosevelt was born on October 27th 1858 to Theodore Roosevelt Sr. and Martha "Mittie" Bulloch in a four-story brownstone in the modern-day Gramercy Park section of New York City. Roosevelt was the second of four children and the oldest son born into this long-established, socially prominent family. The Roosevelts amassed considerable wealth and political power through several businesses, including hardware and plate-glass importing.

Thomas Woodrow Wilson was born two years before Roosevelt on December 28th 1856 to Joseph Ruggles Wilson and Jessie Janet Woodrow in Staunton, Virginia. He was the third of four children and the son, grandson, and nephew of Protestant ministers. As such, he grew up in a pious household, and religion served as one of the greatest influences on his life.

Though these men were born into seemingly different circumstances, the parallels between their lives quickly began to emerge. During their youth, Roosevelt and Wilson suffered from debilitating handicaps that threatened to interfere with their ambitions. Roosevelt had asthma, as well as weak eyesight, and was generally in poor health. His condition was so bad that he had to be propped up in bed at night or had to sleep sitting up in a chair to accommodate his sickness.

Wilson suffered from what was most likely dyslexia, stemming from a congenital brain condition and did not learn the alphabet until he was nine years old. He could not read until he was twelve. Wilson's parents were both troubled and embarrassed by his seemingly dull intellect. Wilson himself acknowledged that he had been "always a slow fellow in mental development."[2] Nobody thought he would get very far in light of this condition.

Both Roosevelt and Wilson refused to be derailed from their ambitions and sought to disassociate themselves from their ailments. Roosevelt often dressed up as a soldier as early as the age of four years, believing this to be the ultimate symbol of power, a persona he dearly desired to take on. He also became involved in many physical activities, with the encouragement of his father, who believed that this would help cure the boy's sickness.

Roosevelt learned how to hunt and also the art of taxidermy; and after discovering a dead seal in a local market, acquiring its head, and creating what he called the Roosevelt Museum of Natural History (with the head functioning as the first artifact on display), Roosevelt used his hunting and taxidermy skills to expand this museum.

Roosevelt began participating in several sports, with his athletic pursuits continuing through college, where he participated in rowing and boxing and at one point won runner-up in the Harvard boxing championship. Overall, his frenzy for the pursuit of glory gave him the strength to overcome his weaknesses.

Wilson handled his impairment by rigorously pursuing academics under the guidance of his father, specifically focusing on enhancing skills that would help him compensate for his troubles with reading, such as developing a fierce concentration and a near photographic memory.

These efforts ultimately led both men to overcome their disabilities, thus enabling them to pursue the positions for which they are now famous. Roosevelt graduated from Harvard University in 1880. Following his graduation, he had a physical examination, leading his doctor to discover what he believed to be serious heart problems and to encourage Roosevelt to get a desk job and avoid any strenuous activity. Roosevelt decided to attend Columbia

Law School; however, he remained there only one year. When he was given the opportunity to run for public office, he immediately dropped out of Columbia in pursuit of this far more exhilarating and glorified career.

In 1881, Roosevelt was elected to the New York State Assembly, making him the youngest person ever to fill that position. Despite his youth, by 1884, he had already risen to the position of minority leader.

Roosevelt's political career suffered a brief hiatus following the death of his first wife, Alice Lee, from Bright's disease (a kidney disease), as well as the death of his mother on the same day, February 14th 1884.

In his diary, Roosevelt drew a giant X over that date and wrote just below it, "[T]he light has gone out of my life."[3] Reacting to this tragedy, he moved out to become a cowboy. It wasn't until Roosevelt lost the majority of his family's fortune two years later that he finally returned to New York City. The mark this tragedy left on Roosevelt likely stayed with him for the rest of his life; he never spoke about Alice publicly, and he didn't even mention her in any of his private writings. Such was the weight of this loss that he sought to shut himself off from it entirely.

When Roosevelt returned to New York City, he ran for mayor in 1886, coming in third. Later that year, he married Edith Carrow. By 1889, Roosevelt was back in politics, having been appointed by President Benjamin Harrison to the United States Civil Service Commission, a position he maintained until 1895. Roosevelt next served two years as president of the New York City Police Board. In 1897, Roosevelt was appointed assistant secretary of the navy, a position that gave him considerable control of men and military machinery; at one point he even became the acting secretary for four hours and used this opportunity to mobilize the United States toward war.

When the United States and Spain went to war, Roosevelt once again deviated from his political career, this time to join the U.S. Volunteer Cavalry Regiment, more popularly known as the Rough Riders, where he served from May through September of 1898.

Roosevelt ran for governor of New York after the war and was elected in 1898. In 1900, he was designated as the vice presidential running mate of William McKinley. When McKinley was elected, Roosevelt served as vice president for six months. After McKinley was shot on September 6th 1901 and died a week later, Roosevelt became President of the United States of

America. In 1904, he was reelected to serve for another term; however, he declined to run again in 1908 and instead went on a safari in Africa from which he did not return until 1910.

While Theodore Roosevelt's more fiery personality led him to pursue his political career nearly from the onset, Woodrow Wilson's more calculated one caused him to leave his political career on the back burner until he felt the time was right to begin pursuing it. Wilson originally attended Davidson College in North Carolina during the 1873–74 school year, but medical ailments prevented him from returning for his second year, and when he eventually went back to college, he attended Princeton University instead, graduating in 1879.

Like Roosevelt, Wilson took an interest in the law, and he attended the University of Virginia law school for one year. Despite never graduating (his poor health once again forced him to withdraw from school), he continued to educate himself in the law, and in 1882 he opened up his own law practice.

Wilson soon tired of the law, but unlike Roosevelt who gave up the law· for politics, Wilson continued to pursue higher education. In 1883 he began doing graduate studies at Johns Hopkins University, receiving his Ph.D. in history and political science a mere three years later.

Even after graduating, Wilson remained an academic for some years, working as a professor at Cornell, Bryn Mawr, and Wesleyan, and finally returning to Princeton, his alma mater, in 1890 to teach. In 1902, the trustees named Wilson the president of Princeton University, and he remained in that position until 1910, when he decided to resign and enter New Jersey state politics.

By that point Roosevelt had nearly completed his political career; however, it seemed to be just the beginning for Wilson. Despite Wilson's late start, his race to the top seemed to take place within the blink of an eye, moving from relative obscurity to world prominence at lightning speed. Wilson was elected governor of New Jersey in 1910, and by 1912 he was running as the Democratic candidate for president of the United States.

It was during this election that Roosevelt's and Wilson's political careers intersected with one another. Upon returning from Africa, Roosevelt craved to be back in the spotlight and regain the presidency, so he decided to run in the 1912 election. Out of favor with the Republican Party, Roosevelt formed his own Progressive or "Bull Moose" Party and proceeded to compete against the incumbent president, William Howard Taft, and the Democratic candidate, Woodrow Wilson. While on the campaign trail, Roosevelt was the victim of an assassination attempt. However, Roosevelt was so frenzied and desperate to get back into politics that he delivered his speech despite the bullet wound.

Wilson's successful campaign for president sounded the death knell for Roosevelt's political career once and for all and served as a crushing blow to the spirit of this seemingly tireless man.

While Wilson was in office, he suffered the same poignant loss that Roosevelt had—his first wife, Ellen Louise Axson, died from Bright's disease in 1914. As her health failed, Wilson spent hours mourning by her bedside. He lamented, "God has stricken me almost more than I can bear."[4]

Though both men's political careers were marked with superficial success— for example, each was awarded the Nobel Peace Prize—these men themselves likely considered their careers to have been failures. Roosevelt, having been abandoned by his own political party and unable to find political success in the aftermath, was never able to regain the glory he so desperately craved. In 1919, Roosevelt died in his Oyster Bay, Long Island, home, first suffering from two and a half months of inflammatory rheumatism and then eventually suffering a heart attack. His last words are said to have been, "[P]ut out the light."[5] It seems that death was a welcome friend after the series of disappointments and chronic illnesses that Roosevelt suffered from in his later years.

Wilson, so obsessed with creating a world order that would end all wars, fought relentlessly for this dream to come to fruition. Having failed to persuade his country to join the League of Nations, which was his ultimate vision for a new world order, Wilson was crushed both physically and mentally. In 1919, he suffered a tremendous stroke, which nearly incapacitated him and permanently left him paralyzed on the left side of his body, as well as blind in the left eye. He spent the rest of his presidential term lurking in the background, and when he finally left office in 1921, he was broken both in health and in spirit. He died in Washington, D.C., a mere four years later, in 1924.

When his time came, Wilson, too, seemed to embrace the end of his dismal journey; his final words, similar to those of Roosevelt, are believed to have been, "I am ready."[6]

In the end, each man considered himself to be a failure: Roosevelt because he lost the limelight at a time in which he thought himself best prepared for it; and Wilson because he lost the League of Nations at a time he thought the world most needed it.

Both radically and irreversibly altered the relationship of government to individuals in America and probably didn't realize it.

Did those alterations make posterity happier, more free, or more prosperous? Or did the work of Theodore and Woodrow set America on a course for massive government that writes any laws and regulates any behavior and taxes any event with utter disregard for the Constitution?

The answers, now explored in this book, are painfully obvious.

Chapter 1

The Bull Moose

Roosevelt's New Party in His Own Image and Likeness

I'll name the compromise candidate. He'll be me. I'll name the compromise platform. It will be our platform.

—THEODORE ROOSEVELT, 1912 REPUBLICAN CONVENTION

[I]t may be concluded, that a pure Democracy, by which I mean a Society consisting of a small number of citizens, who assemble and administer the Government in person, can admit of no cure for the mischiefs of faction. A common passion or interest will, in almost every case, be felt by a majority of the whole; a communication and concert result from the form of Government itself; and there is nothing to check the inducements to sacrifice the weaker party, or an obnoxious individual.

—PUBLIUS (JAMES MADISON), *FEDERALIST* NO. 10

The Constitution makes no mention of political parties. In fact, when drafting the Constitution, our Founding Fathers were very weary of the creation of political factions. They knew that political parties would get in the way of pragmatism and rational thinking. Having political parties would cause party loyalists to cling steadfastly to their party lines and keep the government from protecting freedom. But on another level, they liked the fact that factions in a democracy could clog the government's mechanisms and keep it from doing anything rash. Alexander Hamilton and James Madison mentioned in *Federalist* No. 9 and No. 10 how detrimental political parties would be for the nation, but the factions quickly reared their ugly heads all the same.

Early Political Parties

Over the course of American history, there have been several incarnations of the two-party political system. Initially, during the Constitution's drafting phase there were the Federalists, who were in favor of a strong federal government, and the anti-Federalists, or Democratic-Republicans, who wanted more rights to be retained by the states and a smaller federal government. Even Hamilton and Madison, who wrote No. 9 and No. 10 of the *Federalist Papers*—a two-part exploration of political parties—quickly became factionalized.

The Federalists were led by the nation's first secretary of the Treasury, Alexander Hamilton. He was a strong advocate for a central national bank, tariffs, and muscular foreign relations. Both modern Republican and Democratic parties support all these ideas, each of which has become manifest in extremes far beyond anything Hamilton ever wrote or publicly spoke about.

America's first opposition party was originally born as the anti-Federalists, led by the nation's first secretary of state, Thomas Jefferson. He tried to limit the power of the federal government in the Constitution itself and championed the drafting and inclusion of the Bill of Rights. His party quickly grew into the Democratic-Republicans. That name may sound funny to readers abreast of modern politics, but not to history. Our modern two parties were born out of the same party name.

The Constitution establishes the federal government of the United States of America as a form of government known as a *federal democratic republic*. A *republic* is a nation run by leaders chosen by the people and not solely based on birth; a *democracy* is a type of government where the people have a direct say in who will lead them and what actions those leaders take; and *federal* connotes the union of sovereign entities (those would be our once sovereign states).

The first heads of the Democratic-Republicans were Thomas Jefferson and James Madison. They both understood that having a federal government was necessary to keep commerce regularly flowing between the states, but they also wanted to make sure that it did not jeopardize the rights of the people and the states. It is from the Democratic-Republicans that the modern Democrats claim their heritage, feeling that the nation should always be more of a democracy than a republic, and calling themselves the party of Jefferson, who no doubt would reject the Nanny State that the Democrats have built.

The Federalists were the first major American political party to die off. Their original leaders, in addition to Hamilton, were George Washington and John Adams. They met their demise during the eight-year so-called Era of Good Feelings from about 1816 to about 1824. The nation turned on the Federalists when they did not support the War of 1812, and for that brief period only the Democratic-Republicans were relevant in federal elections.

But that honeymoon wouldn't last. The Democratic-Republicans quickly split in 1824 and 1828 into the Democrats led by Andrew Jackson and the Whigs led by Henry Clay.

The Democrats favored the strong presidential power of their leader, Andrew Jackson, and strongly opposed the Bank of the United States. The Whigs took the name of the common British opposition party and were formed to oppose the principal policies of the Jacksonian Democrats. The Whigs thought that Congress—some of whose members at the time still wore actual wigs—should be supreme over the president, and they favored the strong national bank.

The Whigs were replaced in the 1850s by the Republican Party. This new party continued the economic policies of the Whigs, such as supporting the bank, supporting the railroads, raising tariffs, furthering the nation's homestead policy (making free western land available to Americans who agreed to improve it for a period of five years), and providing further funding for the nation's land grant colleges.

Unfortunately for the Democrats, this period in American history did not serve them well. The first victorious presidential candidate of the new Republican Party was, of course, Abraham Lincoln. He would undoubtedly be happy with the Regulatory State, the Warfare State, and the Welfare State that the Republicans have built.

Andrew Jackson hailed from the South, as did much of the Democratic bloc. When the southern states seceded from the Union, they took with them many Democratic states. The setup of strong anti-slavery Republicans and weakened pro-slavery (until the Civil War) Democrats lasted through the nation's reconstruction and was coming to a close when the Progressive Era began.

Along Came Teddy

Theodore Roosevelt was an old-money Republican. His family had been influential for six generations in politics, business, and society.[1] He grew up in several luxurious Manhattan apartments and a vast country estate in Oyster Bay, Long Island. At a young age he was drawn into politics and joined the family's Republican Party. But his party was a far cry from the Republicans we think of today.

In 1896, as police commissioner of New York City, Roosevelt saved from a heat wave thousands of poor New Yorkers on the Lower East Side that the rest of his party had decided to neglect.[2] He pushed for the idea of giving away free ice to overheated New Yorkers and personally oversaw the proper distribution and use of the ice.[3] He also advocated reforms such as universal health care and women's suffrage.

Another difference between Roosevelt and most politicians of either party of his day was the fact that he was quite the aggressive war hawk. From his youth, he had a tendency for violence, even once shooting his neighbor's dog because his girlfriend dumped him. He had long felt that Americans were the superior race and that the nation was at its strongest when it was at war. His appetite for blood was whetted on hunting trips and during the infamous escapades of the Rough Riders in the Spanish-American War in Cuba in the late nineteenth century.

Roosevelt may have been a Republican, but he wasn't a typical toe-the-party-line Republican by his day's or our day's definition. Before being added to President William McKinley's Republican ticket for McKinley's reelection campaign in 1900, Roosevelt was the very popular governor of New York. He was popular with the citizens of the state, but not with Thomas C. Platt, New York State's Republican Party boss.

During that era, both political parties had bosses who may or may not have held office but were undoubtedly the kingmakers for large and important states. These bosses held large sway over constituencies of voters, or worse, over the people counting the votes, and were able to ensure that their man would be elected. Today, the equivalent of a political boss on the surface is each party's chairman.

Platt controlled the Republican-dominated New York state government and saw Roosevelt as too much of a reformer to be controlled by the political machine of the day. After President McKinley's first vice president, Garret Hobart of Paterson, New Jersey, died, Platt moved to get Roosevelt on the ticket in the powerless position of vice president. Vice president had long been seen as a purely glad-handing position that did not allow its holder to exercise any actual power or influence.

In Platt's view, putting Roosevelt into that slot would kill two birds with one stone. Not only would it remove Roosevelt as governor of Platt's state, New York; it would also silence and neuter Roosevelt. Little did Platt know that McKinley would die less than a year after the election, making the traditional Republicans' worst nightmare, the bellicose Nanny Stater from Oyster Bay, the president of the United States.

Roosevelt knew throughout his presidency that he had gained his position despite his party and not because of it. He consistently pushed for and signed into law measures that he thought were best for the nation and not necessarily what the Republican Party thought was best for the nation. He regulated the railroads, regulated what Americans could eat and drink, personally intervened to resolve a coal strike, kept vast amounts of public land from private ownership, and dissolved many corporate giants. And he didn't care much about following the Constitution.

Roosevelt was one of the first presidents to use the press in his favor. He gave the press its own room inside the White House (he was actually the first president to call it officially the White House).[4] He understood that if he made himself popular enough, it did not matter how much the old Republican guard hated him; he would be their candidate and win election to keep his office in 1904.

Early in Roosevelt's first term there was a dump Roosevelt movement, which put forth Ohio senator Mark Hanna as its candidate. Unfortunately,

Hanna died in February 1904, also killing the movement's shot at wrestling the Republican nomination away from Roosevelt.

As a compromise in return for allowing a Progressive, Roosevelt, to be the 1904 Republican candidate, the conservative Republicans were allowed to pick his vice presidential running mate, Charles Fairbanks. Fairbanks made his millions as a lawyer for the Indianapolis, Bloomington, and Western Railroad. Fairbanks then turned to politics, where he was a member of the U.S. Senate for one term (1897–1905).

Both men were chosen unanimously as the candidates on the first ballot at the 1904 Republican Convention. Roosevelt won a landslide victory. He took every northern and western state, 56.4 percent of the popular vote, and 336 out of 476 electoral votes. He defeated the Democratic candidate, Alton Parker. Parker was the chief judge of the New York Court of Appeals (New York's highest court), and he ran on a platform that primarily supported small government and was sympathetic to the Wall Street banks. He was nominated primarily because he was seen as an affable and smart man who would be a popular candidate, but he was not as popular as Roosevelt.

Upon election to retain his presidency in 1904, Roosevelt vowed that he was retiring from the presidency when his term ended in 1909, after serving as president for seven and a half years. Upon his departure, Roosevelt hand-picked his successor, William Howard Taft.

What About Taft?

Many readers who keep up with the order of the men who ascended to the post of the presidency may have asked early on when opening this book the following question: "What about Taft?" Taft served as a one-term (1909–13) president between the bookends who are the subjects of this book, Theodore Roosevelt (1901–9) and Woodrow Wilson (1913–21). He served four short years during the Progressive Era, but was a clog in the Progressives' gears of change that was quickly thrown out of office when he ran for reelection.

The conservative Republicans would not forget Taft's presidency, and when the next conservative Republican, Warren Harding, held the presidency in 1921, Taft was appointed Chief Justice of the Supreme Court.

Roosevelt selected Taft to succeed him because he had served as his secretary of war and appeared to be the man who would continue his Progressive agenda, but Taft shortly revealed that he did not have the stomach for it. He stayed much truer to conservative Republican principles than Roosevelt had envisioned or enjoyed.

Roosevelt saw the federal government's role as a protector of the people from big business. But Taft felt it was a good Republican's duty to protect persons and corporations *from the government*. When the time came for Taft's reelection campaign in 1912, Roosevelt—the man who just three years earlier had retired from the presidency and sworn never to run again—went back on his word.

Roosevelt felt he had to enter the race because Taft was simply "an agent of 'the forces of reaction and political crookedness.'"[5] The two men were then set on a crash course to meet in a battle to the political death in the Chicago Coliseum for the Republican nomination.

Although it was not a true battle to the death, journalists of the day used similar hyperbole when describing the gravity of the encounter in which the two former friends were now to be engaged.[6] Roosevelt had promised the American people a fair deal, and he felt that Taft was not giving them their deserved fairness. He felt it was his duty to take back the presidency or at the very least remove Taft for the good of the American people.

Taft had thought that Roosevelt stretched the powers of the executive too far, and in a rare move Taft actually reined in those powers and limited his own powers as a sitting president. (As this book will explain in a later chapter, sitting presidents almost never lessen their own powers. The modern Democrats were outraged at the reaches that President George W. Bush made, but President Barack Obama has only reached further since he took office.)

Taft and Roosevelt had a distinct disagreement about the role of the courts. Roosevelt was deeply upset by the fact that the Supreme Court had overturned several of his key pieces of Progressive legislation, such as the *Lochner v. New York* decision, which held that a baker's natural right to work as many hours as he pleased superseded New York's maximum work hours law,[7] thus invalidating laws he sought and signed into law as governor of New York. One of the issues on Roosevelt's platform as he ran for the Republican nomination was the recall of judicial decisions through the popular vote.

Roosevelt was a bully and was willing to use the tyranny of the majority to bully any minority. He felt that if the people wanted something, in a true democracy, they should be able to have it. This was a key theme of Progressivism and led to the multiple constitutional amendments that were enacted during the Progressive Era. A constitutional amendment is the one way that the people can enact legislation that is unconstitutional because it changes the actual Constitution.

Taft and the conservative wing of the Republican Party rightfully viewed Roosevelt as a serious threat to their conservative plans. They feared that if Roosevelt won a third term, he might become a perpetual president, running for a fourth term, a fifth term, and so on until nature or someone more popular took the post from him. He had made the mistake of relinquishing the presidency once and would likely not make it again. Oddly enough, that would happen thirty years later with Theodore Roosevelt's distant cousin, Franklin Delano Roosevelt, who was elected to four presidential terms, but only served three.

Taft said that he feared Roosevelt because Roosevelt firmly had the vote of the "less intelligent voters and the discontented."[8] Taft feared that to appease his base, Roosevelt would initiate "a forced division of property, and that means socialism."[9] The campaign became extremely bitter, with both men calling each other names. Roosevelt called Taft a "puzzlewit," and Taft called Roosevelt a "honeyfugler." While neither name has a direct translation to modern politics, "puzzlewit" roughly meant that Taft was of inferior intelligence, similar to the tactic used by the modern Left to describe Republican candidates such as George W. Bush, Sarah Palin, and Michele Bachmann. The name that Taft gave to Roosevelt, "honeyfugler," has a looser translation. It has the obviously similar sound to several words that cannot be said on television and was most likely intended to have a similar effect. It also had the slang meaning of a person who would stoop to any low in order to get what he wanted.[10]

Neither of these men realized that this feud and the principals of the election of 1912 itself were no accident and were not even in their control. Although Roosevelt and Taft considered themselves politicians, the big bankers regarded them as nothing but puppets. Despite the supposedly anti-trust position of Progressives such as President Theodore Roosevelt and President

Woodrow Wilson, both men allowed themselves to be used as pawns of the big bankers. The presidential election of 1912 is a prime example of the unhealthy relationship between the bankers and the federal government during the Progressive Era.

Theodore Roosevelt's candidacy in 1912 was constructed by financier J. P. Morgan. Bankers and Wall Street were frustrated with President Taft and were obsessed with accomplishing their goal of banking reform. The battle between Roosevelt and Taft created the perfect opportunity for the banking elite to manipulate the election by promoting an unprecedented third party, the Bull Moose Party. Morgan soldier George W. Perkins funded, advised, and managed Roosevelt's campaign and the Bull Moose Party. Perkins covered pre-convention costs, managed the convention, and chaired the party's executive committee. Roosevelt did not realize that he was being used until after he had suffered a humiliating defeat.

Morgan needed someone in the White House who would sign the Federal Reserve bill into law. Taft was clearly not the right person for the job; the big bankers were furious with him and fed up with his trust-busting efforts. Morgan therefore supported Roosevelt's new party, encouraging Roosevelt's candidacy. Thanks to his huge ego, Roosevelt was easily convinced to run again, despite losing the support of the Republican Party. Little did he know, he was only being used as a pawn to get Taft out of the White House and Wilson in. This plan was successful, as Roosevelt took away votes from Taft, allowing Wilson to get elected.

In 1913, President Wilson signed the Federal Reserve bill into law. Although he portrayed himself as a champion of the people, "Woodrow Wilson, far from attempting to rein in the banks via the Federal Reserve Act, was a great champion of the wealthiest of banking elites, especially the Morgans."[11]

The Bloody 1912 Republican Presidential Nomination

Luckily for Taft many states did not have direct primaries at the time, and the nominating delegates were still controlled by the local political bosses. The bosses wanted Taft to win the nomination because he would keep them in power and keep the corporations and fat cats filling their coffers free from regulation. In the few states that did have direct primaries, Roosevelt won nine of the primaries: California, Illinois, Maryland, Nebraska, Oregon, South Dakota, Ohio, Pennsylvania, and New Jersey. The vainglorious Progressive Republican senator Robert La Follette won North Dakota and his home state of Wisconsin, and Taft won only Massachusetts.[12] Roosevelt dominated in the popular vote, winning many states' Republican primaries by wide margins, nearly doubling Taft's vote in California, more than doubling it in Illinois, and more than tripling it in Nebraska and South Dakota.[13] Impressively, Roosevelt even beat Taft in Ohio, Taft's home state, by a wide margin.[14] Roosevelt won the popular vote of all primaries with 1,157,397 votes to Taft's 761,716 and La Follette's 351,043.[15] When the primaries were said and done, Roosevelt won 278 delegates, Taft won 48 delegates, and La Follette won 36.

If the people had any say, Roosevelt was to be the Republican candidate. But Taft dominated the boss-controlled primaries, so when the convention came around, neither man had the necessary 540 delegates to secure the nomination. Going into the convention, Roosevelt led with 411 delegates, Taft had 367, other minor candidates (including La Follette) held 46, and the remaining 254 delegates were still up for grabs.

It seemed that either man could still get the nomination, and it would take a long, drawn-out series of ballots for a true winner to be chosen, but the Republican National Committee was firmly behind its man, Taft. The members awarded 235 of the remaining delegates to Taft and only 19 to Roosevelt, putting Taft far over the threshold of 540 needed to secure the nomination.

At the time it was common for candidates to stay away from the convention, but President Roosevelt barged into the convention with outrage that he had been wronged. Roosevelt rallied his supporters and stormed the Chicago Coliseum, pleading that he deserved "sixty to eighty lawfully elected delegates" be added to his total. He felt that he had rightfully won the support of these delegates in the popular primaries and that if the delegates did not vote for him, they should not be allowed to vote at all.

Roosevelt was so steadfast in his convictions that he concluded his speech to his followers by proclaiming, "Fearless of the future; unheeding of our individual fates; with unflinching hearts and undimmed eyes; we stand at Armageddon, and we battle for the Lord!"[16] Roosevelt was, of course, referring to *himself* as the Lord. It was obvious from the early moments that a definite parting of the ways, and not a peaceful compromise, would be the product of the altercation.

Roosevelt's first action was to force a test vote to remove party chairman Elihu Root and replace him with Wisconsin governor Francis McGovern. Unfortunately for Roosevelt, Taft's man, Root, won via a very close and contentious vote and kept his post. Next, Roosevelt tried to have delegates supporting him get themselves substituted for Taft-supporting delegates during the voting's roll call. When this plan also failed after several contentious states' roll call, Roosevelt accepted the fact that he could not win the 1912 Republican nomination.

There were calls for a compromise third candidate because both Roosevelt and Taft had been too injured by the nasty primary campaign, but Roosevelt refused to accept the compromise. He said, "I'll name the compromise candidate. He'll be me. I'll name the compromise platform. It will be our platform." Roosevelt then took his followers and left the convention. He instructed them not to vote at all for the presidential candidate and instead went "to nominate for a presidency a Progressive on a Progressive platform."[17]

After years of angering his party with his Progressive tendencies and being angered by his party's backhanded support, Theodore Roosevelt finally split from the Republican Party and formed his own party in his own vision: The Progressive Party, also called the Bull Moose Party.

Roosevelt Forms His Own Party

The day after walking out of the Republican National Convention in Chicago, Roosevelt and his followers met to form a new party. Publisher Frank A. Munsey, the largest stockholder of U.S. Steel at the time, and George W. Perkins of J. P. Morgan, a director of U.S. Steel and chairman of International Harvester, were two of the biggest donors of Roosevelt's new party. U.S. Steel was one of the biggest monopolists in the United States, one that Taft had attacked, but that Roosevelt had deemed a "good trust."[18] This is a small example of Roosevelt the trustbuster going back on his word and welcoming some strange bedfellows when his coffers were empty.

Lack of money was not the only problem facing Roosevelt's party in its early days. Of the fifteen most Progressive Republican senators, only five pledged their support to Roosevelt and his new party. Although they may have supported Roosevelt ideologically, they did not want to lose the support of the Republican Party and its machine.

Today members of both parties are afraid to stand up for what they believe in or what they think is right because they are afraid they will lose the support of the national party. Although Democrats were swept into office in 2006 and 2008 to bring sweeping Progressive change, they backed down at every chance possible and compromised more often than not with the Republicans whom they were elected to defy.

Following the 2010 election, when the tides turned and many Republicans were elected to shrink the government, and instead have expanded it, the buck was passed once again back to the Democrats to let their base down with compromise.

Roosevelt's Progressive Party dared to buck the trend of two-party politics, but as is even more the case today, most politicians were reluctant to join him.

While today the Democrats are generally seen as the party of Big Government and Big Government spending, it was the Republican George W. Bush who took federal government spending to unprecedented new heights during his presidency. He increased government spending by 45 percent in the first five years of his presidency alone.[19] That was before the massive bank bailouts and all other spending that took place in a failed attempt to lessen the blow of the 2008 recession. Today both parties are in favor of large government expenditures, the biggest of which is always the military.

Another major development during Roosevelt's Progressive campaign was the Democrats' July 1912 nomination of Woodrow Wilson as their candidate for president. Wilson was the most articulate and most prominent Progressive in the Democratic Party. He was a Progressive in the same mold as Roosevelt, and since he was affiliated with a major party, he was a safer bet for many of the independent Progressives whom Roosevelt had thought were his. There were even some Progressive Republicans who endorsed Wilson over Roosevelt because they thought he had the better chance of defeating Taft.

Although they may not have been as numerous as Roosevelt envisioned, his supporters were very passionate. The Progressive Convention opened in August 1912 in Chicago to great fanfare. More than two thousand delegates attended, many of whom were women. At the time women did not yet have the right to vote on the federal level, but women voting was a Progressive policy that was sweeping the nation, with many states already granting women suffrage.

As open-minded as his Progressive movement seemed at the time, Theodore Roosevelt still excluded blacks from attending his convention. He saw them as a corrupt element sent by the general Republican Party to make his convention and the people of his party look bad. Roosevelt was long a believer that Anglo-Saxon whites were the dominant race, and he did not want that to change by associating "lesser races" with his Progressives.

Roosevelt also hated immigrants, of whom he said,

The one absolutely certain way of bringing this nation to ruin, of pre-venting all possibility of its continuing to be a nation at all, would be to permit it to become a tangle of squabbling nationalities, an intricate knot of German-Americans, Irish-Americans, English-Americans, French-Americans, Scandinavian-Americans, or Italian-Americans.[20]

At the convention, the Progressive Party amassed a platform that included these points:

- a national health service to encompass all existing government medical agencies,
- a form of social insurance for elderly and disabled people (a system similar to what would become Social Security),
- limited injunctions to stop striking workers,
- workers' rights, such as an eight-hour workday and a minimum wage for women,
- a federal securities commission (similar to what would become the Securities and Exchange Commission),
- farm subsidies, workmen's compensation for work-related injuries,
- a tax on inheritance (similar to what would become the estate tax),
- a constitutional amendment to allow federal income tax,

- women's suffrage,
- direct election of senators, and
- binding primary elections for state and federal nominations.

Roosevelt, of course, knew very well that if binding primaries had been in place during the 1912 Republican nomination process he would have been the chosen candidate, and the Republicans would have remained a Progressive party. The Progressive Party also supported several more drastic measures. The platform included numerous provisions to increase direct democracy. The Progressives wanted to institute a recall election process whereby voters could remove any elected official before the end of his term. They also pushed for the referendum coupled with the ballot initiative, where citizens could propose a law and enact it via popular vote.

The recall election, referendum, and ballot initiative have all since been instituted on various state levels throughout the United States. Perhaps the most infamous State to utilize these concepts has been California. In 2003, California held a recall election in which it removed its unpopular governor, Gray Davis, and replaced him with former bodybuilder and movie star Arnold Schwarzenegger, who soon became another unpopular governor. Davis was only the second governor in American history to be removed via recall; the first was Lynn Frazier of North Dakota in 1921 at the height of the Progressive Era.

California voters also used the ballot initiative to get the controversial Proposition 8, banning gay marriage, on the ballot in 2008. Based solely on popular opinion, the people of California effectively reversed a decision of the California Supreme Court that had earlier ruled that marriage is a natural right that does not presuppose the approval of one's neighbors or the state. Although the idea of removing equal rights from a certain group of individuals may not seem like a Progressive ideal, the process through which it was accomplished came directly from the Progressive Party's 1912 platform.

The Progressive platform also called for curbs on the connections between big business and politics. The Theodore Roosevelt crowd called for strict limits and disclosure requirements on political campaigns, a concept that has become a part of American law.

Roosevelt wanted the mandatory registration of lobbyists, and the recording and publication of congressional committee proceedings, all in an effort to enhance transparency and give the lay public more opportunities to make informed votes.

The convention had some controversy when it came to the regulation of large businesses and trusts. The party as a whole approved a trust-busting plank, but Roosevelt himself still held out and felt that instead there should just be strong federal regulation and permanent active government supervision so that the president, through the Department of Justice, could choose which cartels to bless and which ones to condemn. This difference of opinion was never resolved, but Roosevelt and his campaign carried on nonetheless.

His campaign had the general theme of New Nationalism. He felt that a strong government was needed to regulate industry, protect the working class, and carry on great national projects such as building infrastructure, preserving our natural resources or "wonders" as he called them, and strengthening the military.

Although both men were Progressive, in the campaign Roosevelt was the Big Government Progressive, while Wilson proposed a more limited government form of Progressivism known as New Freedom. Wilson had a few target areas that he felt needed reforming—tariffs, big business, and big banking—but falsely stated that he wanted to keep the federal government to a minimum beyond those areas. Neither talked about the Constitution, civil liberties, economic liberties, Natural Law, or the tyranny of the majority.

The Bull Moose Gets Shot in the Chest

The campaign trail was undoubtedly tough for all three men running, but it was especially perilous for Roosevelt. On October 14th 1912, Roosevelt was exiting the Hotel Gilpatrick in Milwaukee, Wisconsin, after dinner and entering his limousine to travel to give a speech that night, when he stopped to wave to the crowd that had assembled. Then a short, pale, blonde-haired man, John Nepomuk Schrank, burst through the crowd and shot the former president in the chest.[21] The bullet went through Roosevelt's overcoat, his jacket, his vest, his double-folded fifty-page speech, and his steel-lined spectacle case and hit one of his ribs. Roosevelt survived, and the bullet remained lodged where it came to rest for the balance of his life.[22]

15

Although Schrank was later declared insane, his stated reason for shooting Roosevelt was a feeling shared by many Americans. Among other less rational reasons for his action, Schrank stated that he wanted to shoot Roosevelt because he did not think that anyone should break the unwritten two-term rule for presidents and serve a third term. This was an issue that definitely affected Roosevelt's campaign, but it was not something that would affect his distant cousin thirty years later.

Roosevelt did not alter his plan to give his speech that night. He began his speech, "Friends, I shall ask you to be as quiet as possible. I don't know whether you fully understand that I have just been shot; but it takes more than that to kill a Bull Moose."[23] Roosevelt then went on to give a rousing ninety-minute speech at the Milwaukee Auditorium before seeking medical attention. From that point forward, the Progressive Party also became known as the Bull Moose Party. Roosevelt was a consummate performer.

The Bull Moose Gets Trampled

If the three candidates for president had to be put on a left/right spectrum, Wilson would fall in the middle between Roosevelt and Taft. He campaigned to change things, but still keep the government small. He was neither a Rough Rider nor a big-business fat cat. He was simply a former professor and college president and sitting New Jersey governor who looked like he knew what he was talking about and was running on a platform that more Americans could agree to agree on than the platforms of the other two men.

None of the three men won a majority of the popular vote. Wilson carried 41.8 percent of the popular vote, Roosevelt was second with 27.4 percent, and Taft was third with just 23.3 percent. Taft's finish was the first and only time that an incumbent president finished third in his reelection campaign. Interestingly, the Socialist candidate whom Wilson would one day prosecute for sedition, Eugene V. Debs, received 6 percent of the popular vote, totaling 901,551 votes. This shows that the time was ripe for radical change, and the Progressive ideal had infected the nation. Debs was by far the most radical of the candidates. He was an unabashed Socialist, and more than one in twenty voting Americans agreed with him.

Roosevelt's exceptional performance as a third-party candidate and Taft's exceptional failure as an incumbent were even more visible in the electoral college. While Wilson won with 435 electoral votes, far more than the 262 then needed for a majority, it was Roosevelt who finished second with 88 electoral votes. Taft, the sitting president, managed to muster only 8 electoral votes, from Vermont and Utah. Other than those two small states, the entire nation chose to fire the incumbent president.

The Progressive platform planks of women's suffrage, the federal income tax, and the direct election of senators all became realities during the presidency of Woodrow Wilson. The Progressives may have lost the battle that was the 1912 election, but by making sure that Wilson and not Taft won in their stead, they certainly won the war.

While neither Roosevelt nor anyone from his campaign came out and said it, they were definitely pleased that Wilson won the election rather than Taft. By entering and remaining in the race after losing the Republican nomination, Roosevelt was able to ensure that even if he was not the next president, it would be a Progressive. Wilson was not as Progressive as Roosevelt, but he was still a Progressive.

Although Theodore Roosevelt branched out of the Republican Party to form his third party, his campaign served a different role of spoiler than other major third-party campaigns. Roosevelt far and away received a larger percentage of popular votes and more electoral votes than any other third-party candidate in our nation's history. Recent third-party candidates have played spoiler for the candidate with whom they are more closely aligned— like Ross Perot, who mostly aligned with Republicans, spoiling the 1992 and 1996 elections for George H. W. Bush and for Bob Dole, respectively, and like Ralph Nader, who is left of most Democrats, spoiling the 2000 election for Al Gore. Roosevelt actually played spoiler to the candidate he would *least* want to be president: The Republican incumbent and his former close friend, William Howard Taft.

Roosevelt was a former Republican, and his staying in the race spoiled it for the Republicans. But his policies were much more closely aligned with the Democrats and Woodrow Wilson. The recent third-party candidates who ran for president had nowhere near the impact on the election that Roosevelt did in 1912.

Conclusion

Theodore Roosevelt was the only third-party candidate who ever had a serious chance of winning a presidential election, and unfortunately, his campaign taught the two parties a very simple lesson: *Never again*. Never again will any part of Roosevelt's Bull Moose run be allowed to happen. The Twenty-second Amendment to the United States Constitution was ratified in 1951. It limits a president to two full terms, or one full term if he served out more than half of a term after elevation from vice president upon the death or removal of the president. This would have stopped Roosevelt from even running in 1912, since he had served three of the four years of McKinley's second term and then won election once himself and served that full term.

Additionally, the parties no longer come to their political conventions without their presidential candidates chosen. The longest recent battle for a nomination was the 2008 Democratic primary between Hillary Clinton and Barack Obama; and even this contest was over by June 3rd 2008, a full two months before the Democratic National Convention that year. That primary was similar to the 1912 Republican primary because although Clinton won the popular vote, like Theodore Roosevelt, she was not chosen as the candidate. Much like Taft, Obama had the support of party insiders, or super-delegates, and was awarded the nomination.

Mrs. Clinton did not, however, go out and form her own party a la Theodore Roosevelt. Since her loss of the nomination was known before the convention itself, her campaign was able to broker a deal where she would go quietly and even campaign for Obama in return for him granting her his highest cabinet position, secretary of state.

Roosevelt's Bull Moose run for president in 1912 not only changed the way presidential primaries and third parties are viewed; it changed America's political framework for a long time. When Theodore Roosevelt left the Republican Party, he took with him its Progressive wing. They may not have all jumped immediately to his Bull Moose Party, but they all were gone in spirit. Many jumped to support Wilson in the 1912 election; others remained Republicans but stayed quiet.

The lasting takeaway from the 1912 election and Roosevelt's split is that it was the moment when the Republican Party became the party of smaller government and less regulation. The seeds of the Barry Goldwater Republicans and the modern libertarians were born from the remnant after the exit of Theodore Roosevelt. Republicans remained purely about small government until they started their unlawful and unnecessary wars. The first was Nixon's and later Reagan's and Bush's War on Drugs, and the second was George W. Bush's War on Terror. These wars enlarged government, increased spending, enhanced regulation, took away the rights of the American people, and were largely ineffective.

From an early age, Theodore Roosevelt thought that he could single-handedly save America. He personally led his brigade of Rough Riders to victory up San Juan Hill in the Spanish-American War and intended to bring the same attitude to his presidency. After he had served the customary length of time, he momentarily relinquished his power, but then quickly regained his thirst and fought for it again. Even after he was rebuked both by his party and by a gunman, he continued to fight onward to regain his post as an "elective king."

Roosevelt's unrelenting fight directly led to the presidency of Woodrow Wilson. Wilson ran a campaign that seemed reasonable in relation to Roosevelt, but quickly became just as, if not more, Progressive. Wilson campaigned for small government with few exceptions and quickly created a large government with few exceptions. He campaigned for isolationism, but extended Roosevelt's nation building and pushed our nation into the first world war.

Although one was a Democrat and the other a Republican, Wilson and Roosevelt worked together to push our nation in a more Big Government direction. They moved the nation away from its minimalist beginnings and into the modern era of overarching government control—a system that both parties, despite their petty squabbles, have consistently worked together to grow.

From banks to schools, the Progressives reworked society to their image. If they could control money, how about young minds? We move next to the methods and motives behind compulsory state education.

Chapter 2

Reeducation Camps

Compulsory Education

The parent is viewed as a backward and harmful influence in the formative years of the child's upbringing, an influence that must be corrected for and replaced by the "enlightened" professional teacher who has been trained, appointed and funded by the state. The public school, therefore, is a "reeducation camp" in which the child is to be remade in the proper "politically correct image."

—Professor Richard M. Ebeling[1]

Separation of the (Catholic) Church and the (Progressive) State

Alfred Roncovieri was a French-Italian Catholic who was elected superintendent of schools in San Francisco in 1906. After more than a decade of Progressive politics and anti-Catholic and anti-immigrant hostilities in San Francisco, he lost his job.

One of his biggest mistakes was holding the view that public schools were not the appropriate place to teach children about sex and morality. Because he thought these subjects should be left to the family or the church to teach, and because he was a European Catholic, Roncovieri was pushed out of his position by local Progressives. They launched a campaign to get him fired and to change the system to make it more responsive to the Progressive agenda.

It was during this time that the San Francisco school system went from locally elected superintendents to an appointment system that would leave the educational bureaucracy in charge of appointing a more powerful superintendent.

Murray N. Rothbard, a seminal libertarian thinker, noted that "[t]he removal of the Board of Education and school superintendent from direct and periodic control by the electorate had effectively deprived parents of any significant control over the educational policies of public schools."[2] In addition to becoming a more powerful position, the superintendent could now be appointed by San Francisco's political and educational elites instead of elected by voters, taking away any control that parents had over their children's education.

The San Francisco case is a good example of the push for compulsory education in the Progressive Era. In the midst of intense religious and ethnic conflict, San Francisco Progressives were using public schools as a way to Americanize and homogenize immigrant children. As Theodore Roosevelt stated in a speech in Boston, Massachusetts, in 1893, "In our public schools the lessons should be conducted in no language but in English, neither in German, French, Spanish, or any other, exactly as the children should be taught to speak United States and to think United States, and to be United States."[3] The demise of the career of Superintendent Roncovieri was analogous to the push for compulsory education during this time period, which was rooted in anti-immigrant sentiments and the Progressive political agenda.

Through compulsory education in state-owned schools, Progressives gave the state a firm hold on the development of the child. Presidents Theodore Roosevelt and Woodrow Wilson were among the Progressives advocating for compulsory education (hardly a federal issue), because they wanted to ensure that every generation of Americans would be brainwashed at an early age. As Roosevelt opined in 1893, "[T]he public schools are the nurseries from which spring the future masters of the commonwealth. . . . We have a right to demand that every man, native born or foreign born, shall in American public life act merely as an American."[4] Wilson believed that it was the government's job to educate children and that "the chief object of education is discipline."[5]

It turns out that compulsory education, a feat accomplished during the

Progressive Era, was also a compulsory indoctrination into Progressive thought and twentieth-century Protestantism. Arthur Calhoun stated in 1919, "The fondest wish of Utopian writers was coming true, the child was passing from its family into the custody of community experts."[6] The power to shape children's futures was taken from their parents and put into the hands of the government. Starting in this era, as John Swett, the founder of public education in California, stated, schoolchildren belonged not "to the parents, but to the State, to society, to the country."[7]

The Progressive Interest in Education

Every politically controlled educational system will inculcate the doctrine of state supremacy sooner or later, whether as the divine right of kings, or the "will of the people" in "democracy." Once that doctrine has been accepted, it becomes an almost superhuman task to break the stranglehold of the political power over the life of the citizen.

—Isabel Paterson[8]

When viewed through the rosy lens of history, statewide compulsory education was a positive step forward in the Progressive Era. It was a way to get children out of dangerous factories and into safe and nurturing class-rooms. The choice between child labor and public school is seemingly an easy one. However, the real story of the push for compulsory public education is much darker. It was actually rooted in anti-immigrant sentiment and was fueled by a desire to push the Progressive agenda onto the youngest generation. One of the main goals of the Progressive Era reformers was to coax immigrant (specifically Catholic) children out of their homes as early as possible, so that they could be influenced by the state instead of their parents.

The anti-immigrant impetus behind the push for compulsory education conforms with President Woodrow Wilson's outright and well-documented racism. Wilson stated prior to taking office, "Our problem is not merely to help the students to adjust themselves to world life . . . [but] to make them as unlike their fathers as we can."[9] This thinking shows Wilson was an elitist and racist who looked down on anyone who did not share his Progressive beliefs. He genuinely believed that the only way to fix the "problem" that immigrants presented was to brainwash their children in public schools.

Theodore Roosevelt shared Wilson's anti-immigrant sentiment. He publicly complained about "hyphenated-Americans," such as Italian-Americans and Irish-Americans. He even went so far as to applaud the brutal murders of a group of Italian-Americans in a prison in New Orleans in 1892, many of whom were in custody despite the fact that they had been exonerated of the crimes with which they had been charged. Roosevelt actually called these mass lynchings a "rather good thing" and bragged that he made this statement in front of a group of "various dago diplomats."[10]

For Wilson and other Progressives at this time, the idea behind compulsory education was not to provide children with a well-rounded education, but to make them wards of the state.

The use of schools as a breeding ground for Progressive thought continued from the late 1800s to the 1930s. In 1933, Max Mason, the president of the Rockefeller Foundation, outlined a plan to control human behavior that involved the school system. This plan would attempt to control "human breeding" by determining which people were fit to reproduce.

Public schools were an ideal place to weed out students in order to create an elite class of people, while relegating the rest to their rightful position in life. Woodrow Wilson stated in a speech to a group of businessmen prior to World War I, "We want one class of persons to have a liberal education, and we want another class of persons, a very much larger class of necessity in every society, to forgo the privilege of a liberal education and fit themselves to perform specific difficult manual tasks."[11]

Clearly, Wilson did not want compulsory education to give all children an equal opportunity. He genuinely believed that children could be divided into elite and non-elite classes, and that their roles in society could be predetermined based on their class.

Louis Alber, an executive director of the National Education Association, announced in 1933 that his organization expected "to accomplish by education what dictators in Europe are seeking to do by compulsion and force."[12] Schools were seen as places for the state to have greater control over the population and decide which students would be successful and productive members of a

Progressive society. Fortunately, in the wake of World War II, these types of plans (also advocated in Europe by Adolf Hitler and Benito Mussolini) became unpopular. Many ideas advocated by Roosevelt and Wilson were not far off from those of some European dictators of the time. Roosevelt and Wilson were just better at hiding their extremist views through bombastic (in the case of Roosevelt) and clever (in the case of Wilson) rhetoric and through control over the press (in both cases).

From Free Choice to Compulsory Education

Prior to the Progressive Era, schools in America were run by families, churches, and local communities. By 1850, every state had a system of public schools; however, compulsory education did not begin to spread until the 1870s and 1880s. While the benefits of "free" education for the underprivileged cannot be denied, taking the decisions of when, how, if, and by whom to educate a child out of the hands of the parents and put under control of the state contradicts the principles of individual liberty upon which this country was founded. Thomas Jefferson stated, "It is better to tolerate the rare instance of parent[s] refusing to let their child be educated, than to shock the common feelings and ideas by the forcible transportation and education against [their] will."[13]

Following a long history of educational regulation in the Puritan tradition, Massachusetts became the first state to pass compulsory attendance laws in 1852. By 1918, at the height of the Progressive Era, every state required that children attend school.

Although the states regulated and generally paid for education, there was also a federal push toward compulsory education. The Smith-Hughes Act, passed in 1917 and signed into law by Woodrow Wilson, provided one million dollars to any state that agreed to improve its public schools by providing vocational education programs. After facing judicial obstacles in passing federal laws to prohibit child labor, supporters of the Smith-Hughes Act hoped to encourage education as an alternative to child labor.

Of course, under the Constitution, education of children is an area of human behavior reserved to the people and the states, and not delegated to the federal government.

This represents the beginning of the federal government's use of Congress's spending power to coerce the states into uniformity. Today, when Congress comes across an issue that it wants to regulate but over which it lacks constitutional authority, it conditions grants of federal money on the states' compliance with congressional will.

For example, Congress compelled the states to set their minimum drinking age at twenty-one in order to receive federal highway funds. These types of coercive tactics were approved by the Supreme Court in 1987 in *South Dakota v. Dole*.[14] This leaves Congress with almost unlimited power to regulate all aspects of American life, a significant departure from the enumerated powers that were set out in the Constitution. This is also a form of bribery.

Give the State Your Children

As evidenced by the political demise of Alfred Roncovieri in San Francisco, it is clear that there was more to the story than simply getting children out of factories and into schools. As Edward Alsworth Ross, a favorite of Theodore Roosevelt, stated, the role of a public official and teacher is "to collect little plastic lumps of human dough from private households and shape them on the social kneading board."[15] The reform of education was a way to indoctrinate children (specifically immigrant children) into the Progressive way of thinking.

For example, although the Prohibition Amendment would not be ratified until 1920, public schools were instructing children in the evils of alcohol years before that. By 1901, every state required instruction in temperance. This was also a veiled attack on groups such as Irish-Americans and Italian-Americans, for whom alcohol was an integral part of family culture.

The "Right" Religion

These public schools did not separate church and state. Instead, they hoped to emphasize Protestant teachings over other religions, specifically, Catholicism. As the archbishop of the Roman Catholic Archdiocese of New

York, John Cardinal Hughes, explained, public schools taught children that "Catholics are necessarily, morally, intellectually, infallibly, a stupid race."[16]

Although the practice of religion in public schools is now strictly regulated, public schools during the Progressive Era were actively trying to convert young children to Protestantism. Schools banned other religions while emphasizing Protestantism. Schools required Protestant teachings, teachers, prayers, ceremonies, songs, and Bible readings. The textbooks that were issued often contained an anti-Catholic slant.[17]

Any efforts to take Protestant teachings out of public schools were met with hostility. For example, an attempt to take the Protestant Bible out of public schools in Cincinnati led to the Cincinnati Bible Wars. In 1869, the Cincinnati Board of Education decided to take the Bible out of public curriculum in order to appease Catholic complaints. Protestants fiercely objected, employed protests and petitions, and even brought a lawsuit to challenge the board's decision.

The tension came to a head in 1872 in the Ohio Supreme Court in the case of *Minor v. Board of Education of Cincinnati*, where the decision of the board was upheld.[18] However, this decision was met with continued hostility from Protestants, who attempted to exert their influence on education without using the Bible through songs, literature, and Protestant teachers.[19] The goal was to educate children in the morals and beliefs that were considered the norm at the time. It was not enough that children receive an education in academic subjects. Changes in religious and moral values were integral to the goals of the compulsory education movement.

Both Theodore Roosevelt and Woodrow Wilson were proponents of education through Bible study. Roosevelt proposed, "The teachings of the Bible are so interwoven and entwined with our whole civic and social life that it would be literally impossible for us to figure to ourselves what that life would be if these teachings were removed."[20] In 1912 in a speech on the importance of Bible study, Wilson proclaimed that "no great nation can ever survive its own temptations and its own follies that does not indoctrinate its children in the Word of God."[21] Through compulsory public education, Roosevelt and Wilson hoped to control not only children's academic education, but also their religious education, an endeavor that is traditionally left to parents.

The saving grace for private and parochial schools did not come until 1925. In Oregon in 1922, an initiative was passed that amended the state's compulsory education law by taking out the exception for children who attended private schools. This initiative was challenged by private and religious schools, fearing that the new law would force them out of business.

The situation in Oregon led to the landmark 1925 Supreme Court case *Pierce v. Society of the Sisters.*[22] The Supreme Court ruled against attempts to compel all children to attend only public schools because "the fundamental liberty upon which all governments in this Union repose excludes any general power of the State to standardize its children by forcing them to accept instruction from public teachers only."[23] This case affirmed that parochial and private schools had to be an option, despite compulsory education laws. It was also a response to the attempts to mold and homogenize all American children with the same religious values. Despite the intense anti-Catholic sentiments of the time, this ruling was a triumph for Catholic schools.

The Legal Justification

Today, compulsory education requirements vary from state to state. Ages of required enrollment vary from five to eight years old. Although all states require high school education, the ages of legal withdrawal vary. Students are given the option of homeschooling or public or private education.[24]

Judicially, the right of parents to raise their children was confirmed by the Supreme Court in 1923 in *Meyer v. Nebraska.*[25] This case involved the prosecution of a teacher, Robert T. Meyer, for teaching reading to a fourth-grade student in German rather than in English. This violated Nebraska's Siman Act, which banned teaching foreign languages. This Act followed a national push to ban all things German in the midst of World War I. Meyer's conviction was upheld by the Nebraska Supreme Court. The Supreme Court of the United States overturned this decision in 1925, holding that liberty includes the right "to marry, establish a home and bring up children." This decision established the right of parents to decide what their children were being taught and who shall do the teaching.

However, since the dawn of compulsory education during the Progressive

Era, the Supreme Court has consistently reiterated the interest of the state in regulating education. This principle has been upheld in Supreme Court cases such as *Pierce v. Society of the Sisters* in 1925 (establishing that private and religious schools must be an alternative to public schools), *Brown v. Board of Education* in 1954 (holding that although states had a right to regulate education, schools could not be segregated based on race), and *Wisconsin v. Yoder* in 1972. In *Wisconsin v. Yoder*, the state claimed two specific interests in compulsory education.[26] The first is to ensure that children receive enough education to prepare them to participate in the democratic process. The second is to ensure that children receive enough education to be self-sufficient members of society.

The interest of the state must also be balanced with the constitutional rights of the parents to make child-rearing decisions. Here the Supreme Court stated in *Wisconsin v. Yoder*, "[A] State's interest in universal education, however highly we rank it, is not totally free from a balancing process when it impinges on fundamental rights and interests [of the parents]."[27] In order to uphold the constitutionality of compulsory education laws, it must be proven that the state's interest outweighs the fundamental rights of the parent. Yet it is rare that a parent's rights are held to outweigh the state's interest.

But *Yoder* is just such a rarity. There a group of parents in the Old Order Amish religion challenged Wisconsin's compulsory education laws because they conflicted with their religious beliefs. Three separate families refused to send their children to a public high school. Although these Amish parents did not object to schooling, they did not believe in sending their children to school after eighth grade. According to them, the public high school tended to "emphasize intellectual and scientific accomplishments, self-distinction, competitiveness, worldly success, and social life with other students."[28]

These Amish parents did not want to emphasize these goals in raising their children. Instead, they wished to emphasize agrarian and Amish religious and social values during their children's formative years. The right of these Amish parents not to send their children into formal education after eighth grade was upheld in this case based on the Free Exercise Clause of the First Amendment.

While this case represents a victory for parents' rights to make educational decisions, it is narrowly tailored and based on their First Amendment right to freedom of religion and parents' interests in their children's religious upbringing. This victory and the right to free exercise did not come easily. These parents were forced to engage in a time-consuming litigation that went to the Supreme Court before they were able to exercise their freedom. This was an especially difficult task, as part of the Amish religion also prevents them from fighting and preaches that they "turn the other cheek." However, when the government is your enemy, you have no choice but to fight, even if it is costly or dangerous to be right when the government is wrong.

For parents who do not have a religious reason for wanting to control their child's education, there are no options that are outside the government's control. As the Court held in *Wisconsin v. Yoder*, "A way of life, however virtuous and admirable, may not be interposed as a barrier to reasonable state regulation of education if it is based on purely secular considerations."[29] By making this distinction, the Court is making value judgments regarding when parents have legitimate reasons to want to control their child's education (religion) and when these reasons are illegitimate (everything else). Wouldn't the same First Amendment that is the basis for Yoder's victory also prevent any government from requiring a religious belief in order to be free from state regulations? It is not the proper role of the Court to be making these kinds of distinctions.

Today: Nanny Staters Are Literally Nannies

The courts have established that parents have no right to educate their children free from governmental regulation.[30] Today parents have the option of public schools, private schools, or homeschooling, but each option is regulated by the government in some way. This is the legacy that Wilson and Roosevelt have left us. For many families, private school or homeschooling is not a viable option. Parents who choose to send their child to private school end up paying for public schools through taxes, in addition to the cost of private school tuition. Therefore, private schools are a significant financial burden. Even private schools are subject to minimum standards, a way to ensure that the state has some say.[31]

Homeschooling may give a parent more control over the child's education, but the government still has a right to pre-approve the planned curriculum. In 2008, the United States Court of Appeals for the Third Circuit addressed this issue in *Combs v. Homer-Center School District*.[32] There, parents in Pennsylvania claimed that state review of homeschooling curriculum interfered with their religious beliefs. In Pennsylvania, even homeschooling is subject to restrictions set by the state. Parents are subject to regulations that set a minimum number of hours and days and certain subjects that must be taught. The state then monitors the parent to ensure that he or she is complying with the regulations. If these reviews produce unsatisfactory results, the child may be forced into a public or private school.

Homeschooling parents challenged these regulations on religious grounds; however, they were still upheld by the court. This decision proves that even in the case of religious beliefs, governmental control of education is almost limitless.

There is no way to escape interference from the state when educating your child. As this case demonstrates, although freedom of religion is respected in regard to compulsory education, even this First Amendment guarantee is not unconditional. The decision in this case shows that it is not always an option for parents to homeschool their child, for religious reasons, without any interference from the state.

Homeschooling is also not an option for parents who work full-time or do not have the means to educate their children themselves. This leaves a majority of American children in public schools. Public schools are regulated and funded by the state and are often subject to federal regulation as well. This structure leaves very little, if any, parental control over the educational experience of their child. The curriculum and values that are being taught are pre-determined.

During the Progressive Era, public schools were used as a vehicle to further Progressive goals. This continues today. Schools continue to take children out of their homes and influence and change their habits.

One modern example of values being forced upon school-age children is the current push for regulation of food in schools in order to impose a healthier lifestyle on children and combat childhood obesity. This push is oddly reminiscent of Roosevelt's campaign for food and drug regulation during the Progressive Era. The underlying theme is the government deciding what you should or should not eat or drink.

In many states public schools are beginning to regulate what students can eat. A national initiative pushing healthy eating in schools is being led by First Lady Michelle Obama. Mrs. Obama's "Let's Move!" campaign has led to increased governmental control over what children can eat while they are in school.[33]

As in the Progressive Era, many schools have been making changes at a local level, based on this federal push, for example, by getting rid of soda and candy machines or eliminating government-disliked options such as French fries.

This has turned from a campaign to a federal law. Passed in 2010, the Healthy, Hunger-Free Kids Act gives the federal government the power to regulate what is sold in vending machines, on campus, and at fund-raisers during school hours.[34] Any food that is served during school hours now must fit into nutritional guidelines that will be set by the U.S. Department of Agriculture.

The push for national compulsory education in the Progressive Era has led to a culture of using public schools as a place to impose political ideals and values onto children. Just as Woodrow Wilson believed that the government was responsible for making children "unlike" their parents, the Obamas have decided to take it upon themselves to tell children what they can and cannot eat. Woodrow Wilson and Theodore Roosevelt believed that the government and government agents were better at raising children than parents. The "Let's Move!" initiative embodies that spirit by attempting to force values onto children instead of leaving this job to their parents.

Check Your Rights at the Gate

Since the dawn of compulsory education in the Progressive Era, the public school system has increasingly created an environment where the government may impose its will upon Americans in their formative years. Despite the standard set out in the Supreme Court case of *Tinker v. Des Moines Independent Community School District* in 1969[35] that it "can hardly be argued that either students or teachers shed their constitutional rights to freedom of speech or expression at the schoolhouse gate," students across America would probably tell you otherwise. In public schools, students lose many of their rights to free speech and expression and many other constitutionally guaranteed rights. Students are subjected to drug testing before participating in school clubs or sports. School officials may conduct searches and seizures of their private property without the Fourth Amendment's protection against unreasonable searches and seizures.

In *New Jersey v. T.L.O* (1985),[36] the Supreme Court established that although students still had some protection under the law in a school setting, the warrant requirement and probable cause requirement of the Fourth Amendment to the U.S. Constitution do not apply. The same goes for random drug testing. As decided in the 1995 case *Vernonia School Dist. 47J v. Acton*,[37] there is a different, lessened standard for unreasonable searches and seizures for students and specifically athletes. Governmental coercion starts early for student athletes, who in many places must submit to random drug testing in order to participate in school sports. Although these students technically have the option, they are forced to choose between playing sports and giving up their individual liberty without just cause. It can hardly be said that absent other evidence, participation in school athletics gives school officials any reason to suspect that a student is using illegal drugs.

In 1977 in *Ingraham v. Wright*[38] the Supreme Court ruled that students do not enjoy the protection of the Eighth Amendment against cruel and unusual punishment and refused to intervene after a student was brutally beaten in a public school by a school official. The student was not afforded due process before the corporal punishment was administered. The beating was so bad that the student was unable to attend school for several days due to the injury. However, the Supreme Court decided that local tort remedies and community supervision of public schools could adequately compensate the student for his loss of liberty.

Students may also be punished for the language or views that they promote while on school grounds. In the 1986 Supreme Court case *Bethel School District No. 403 v. Fraser*,[39] a student's speech was deemed "lewd" and "indecent" and therefore warranted absolutely no First Amendment protection.

Free speech is also hindered in schools through the use of prior restraint. It is a generally accepted principle of First Amendment jurisprudence that preventing someone from exercising his right to free speech before he has a chance to speak (for example, not allowing a newspaper to publish a story) is only acceptable in extremely limited circumstances.

Yet in the 1988 Supreme Court decision in *Hazelwood School District v. Kuhlmeier*,[40] the First Amendment claims brought by a group of students who published a high school newspaper were shot down. It was held that in a school setting, the principal had the right to impose "reasonable" restrictions on the content published in a school newspaper, and he was exercising legitimate authority in vetoing two stories before the paper was published.

All these examples show that not only does the government regulate education but it also heavily regulates the speech and activities of students and takes away crucial rights. Although students may not lose all their rights when walking through the schoolhouse gate, they are offered watered-down, modified versions of their guaranteed rights, if at all.

Reaching Outside School Grounds

Today, students' rights are being stripped away from them, even when they are engaging in an activity that takes place off campus. In the 2007 Supreme Court case of *Morse v. Frederick*,[41] a student was suspended for waving a banner containing the phrase "Bong Hits 4 Jesus" at a school-sponsored event that took place off school grounds. Although the Ninth Circuit found that the student's First Amendment rights were violated, the Supreme Court reversed, holding that since this student's speech could be construed as promoting illegal drug use, and since the event was sponsored and authorized by the school, this speech could be regulated by the school.

Despite the eloquent statement in *Tinker v. Des Moines Independent Community School District* that students and teachers do not lose their rights just because they walk through a schoolhouse gate, this does not always apply, particularly if the student or teacher is saying something that the school does not approve of. In this case, the student did not even have to enter the schoolhouse gate to be punished for attempting to engage in free speech.

This issue is becoming particularly relevant in the age of the Internet. First Amendment issues are exacerbated by the use of the Internet in countless ways. Consider the situation of a student, on his grandmother's computer, using pictures of a principal found on a school website to create a fake Internet profile. The student is completely off campus and not engaged in a school-related activity. The website is in the public domain, and the pictures and information there are available to the public. The student is using this fake Internet profile to engage in lewd and offensive speech revolving around the school principal.

This was the situation in the 2011 case, *Layshock ex rel. Layshock v. Hermitage School District*.[42] The United States Court of Appeals for the Third Circuit declined to allow a school to regulate an activity that took place online, in the home of a child's parents. This case represents the problems of boundaries and free speech that the Internet may pose. Although students may be engaging in speech at home, it is still readily accessible to teachers, school officials, and other students when it is online. It may not be long before the government finds a way to regulate students' online speech as well.

This decision solidifies the First Amendment right to engage in speech, however unpopular, even if it involves something that is school related. Given that education is compulsory in every state, there is a danger in allowing schools freely to regulate speech whenever it takes place on school grounds or at school activities or involves school officials or teachers. Recently, authorities at Columbia High School in Maplewood, New Jersey, shut down a student comedy show because one teacher did not want to be parodied. Allowing this to go too far would mean that all American students may not enjoy their rights to free speech during their formative years, during which they must receive a formal education. Although Progressives wanted schools to Americanize immigrants, taking away individualism and free speech in schools is directly contrary to the core values upon which this country was built.

Conclusion

The move toward compulsory education was rooted in the Progressive Era, and the former police commissioner and the former college professor nurtured those roots from their perches in the White House. Today, public schools still afford the government the opportunity to foist values and ideals onto children. The Progressive push for compulsory education has led to an immense industry in public education. The public school system currently employs three million people and spends $400 billion annually to educate nearly forty-nine million students nationwide.[43] That is more than $8,000 per pupil, per year. This is funded by taxpayers, even if they do not have children attending public schools. The Progressive Era has allowed the government to dominate the "business" of education.

The government's involvement in the business of education gives it an unfair advantage that diminishes the value and quality of education. As Murray N. Rothbard states, "The problems of schooling . . . are examples of what happens when government, instead of private enterprise, operates a business."[44] The government has guaranteed funds from the taxpayers and guaranteed customers in students. These guarantees decrease its account-ability, because regardless of whether the "consumers" are happy with the product, the government will remain in the business of providing education.

Although private and parochial schools are an option for students, tax-payers cannot opt out of paying for public schools also. Allowing taxpayers to opt out of paying for public schools would lead to increased competition, lower prices, and a better quality of education. Once again, the Progressives, specifically Theodore Roosevelt and Woodrow Wilson, have left us with a system that takes away our freedoms and increases governmental control over our private lives.

The goal of compulsory, government-managed, and government-delivered basic education is not good people, but good (from the government's view) citi-zens. It is state indoctrination; and it has been perfected in America, as has its cousin to which we now turn our attention, the regulatory state. Public educa-tion enabled the government to control minds, and the regulatory state enabled it to control bodies.

Chapter 3

Quiet Men with White Collars

The Rise of the Regulatory State

The greatest evil is not now done in those sordid "dens of crime" that Dickens loved to paint. It is not done even in concentration camps and labour camps. In those we see its final result. But it is conceived and ordered (moved, seconded, carried, and minuted) in cleaned, carpeted, warmed, and well lighted offices, by quiet men with white collars and cut fingernails and smooth-shaven cheeks who do not need to raise their voice. Hence, naturally enough, my symbol for Hell is something like the bureaucracy of a police state or the offices of a thoroughly nasty business concern.

—C. S. Lewis, *The Screwtape Letters*[1]

In April 2010 the Food and Drug Administration (FDA) raided the farm of Pennsylvania Amish farmer Dan Allgyer.[2] This raid was complete with armed federal agents, two federal marshals, and a state trooper, all to invade an Amish farm called Rainbow Acres.[3] The reason for this armed federal raid? Allgyer was openly and notoriously selling raw milk to customers who wanted to purchase it.

Prior to this raid, the FDA had spent a full year and taxpayer money investigating Allgyer for selling unpasteurized milk to informed customers. These agents had been issued a warrant that allowed them to use reasonable force in order to gain entry to any part of his farm they were authorized to search.

These customers, like many others in the United States, made the informed decision to buy and consume this unpasteurized milk. Allgyer was not attempting to deceive or poison his customers. There is demand for raw milk because many people believe it is healthier than pasteurized milk.[4] Many consumers cannot tolerate pasteurized milk for health reasons. Governmental regulations force them to go underground to purchase raw milk that they can actually drink.

If this sounds ludicrous, thank President Theodore Roosevelt. He and the Progressives left us this legacy through the Pure Food and Drug Act, which gave us the Food and Drug Administration.

Today, the federal government's administrative agencies and regulations govern every aspect of our lives in America. There are few areas in a person's public or private life that the government does not control in some way. Through food and drug regulations, the government dictates what we can eat or drink, and what medicine we can or should take. Economic regulations govern the way that private companies and employers do business and the hours and wages that their employees must abide. These federal regulations are promulgated by federal agencies that are comprised of unelected and therefore unaccountable bureaucrats. The foundation for this type of regulatory state was set during the Progressive Era.

Progressive policies set out during the presidencies of Theodore Roosevelt and Woodrow Wilson created the Nanny State that we live in today. Progressives wanted to increase the size and power of the federal government and to substitute their judgment for ours. This increase in the scope of federal governmental power has taken us far from where the Founding Fathers envisioned our country and far away from the Constitution that they crafted.

The Birth of Food and Drug Regulation

If we are not even free anymore to decide something as basic as what we wish to eat or drink, how much freedom do we really have left?

—RON PAUL[5]

Today, the FDA oversees the production and approval of most foods, drugs, medicines, cosmetics, tobacco products, and vaccines in the United

States.[6] The modern FDA developed from the Pure Food and Drug Act of 1906, a law that was enacted during the Progressive Era under President Theodore Roosevelt and in which Congress gave *to itself* the power to regulate food and drugs.

At the time it was passed, the Pure Food and Drug Act was an unprecedented example of federal interference into the lives of producers and consumers. Although proponents of governmental food and drug regulations would have you believe that it is in the interest of the consumer, history shows that the Progressives had other motives.

Dairy farmer Allgyer's modern situation exemplifies how the Pure Food and Drug Act is currently utilized. Following the legacy of the Progressive Era, the federal government has almost unlimited power to regulate what goods are made and consumed, regardless of whether they are actually harmful to the consumer. This completely undermines the freedom of both the producer and the consumer, and gives the federal government the power to make judgment calls on what we are allowed to eat and drink.

The actions of the modern FDA are not surprising, considering that the history of the Pure Food and Drug Act is rife with corruption and deception. One of the influential Progressives behind this Act was Harvey Washington Wiley, the chief chemist at the U.S. Department of Agriculture during much of the Progressive Era. He is affectionately known as the "father of the Pure Food and Drug Act" and rightly so, as he was a consummate Nanny Stater. Although Wiley had been appointed commissioner of agriculture in 1883, it was not until Theodore Roosevelt came into office in 1901 that he was able to finally put his crazy ideas into action.

Wiley was a champion for food and drug regulation within the federal government. In his campaign for national food and drug regulation, he crusaded against adulterated foods and food additives.

In 1902, in an attempt to draw attention to his theories, Wiley conducted a "scientific" study to test food additives using a Poison Squad. This Poison Squad consisted of twelve healthy men who were used to test the effects of adulterated food by consuming large quantities of various food additives for five years. Unlike a typical scientific study, however, there was no control group. Therefore, he had no data with which to compare his results. Wiley was given five thousand dollars of taxpayer money to pay for this study. It is no coincidence that this waste of time and taxpayer funds was approved under Roosevelt's administration, just a year after he took office.

In another effort to bring attention to the "problem" of adulterated food, Wiley decided to join forces with the makers of straight whiskey, who wanted to knock out their competitors that produced watered-down whiskey, which was cheaper to produce and sell.[7] Wiley even tried to convince doctors to prescribe straight whiskey as medication. Although he had no proof, Wiley manipulated the public into believing that watered-down whiskey was deleterious to their health and that only pure whiskey was safe to drink.

Several food industries supported Wiley, and he attempted to ban their competitors by using his theories about adulterated foods. For example, he attempted to pass legislation against foods such as margarine and glucose in order to please the dairy and sugar industries' lobbyists.[8]

Wiley promoted a federal ban on food additives only after his friend Henry John Heinz was able to find a way to make ketchup without additives. Wiley's connections to big business were the driving force behind his alleged health regulations. He put off his own agenda until his friend would be exempt and left Heinz with a virtual monopoly.[9]

Thanks to the efforts of Wiley, Roosevelt, and muckraking journalists such as the Socialist writer Upton Sinclair, the Pure Food and Drug Act of 1906 was passed. Roosevelt had even personally pleaded with Congress to pass the Act, stating, "I recommend that a law be enacted to regulate interstate commerce in misbranded and adulterated food, drinks, and drugs. . . . Traffic in foodstuffs which have been debased or adulterated so as to injure health or to deceive purchasers should be forbidden."

This act prohibited "poisonous" or "deleterious" food and drug additives, adulterants, and unsanitary manufacturing processes in food and drug factories. Theodore Roosevelt signed the Act, which was accompanied by a budget of three million dollars.[10]

The Pure Food and Drug Act's constitutionality was upheld in the 1911 Supreme Court case *Hipolite Egg Co. v. U.S.* under Congress's power to regulate interstate commerce. In this case, fifty cans of preserved whole eggs were seized because they contained boric acid, a "deleterious" ingredient. Boric acid is actually no more toxic than table salt.[11] These eggs were purchased by a baking company and shipped across state lines so that they could be stored and then used as an ingredient in baking goods. Therefore, these eggs were not even actually for sale to consumers in interstate commerce. Yet the Court still upheld the Pure Food and Drug Act.

After the Pure Food and Drug Act was enacted in 1906 and upheld in the *Hipolite Egg* case, Wiley gained the political and legal power to back his biased and unsupported claims. For example, the Pure Food and Drug Act was used to prosecute ketchup manufacturers, as illustrated in the 1914 Supreme Court case *United States v. Two Hundred Cases of Adulterated Tomato Catsup*.[12] In this case, two hundred cases of ketchup were seized by the government for being "decomposed and adulterated." This conviction was upheld, although the Court admits there was no proof that the ketchup would have been detrimental to the health of the consumer.[13]

This case also relates back to Wiley's relationship with Heinz, a manufacturer who was able to produce ketchup without additives. This is an example of corrupt government agencies picking winners and losers in the market. This was purely regulation for the sake of federal control and power. In practice, there was actually little concern over consumer health.

Wiley also had a legal vehicle to attack Coca-Cola for its use of caffeine. He simultaneously argued that caffeine was still acceptable in coffee and tea, which actually contained higher levels of caffeine than Coca-Cola. Wiley's crusade against the caffeine in Coca-Cola is almost inexplicable, because despite his desperate attempts to prove the harmful effects of Coca-Cola, he continuously failed to prove that this soft drink was unhealthy. He even expressed paranoid and delusional concerns to a friend that Coca-Cola's use of caffeine would lead to caffeine being added to milk, bread, and meat in order to make them more popular.[14]

Wiley's crusade eventually led to the 1916 Supreme Court case *U.S. v. Forty Barrels and Twenty Kegs of Coca-Cola*.[15] Acting under Wiley's direction, the federal government seized the barrels and kegs of Coca-Cola and charged that the product violated the Pure Food and Drug Act because it was misbranded and contained the added ingredient of caffeine.

Chief Justice Hughes described in the opinion, "[T]he allegation of adulteration was, in substance, that the product contained an added poisonous or added deleterious ingredient, caffeine, which might render the product injurious to health."[16] Another allegation was that Coca-Cola did not contain enough "coca" and very little "cola"; therefore, the name was misleading.

It is clear that caffeine is not a poisonous ingredient and that it is necessary to remove parts of the coca plant in order to avoid adding cocaine, an illegal substance. Caffeine was not illegal, and there was absolutely no evidence that any consumer had been harmed by consuming it. These allegations had no merit, and yet the government's behavior in this case took it to the Supreme Court of the United States.

Wiley was hoping that this case would bring publicity to his cause and, even if he did not win the case, the bad publicity and legal fees would harm the company.[17] This case ended up being a circus, with Wiley and the government on one side, and the powerful Coca-Cola Company on the other. Wiley's plan to destroy the Coca-Cola Company was unsuccessful and actually backfired against him. Coca-Cola was able to tarnish his reputation in court. Coca-Cola subsequently negotiated a settlement with the government which permitted it to continue to use caffeine in Coke.

President Theodore Roosevelt knew that Wiley's opinions and crusades were ridiculous. Roosevelt stated of Wiley,

> The trouble with Doctor Wiley is that to my personal knowledge he has been guilty of such grave errors of judgment in matters of such great importance as to make it quite impossible to accept his say-so in a matter without a very uneasy feeling that I may be doing far-reaching harm to worse than no purpose.[18]

Wiley even admitted in his autobiography that Roosevelt "never had a very good opinion of me."[19] Yet this crackpot was able to influence legislation that dictated what people could eat and drink and forced businesses to conform to regulations that were based on his largely unscientific theories. Roosevelt acknowledged that "Dr. Wiley was of the utmost service in creating sentiment that secured the passage of the act."[20]

This campaign illustrates Progressive Era politics. Increased governmental regulation was portrayed to the public as necessary for their health. Yet the statute was arbitrarily enforced and was used to punish certain companies and industries. Meanwhile, industries that were friendly to the government benefitted. Citizens and consumers had nothing to do with all of this political maneuvering.

Sinclair and *The Jungle*

Upton Sinclair is often lauded as a hero of the working class. His 1906 novel, *The Jungle*, portrayed the allegedly horrendous conditions of the meat-packing industry in Chicago during the Progressive Era. According to popular legend, Theodore Roosevelt was so horrified by Sinclair's tales that he immediately sent out his own team of investigators, comprised of Labor Commissioner Charles P. Neill and social worker James Bronson Reynolds, to corroborate these stories. Roosevelt then led the crusade for a change in working conditions, which culminated in the Pure Food and Drug Act and the Federal Meat Inspection Acts of 1906. In reality, Roosevelt did not even release the report that Neill and Reynolds gave him because it did not corroborate Sinclair's fictional account.

Both Roosevelt and Sinclair are portrayed as heroes in these stories, men who dared to stand up for the common man and against big business. However, similar to Harvey Washington Wiley, Sinclair had his own agenda. Yet his novel, along with Wiley's theories, was used to justify regulation that increased governmental control over the food industry.

Upton Sinclair was actually a struggling fiction author. He was unsuccessful in his early career and became increasingly frustrated with the literary world. He complained of this rejection in a "letter to the world," stating, "You may sneer . . . but you will live to blush for that sneer."[21] Sinclair was determined to become a successful author and he wanted anyone and everyone who had rejected him to regret it.

He also had little tolerance for working-class people. While writing a Civil War novel, Sinclair moved to Princeton, New Jersey, where he complained of his neighbors that "the families . . . contained drunkards, degenerates, mental or physical defectives, semi-idiots, victims of tuberculosis or venereal disease and now and then a petty criminal."[22]

During this time of rejection, he turned to socialism, becoming friends with influential Socialists such as writer Jack London and clergyman and proponent of the Social Gospel George Herron. He began working for the Socialist weekly magazine *Appeal to Reason*, whose publisher sent him to Chicago to conduct an exposé of the meat-packing industry. The product of this assignment was his infamous fiction, *The Jungle*.

The Jungle was the perfect storm for a dramatic man who simultaneously craved a successful career as an author and a crusader. Although his original intention was to focus on the terrible working conditions, the public was more intrigued by the quality of the meat that was being produced at these factories.[23] Among the more horrifying depictions in the book, Sinclair described rats and workers falling into rendering tanks and being ground up with the meat, which was eventually sold. He produced no evidence that these events actually took place.

Six publishers turned down Sinclair. A consultant at Macmillan Publishing wrote, "I advise without hesitation and unreservedly against the publication of this book which is gloom and horror unrelieved. One feels that what is at the bottom of his fierceness is not nearly so much desire to help the poor as hatred of the rich."[24]

Nevertheless, Doubleday realized how profitable his sensationalism could become and published *The Jungle*. In its first year the book sold nearly 150,000 copies, and Sinclair received $30,000 in royalties.

Although Roosevelt is often portrayed as quickly jumping on the bandwagon, he actually despised Sinclair and rightly believed that his book was mostly fabrication. He stated, "I have an utter contempt for him. He is hysterical, unbalanced, and untruthful. Three-fourths of the things he said were absolute falsehoods. For some of the remainder there was only a basis of truth."[25]

Yet Roosevelt capitalized on the public hysteria in order to promote the Pure Food and Drug Act and the Federal Meat Inspection Act of 1906. He realized that the public was upset by the novel and that supporting this legislation would increase his popularity and federal control of another industry.

Roosevelt also had an issue with the meat industry stemming from an event that took place during the Spanish-American War, in which Roosevelt was a lieutenant colonel of the First U.S. Volunteer Cavalry. The meat packers who unloaded their meat in Cuba warned that the meat needed to be kept on ice while it was transported to the soldiers. Their instructions were not followed, and the soldiers were fed spoiled meat. Roosevelt irrationally decided that the meat-packing industry was trying to poison American troops and developed a personal vendetta against it.[26]

Although the Progressives manipulated the public into believing that federal food regulation was necessary to life, the American food industry was actually becoming safer due to competition *before* the Pure Food and Drug Act was passed. Jim Powell, author of the Roosevelt exposé *Bully Boy*, stated, "Like the rest of American business, the food industry was intensely competitive, and the trend was toward more competition—a strong incentive to improve the quality of food and cut cost for consumers."[27]

The bigger companies were able to improve conditions in their factories. According to Robert L. Rabin, writing in the *Stanford Law Review*, "The large meat packers, well aware of the ill-will on all sides and cognizant of their comparative advantages over smaller competitors in complying with federal standards, did not fight comprehensive regulation."[28] The large packers wanted federal regulations to cripple their smaller competitors who could not afford to invest in newer facilities or technology.[29] The added cost of the meat inspections across the country would not be on the meat packers, but on the taxpayers. Therefore, although Roosevelt and Sinclair are lauded as heroes to the common man, their legislation only helped big companies, harmed small companies, and passed the cost of all of this onto the taxpayers and consumers.

The Theory of the Living Constitution

One way that the immense amount of federal regulatory agencies and administration was justified during the Progressive Era was the theory of the living Constitution. This theory sets out the idea that the Constitution has to be read and interpreted based on current developments and changes in societal conditions. According to David Dieteman, this theory purports that "the federal constitution means whatever it ought to mean at a given time. It necessarily follows from this that it will not mean the same thing at different times."[30]

This theory was developed during the Progressive Era. One of the most influential proponents of the living Constitution theory was President Woodrow Wilson. In his book *The New Freedom*, Wilson set out the theory that the Constitution should be interpreted in light of changing times and the theory of Darwinism.

He wrote, "All that progressives ask or desire is permission—in an era when 'development,' 'evolution,' is the scientific word—to interpret the Constitution according to the Darwinian principle."[31] This theory also allowed him to justify circumventing the traditional separation of powers in order to allow the government to become more responsive to the Progressive agenda.

This theory gave rise to the legal justification for federal agencies, something that was not accounted for in the Constitution. Theodore Roosevelt and Woodrow Wilson knew what they wanted to accomplish and found ways around Congress and the Constitution. They utilized this theory in order to justify their support of federal agencies, regulations, anti-trust laws, and labor reform. Much of the Progressive platform was recognized as unconstitutional during this time, yet Wilson and Roosevelt were able to manipulate Congress and the public by destroying traditional notions of constitutionality in order to change with the times.

This legacy can be seen in modern-day jurisprudence, as vast amounts of legislation today are passed by finding a way around the Constitution. For example, Congress has attempted to use the Commerce Clause to justify laws regarding domestic violence and personal use of medical marijuana and its spending power to regulate speed limits and alcohol use.

Giving the Federal Government Total Control

During the Progressive Era, in addition to regulating food and drugs through the Meat Inspection Act and the Pure Food and Drug Act, the federal government gained control over the economy through countless federal regulations. These were promulgated not by Congress but by the administrative agencies, like the FDA and the FTC (Federal Trade Commission), that Congress established.

In 1903, under President Theodore Roosevelt, the Department of Commerce and Labor was created. This department contained a Bureau of Corporations, which would investigate private corporations. Roosevelt stated, "I have always believed that it would be necessary to give the National Government complete power over the organization and capitalization of all business concerns engaged in inter-state commerce."[32]

During President Woodrow Wilson's administration, the Federal Trade Commission Act of 1914 empowered the Federal Trade Commission (FTC) to assist in the federal government's crusade against big business. The FTC regulated large corporations by issuing cease-and-desist orders to end "unfair trade practices." This once again gave way to corruption and put unelected members of the federal government in a position to pick winners and losers in the market. Together, Roosevelt and Wilson were attempting to gain complete control over the private sector of the economy.

The Interstate Commerce Act of 1887 was amended and enhanced through the Hepburn Act in 1906 and the Mann-Elkins Act in 1910. The Hepburn Act gave the Interstate Commerce Commission (ICC) the power to set maximum rates for railroads and extended the agency's authority to cover bridges, terminals, ferries, sleeping cars, express companies, and oil pipelines. The Mann-Elkins Act strengthened the ICC's authority over railroad rates and expanded its jurisdiction to include regulation of telephone, telegraph, and cable companies.

Roosevelt had no problem manipulating Congress into submitting to his will. In a law review article, Stanford Law School professor Robert L. Rabin explains, "It took vigorous intervention by Roosevelt to prevent Congress from including a judicial review provision that would have explicitly vested final authority over rates in the courts."[33] Roosevelt was power hungry, especially in regard to regulating the economy. Similarly, in 1916, Woodrow Wilson begged Congress to reorganize and enlarge the power of the ICC for purposes of "regulation, prevention, and administrative efficiency."[34]

These efforts represent Roosevelt's attempt to gain control over the railroad industry. However, according to Frostburg State University professor William L. Anderson, "Instead of independently 'regulating' the railroads, the ICC, which was staffed by people with ties to rail companies, worked hand in glove with the entities it was supposed to be overseeing."[35]

The results of Roosevelt's actions were higher prices, poor service, lost profits, and diminished competition. Clearly, these types of regulations were enacted not to protect the consumer, but to allow the federal government to take control of the free market. This was the beginning of a system of corrupt agencies that only benefitted people with political ties.

An Excess of Agencies

Pick an issue, any issue, no matter how small or insignificant, and—*poof!*— our [American] progressive government creates *ex nihilo* another government ancillary to appease the sheeple's concern that *something is being done* to address it.

—Ron Shirtz[36]

The Progressive Era also saw a rise in administrative agencies that were used to carry out all of these new regulations. Some of the agencies established during this time period include, in addition to the Food and Drug Administration (a product of the scheming of Roosevelt and Harvey Washington Wiley), the Interstate Commerce Commission, the National Civic Federation, an early version of the Federal Bureau of Investigation (FBI), the Federal Trade Commission, and the Internal Revenue Service.

Theodore Roosevelt and Woodrow Wilson were the driving forces behind many of these agencies. In addition to the Food and Drug Administration, Roosevelt expanded the power of the Interstate Commerce Commission and was the impetus behind the creation of the FBI. Wilson created the Federal Trade Commission in 1914 and necessitated the use of the Internal Revenue Service after the enactment of the Sixteenth Amendment during his administration in 1913.

These administrative agencies, along with countless others, "were the product of a political climate that was receptive to a variety of particularized complaints that the market needed to be policed with greater vigor."[37] Today, the government has [15] major departments and more than 450 supporting and independent agencies.[38] These same federal agencies regulate every aspect of our lives.

The agencies created during the Progressive Era have a long history of corruption and connections with big business and even criminals. For example, the FBI began as a force of special agents created in 1908 under President Theodore Roosevelt. The creation of this agency was controversial at the time because law enforcement was traditionally a function of state and local governments. However, Roosevelt could not resist having a federal police force within the Department of Justice to do his bidding. Although the federal government had used investigators in the past, they were only employed temporarily. Roosevelt felt he did not have enough control over this system. Even though Congress rejected his proposal for a national police force, Roosevelt ordered Attorney General Charles J. Bonaparte to use discretionary funds to create a force of federal agents to work in the Department of Justice.

As Llewellyn H. Rockwell, Jr. states, "Nothing in the Constitution permits the federal government to have its own police force. But the FBI claims the right to intervene in any local criminal issue, trumping the rights of state and local law enforcement."[39] Yet Roosevelt lobbied and manipulated Congress in order to get this measure passed. Roosevelt denounced his critics, stating, "There is no more foolish outcry than this against 'spies'; only criminals need fear our detectives."[40] His desperate need to develop an unconstitutional federal police force has led to shocking abuse of power and destruction of liberties by the FBI.

President Woodrow Wilson utilized the FBI during World War I in order to enforce the Espionage and Sedition Acts and the Selective Service Act. These Acts took away essential liberties such as freedom of speech and freedom of association. The Selective Service Act, which was directly prohibited by the Thirteenth Amendment, allowed a draft during the First World War, forcing young men to serve the U.S. government.

Wilson also utilized the FBI to investigate "enemy aliens" such as anarchists and Communists. Thousands of these "radicals" were arrested and some were even deported for disagreeing with the government, having radical views, or exercising freedom of speech.[41] Even in its earliest form, Wilson used the FBI to enforce national laws that were actively depriving citizens of their freedoms.

The FBI has also been entrenched in scandal and has gained increasing power to violate our civil liberties since its formation. As Tom Burghardt describes, "Like a vampire rising from its grave each night to feed on the privacy rights of Americans, the Federal Bureau of Investigation is moving forward with programs that drain the life blood from our constitutional liberties."[42]

For example, in the 1960s, the FBI launched into an investigation of Dr. Martin Luther King Jr., referring to him as the "most dangerous and effective Negro leader in the country."[43] The FBI spied on King, collected private information with which to blackmail him, and ended up with a file that contained seventeen thousand pages of information on his day-to-day activities.[44]

In June 2011, the FBI announced its new rules that would allow its agents greater leeway in administering lie detector tests and looking through the trash of people who are not even under investigation.[45] This means that the FBI authorized itself to search through an innocent person's trash. The goal is to gain information that could be used to coerce these people into becoming informants.

The FBI also uses a vast system of gaining information which allows its agents to obtain customer information from various companies, such as hotels and telephone service providers.[46] When the FBI gives itself powers not even vested by the Constitution in the federal government, it violates our civil liberties and uses taxpayer money to do it.

A recent report by the Electronic Frontier Foundation (EFF) showed that since the tragedy of September 11th 2001, the FBI has been responsible for at least 40,000 violations of the law.[47] Under the Patriot Act, the FBI has utilized more than 200,000 self-written search warrants known as national security letters in order to allow their agents to invade privacy rights without the permission of a judge. Like many other legacies of the Progressive Era and Theodore Roosevelt, the FBI exemplifies how the creation of federal agencies with immense power can lead to corruption and the destruction of our liberties.

The Non-Delegation Issue

The Progressive Era was the beginning of what has become known as an administrative state in America. The regulations and agencies created to carry them out allowed each branch of government to pass on its duties and powers to "experts" who are not democratically elected. This directly contradicts the Constitution, in which a non-delegation doctrine is implicit. According to Article I, Section I, of the Constitution, *"All* legislative Powers herein granted shall be vested in a Congress of the United States, which shall consist of a Senate and House of Representatives."[48] Congress may not delegate its lawmaking powers to another branch of government.

There is a reason for this. Members of Congress are elected and should be directly accountable to their constituents. This arrangement is supposedly the core of our political system. By passing along its power to administrative agencies and simply calling them regulations instead of laws, Congress is allowing unelected bureaucrats to do its job.

The power given to administrative agencies has been generally upheld by the Supreme Court, with very few exceptions. Today's general standard was set out in the 1928 Supreme Court case *J. W. Hampton, Jr. & Co. v. United States.*[49] This case challenged the constitutionality of the Tariff Act of 1922, which delegated the authority to set and impose customs duties on imported goods to the president. This Act also created the Tariff Commission to investigate and then advise the president on appropriate rates.

In that case it was held, "If Congress shall lay down by legislative act an intelligible principle to which the person or body authorized to fix such rates is directed to conform, such legislative action is not a forbidden delegation of legislative power." Seemingly, this delegation of power to the president and his commission skews the balance of powers set out in the Constitution. However, the Court validated this delegation by setting out the extremely vague "intelligible principle" standard that is followed to this day.

This standard has been used to invalidate a delegation of power only twice, in *Panama Refining Co. v. Ryan* in 1935[50] and *A. L. A. Schechter Poultry Corp. v. United States* in 1936. In *Panama Refining Co.*, the Supreme Court invalidated a provision of the National Industrial Recovery Act of 1933 (NIRA), which allowed the president, through the secretary of the interior, to prohibit trade in petroleum goods in excess of state law or regulation. The Court struck down this provision as an unconstitutional delegation of power, as it did not provide sufficient guidelines and would "invest him [the president] with an uncontrolled legislative power."[51]

In *A. L. A. Schechter Poultry Corp.*, the Court invalidated another section of the NIRA which allowed the president to approve codes of fair competition.

This case specifically involved the Live Poultry Code, which set regulations for poultry slaughterhouses. These codes gave the president the power to regulate weekly hours, wages, and ages of employees.

Today the federal government is made up of countless regulatory agencies that control every aspect of society, from drugs to education to the environment. These agencies are given broad rule-making and decision-making powers, yet are in no way accountable to the people. An example of an agency that has taken on broad powers is the United States Sentencing Commission.

The constitutionality of the United States Sentencing Commission was challenged in the Supreme Court case of *Mistretta v. United States* (1989).[52] This case involved the constitutionality of the Sentencing Reform Act of 1984, which created the commission. This commission is an independent body within the judicial branch that has the power to set binding sentencing guidelines. Although the commission is technically a part of the judicial branch, commissioners are appointed by the president and approved by the Senate. The commission allegedly only creates guidelines, but these guidelines have the effect of laws. Judges who do not follow them can be overruled upon appeal.

Upon its creation, the United States Sentencing Commission upped the sentences for white-collar crimes such as anti-trust violations and imposed stricter control over the issuance of parole and imposition of fines.[53] Basically, the commission made "value judgments and policy assessments." These guidelines took away the traditional deference to the trial court judge in determining the details of a criminal's sentence, fines, and parole. The prior theory was that the trial judge has the best perspective on the case and is in the best position to make these decisions.

In December 1987, John Mistretta was indicted on three counts of selling cocaine. He was sentenced under the guidelines to eighteen months' imprisonment and a three-year term of supervised release. Mistretta charged that this commission violated the separation of powers and was delegated excessive authority in structuring these guidelines. The Supreme Court ruled that this was a valid exercise of legislative delegation.

However, Justice Scalia, in a lone dissent, articulated nicely the theory that Congress was excessively delegating its lawmaking powers to the executive branch, and expressed concern over the future implications of this decision. He stated, "Except in a few areas constitutionally committed to the Executive Branch, the basic policy decisions governing society are to be made by the Legislature. Our members of Congress could not, even if they wished, vote all the power to the President and [then] adjourn."[54]

According to Justice Scalia, Congress is abdicating its authority and diminishing its accountability to its constituents by allowing an independent body that is part of both the executive branch and the judicial branch to *make* laws. This also ignores the careful calculation and balance of powers that was established by our Founding Fathers when creating the Constitution. Justice Scalia states that recent separation-of-powers jurisprudence regards the Constitution "as though it were no more than a generalized prescription that the functions of the branches should not be commingled."[55]

The *Mistretta* case represents the immense development of power of administrative agencies since the Progressive Era. Although since 2005 the Supreme Court has lessened the impact of these guidelines by allowing judges to deviate from the minimum sentencing guidelines, this commission still exists. In *Mistretta*, the Supreme Court of the United States allowed an independent, unelected commission comprised of seven people to determine something as grave as prison sentences.

Another example of a modern regulatory agency that has accumulated an excessive amount of power is the Environmental Protection Agency (EPA). The EPA releases countless regulations, many of which serve little purpose but to burden hardworking Americans. In 2011, the EPA actually went so far as to enact regulations that Congress declined to enact. These regulations were the Ozone National Ambient Air Quality Standards, which proposed rules regulating emissions of mercury, greenhouse gases, and other pollutants.

President Barack Obama was forced to direct the EPA to withdraw these standards because they unduly burdened small businesses. Even Pennsylvania's Department of Environment Protection secretary Mike Krancer, a member of the Pennsylvania Ozone Transport Commission, cast doubt on the necessity of these regulations, stating,

> The standard would have created needless regulatory uncertainty in the business world and was not supported by the best science. If EPA is so far out of scientific step in this rule that the president had to step in, it raises questions about other EPA rules, proposed rules and positions.[56]

This is just another example of how the regulatory state in America has grown to the point that these administrative agencies are completely bypassing the legislative process. Thanks to Progressives such as Theodore Roosevelt and Woodrow Wilson, we are now living under a system where the president is forced to step in to stop a regulatory agency from promulgating regulations that Congress refused to enact.

Conclusion

Today, it seems that there is no limit to what the federal government may control. Although the Constitution of the United States granted specific powers to each branch of the federal government, this changed radically during the Progressive Era. Theodore Roosevelt and Woodrow Wilson set the standard for finding ways around the Constitution in order to claim more power for the federal government and themselves. Their ways have been manifested in the massive amount of federal regulation and federal agencies that we have today.

One effect of finding ways to get around the Constitution is diminished accountability and loss of freedom. You may be sentenced to jail or denied probation based on the guidelines set out by a group of experts that you did not elect, have your garbage searched by a federal agent without a warrant, or be punished for attempting to sell unpasteurized milk to those who want it.

The Progressives have left us with a huge federal government with almost unlimited power and reach into our daily lives, including our minds and our bodies. Next we will see how the micro-managers got into our bank accounts.

Chapter 4

The Government's Printing Press

The Federal Reserve

You already have under consideration a bill for the reform of our system of banking and currency, for which the country waits with impatience, as for something fundamental to its whole business life and necessary to set credit free from arbitrary and artificial restraints. I need not say how earnestly I hope for its early enactment into law. I take leave to beg that the whole energy and attention of the Senate be concentrated upon it till the matter is successfully disposed of. And yet I feel that the request is not needed—that the Members of that great House need no urging in this service to the country.

—WOODROW WILSON, STATE OF THE UNION ADDRESS, 1913[1]

The Story

In the dark of the night, undercover, a cast of characters largely unknown today met in secret on Jekyll Island, Georgia, in November 1910. This all-male group included Senator Nelson W. Aldrich, the Senate Republican whip; Abraham Piatt Andrews, the assistant secretary of the Treasury; Frank A. Vanderlip, the president of National City Bank of New York (now Citibank), who represented John D. Rockefeller as well as the international investing house of Kuhn, Loeb & Company; Henry P. Davidson, a senior partner of J. P. Morgan Company; Benjamin Strong, the head of J. P. Morgan's Bankers Trust Company; and Paul M. Warburg, a partner in Kuhn, Loeb & Company, who as well represented the financial titans, the Rothschild family. These men represented one-quarter of the entire world's wealth in 1910.

These bankers and politicians were meeting in secret because if the truth of their rendezvous were exposed to the world, their master plan would certainly be defeated. In a quest for global dominance, these few men conspired with one another to form an otherwise illegal cartel through a partnership of government and banking. They traveled under cover of darkness, donning disguises and using fake names. They rode in Senator Aldrich's personal train car. It was attached to a train running from Hoboken, New Jersey, to Jekyll Island, Georgia, once all other passengers were aboard the train so that no one knew of their presence. At the other end it was detached the same way.

No one but these few men could know where they were going or even who they were. They needed to maintain this incredible secrecy because they knew that the organization they would eventually set up and have blessed by the government was to become a dominating force in the world not only financially but also politically. The plans were drafted for the implementation of a third central bank in America; this one, unlike its predecessors, destined to last more than a generation.

These men, in their quest for power and money, would now solidify what had failed twice before, a central bank in America. The Federal Reserve Bank is the tool by which banks make great profits and America can exert its dominance as a global power. But the bank's money is legally counterfeited and stolen.

As they did with every ill-fated Progressive Era reform, both Theodore Roosevelt and Woodrow Wilson championed the creation of a central bank in the United States and fully supported the corporate leaders who met secretly at Jekyll Island. Theodore Roosevelt stated, "[T]here exists an imperative need for prompt legislation for the improvement of our national currency system," and "The issue of currency is fundamentally a governmental function."[2]

As president, Wilson fiercely lobbied for the passage of the Federal Reserve Act. Speaking to Congress in June of 1913, Wilson opined, "It is absolutely imperative that we should give the business men of this country a banking and currency system by means of which they can make use of the freedom of enterprise and of individual initiative which we are about to bestow upon them."[3]

How Money Developed

Money is power in a capitalist system, both for banks and for government. If the two forces could combine, each would reap benefits from the other. Yet money is not a simple concept to understand. Its development has taken millennia, and we are increasingly in a complex system of paper money, computer digits, and exotic financial instruments. The complexity of the system veils the inner workings of the financial industry and, more important, the utter lunacy of the partnership that the industry shares with the government. The government can steal our wealth through inflation, which is caused by the Federal Reserve and our banking system, all while the banks reap huge profits and retain customers.

We must trace the origins of money itself in order to understand the vastness of this financial quagmire, and its unhappy and untimely birth during the Progressive Era.

Bartering was the most primitive form of human trade. In a system of bartering one person trades a good or service in exchange for another's good or service. If you imagine that I am a farmer and you are a landscaper, we would each agree to trade services directly. I might deliver you food if you mow my lawn; no money is exchanged. As the size of a society grew, bartering quickly became ineffective as a means of trading goods and services.

Commodity money developed next. A commodity is something that people can agree to trade because it has inherent value. There are many instances of commodity money throughout history. For example, jewels, metals, and even cigarettes have been used.[4]

In the typical case, commodity money is something that is not only valuable but is also durable. The ability to last throughout time makes a commodity trusted and an easily recognizable medium of exchange. One only need consider that gold from ancient times still exists in its shining glory today to understand how useful a commodity becomes when it is consistent and lasting.

For these and many other reasons, gold has been, and continues to be, the premier form of commodity money. Gold has been recognized by humans as having inherent value for thousands of years. The reasons why we love gold so much is a question I will not be addressing in this book; yet it is sufficient to say that for thousands of years humanity has agreed that gold is valuable and worth something just by being gold. Do you know anyone who doesn't like gold?

In an economy where money is a commodity that has inherent value, the goods or services are paid for with the commodity. Using our example from before, I may agree to sell you food for one ounce of gold. You may agree to mow my lawn for one-quarter of an ounce. The free market determines the true price one can charge for a good or service. Therefore, if you are an exceptional landscaper and people value your services, you may be able to charge someone more gold than a landscaper of lesser quality. The main point is that when using commodity money, rather than trading the actual services or goods with one another, we agree to use some other medium of exchange; in our example, not paper money, but gold.

Once people deal in commodities, another system known as *receipt money* quickly dominates the financial markets. With receipt money, rather than trading the actual commodity, we agree to trade a piece of paper, a receipt that carries the value of that commodity because the receipt can be exchanged for the commodity at any time.

Once commodity money was used, it was natural to want to protect that commodity; in our case, gold. Metal workers such as goldsmiths or white-smiths stored large amounts of valuable metals in their vaults as a necessity of their business. Thus, these artisans provided a safe and secure place for one to store commodity money. These artisans began storing other people's commodities, such as gold, in their vaults for a fee. One would deposit commodity money into the artisan's vault and receive a receipt, also called a note. The receipt allowed the depositor to go back at any time and withdraw the gold from the vault.

People quickly trusted this system of receipt money and traded the notes as though they were the commodities. They understood that at any time they could take the note to the storage vault and receive the commodities that the note represented. Using our example, you could simply give me a note that allowed me to go to your bank and pull out the amount of gold you "paid" me for the food I sold to you.

Eventually, a system of banking developed called *fractional reserve banking*. Those who stored the commodity, in our continuing example, the gold, realized that most of the time the commodity laid unused in their vaults. The owners of these vaults started lending those dormant commodities to other customers. Thus, at any time in the vaults there was only a small fraction of the commodities compared to the notes that people were trading. The owners of the vaults were becoming bankers, and they could do this because there was rarely a time when people demanded all their commodities—their gold—from the vaults in sufficient quantities for anyone to notice what the lenders were doing. The banks transferred the gold to other customers in return for interest payments on the loan, thereby creating a profit for the banks; profit that was derived from using someone else's stored commodity.

The banks devised clever accounting tactics to handle this system. The money someone deposited for the banks to hold was counted as an asset. An asset represents something that the banks *own*. In our example, where you are a landscaper, the tools and equipment that you own and operate to run your business would be your assets. Banks also then lend out their assets, which are really your monies, to someone else and count it as a liability. A liability represents a debt that the banks *owe*.

In our example, a liability in your landscaping business would be a loan you take out to finance the purchase of a new piece of machinery. By counting the money you deposit as an asset, and lending it to someone else and counting the loan as a liability on their books, the bankers' books appeared balanced. The banks derived profits from the interest payments on loans, their liabilities, which were made with their assets, which were the money of their depositors. They did this while keeping only a small fraction of the overall commodities (gold) in their vaults.

In this system of banking, the incentive is to loan as much money as possible. The more money a bank can loan, the more interest it will receive and the more profits can be generated. This is termed *leverage*, meaning how highly one party, the bank, uses someone else's money, in the form of debt, to generate profit. Banks that hold more money in the vault than a competitor are losing opportunities for profit compared to their competitor, but are in a much safer position and better able to weather a financial downturn should depositors wish to have their gold.

It was not until a lender of last resort was established that banks were free to make insanely risky loans. Before that time, banks had to consider carefully the banking industry, the potential lender, and how highly they could leverage themselves without going out of business.

Today the Federal Reserve, as the lender of last resort, takes care of this concern and allows banks to make loans that are riskier than they would otherwise be able to make.

The important effect of fractional reserve banking is in how it grows or shrinks the money supply.* In fractional reserve banking, banks accept deposits, lend out nearly all of that money, derive income from the interest on these loans, and then lend the interest to others. The cycle repeats itself many times over, each time generating new money and therefore increasing the money supply.

This is true since whatever amount of money the bank has been given is used to generate more money in the form of interest, but there is no new commodity to back that interest. The interest, therefore, is money from thin air. At this point in the story people have become comfortable trading in paper notes, receipt money, but the commodity money really exists only in small quantities in bank vaults. If everyone who possessed a receipt note were to cash in his or her receipt money, it would quickly become apparent that the actual amount of receipt money in circulation far exceeds the amount of commodity money in the banks. However, since the commodity money ultimately backs the money supply, even if only by a small amount, there is still a limit on how much the receipt money can exceed the commodity money. What is truly occurring is that the value of each note is decreasing, but the banks are gathering a greater share of the overall wealth through the interest collected by lending other people's money.

The final development in our money system is fiat money. This is what we use today. Fiat money is money that in and of itself has nothing backing it. After President Nixon destroyed the gold-exchange standard by unilaterally abrogating both a treaty and the innumerable contracts and agreements the federal government had in place to exchange gold for cash, there was no longer any commodity backing American dollars.

---

* *Money supply* is the amount of money in an economic system. I use *money* here loosely. Incredibly, today there is no agreed-upon definition of just what constitutes money. In the complex system of credit cards, loans, stocks, bonds, swaps, and all other types of financial instruments it is difficult to even say what money is anymore. For the purposes of this book, when I use *money* from here on without qualifying it (such as commodity money or receipt money), think of the term as you would in everyday life, and the principles that I highlight will make sense.

In fact, the Treasury stopped issuing American currency; the Federal Reserve now issues it. If you look in your wallet, you will see printed on any denomination of currency "Federal Reserve Note" on top (unless you have an old dollar which was issued by the U.S. Treasury). Through the magic of the Mandrake Mechanism, which is essentially a method by which the Federal Reserve creates money out of thin air, the Federal Reserve buys government debt and turns it into currency. There is no gold, just debt. This method was named after a 1940s comic book character, Mandrake the Magician, whose specialty was creating things out of nothing and then making them disappear again. This is basically the same way the Fed creates and distributes money, by creating money out of nothing and getting it paid back in interest. It may be shocking to hear, but all of our money is literally debt. If we were to pay back all our debts, there would literally be no money; there would be no dollars.

The process is quite complex and more smoke and mirrors than anything else. Here's how it works: First, the Treasury issues a Treasury note to the Federal Reserve. This note is a promise to pay money at some future date. Then, at the Federal Reserve, the note becomes a securities asset. This security is a promise made by the government to pay the Federal Reserve, and it is backed by the "full faith and credit" of the U.S. government, meaning our tax dollars.

The Federal Reserve, now having a securities asset, creates for itself a liability by issuing a Federal Reserve check to the U.S. government. However, there is nothing to back this liability because the Federal Reserve is issuing a check to the government which itself promises to pay back the money it lent to the Federal Reserve. No commodity was deposited. The only backing at this point is the full faith and credit of the United States, our tax dollars. So, because the government promises to generate tax revenue and pay the Federal Reserve the money it owes to the Fed, the Federal Reserve gives a check to the government. As we will see, this is complete nonsense because the latter steps of the Mandrake Mechanism result in the creation of dollars in the first place. Literally, the Federal Reserve is creating money from nothing. You and I cannot legally do this, but the Federal Reserve, a private bank, can.

The government now endorses this check and sends it to one of the Federal Reserve banks throughout the country where it becomes a government deposit. This deposit is then used to pay government expenses in the form of government checks; those off-green ubiquitous checks bearing the image of Lady Liberty that all of us have seen.

These government checks create our fiat money. Recipients of these checks deposit them into their own banks. The banks then have commercial bank deposits.

Now, the banks use these deposits as assets within the fractional reserve banking system and lend out most of the deposits, thereby creating a liability. The money kept in the vaults (although often just computers today) is called the bank reserves. The Federal Reserve sets the amount of reserves the banks must maintain; currently it is only 10 percent. This means that a bank can lend up to 90 percent of its assets! This is made possible by the system of fractional reserve banking discussed previously.

The deposits that the banks do not have to hold as reserves are called *excess reserves* and are lent out to earn interest as loans. Those loans are made to you, me, companies, governments, other banks, anyone and everyone. We then pay other people, and they then deposit the money into their banks. Those banks then hold the 10 percent of the money deposited and lend out the other 90 percent. Through the Federal Reserve and fractional banking, nine times as many dollars are created than initially authorized! Those initial dollars were simply exchanges between the Federal Reserve and the Treasury; no tangible asset backs any of this, purely debt.

The reason to create such an elaborate system is for inflation. Inflation is the increase in money supply, and it is simply a tax on the American people perpetrated by the government and the Federal Reserve. Since there is nothing backing any of our money other than the government's debt, the government is free to keep conducting this smoke-and-mirrors show as long, and as many times, as it wishes.

Most Americans have no idea that this is occurring; all they see are prices rising. In reality, it is not prices rising but a loss of purchasing power that is happening. The goods that could be purchased with one dollar only a year ago cannot be bought for one dollar today. Thus, while people like to talk in terms of prices rising, it is in actuality the decreasing dollar, because of the government increasing the money supply, which is the problem.

All of this is to prove that the government is paying its expenses through creating money and inflating the currency using the Federal Reserve as its tool for accomplishing this goal. I say that this inflation is a tax because the government is extracting wealth from its citizens through inflation.

In my example above, one dollar cannot buy the same amount of goods from one year to the next because the money supply grows. But the money supply grows when the government issues debt to the Federal Reserve. It uses the Mandrake Mechanism to create new money that it uses to pay its bills. Therefore, the money supply is inflated, and we lose purchasing power because the government is paying its bills with money it otherwise did not have.

Thus, when all is tallied, the amount of purchasing power you and I lose to inflation is literally the amount spent by the government! Taxes are unpopular, and for this reason the government pays its debts through inflation and theft of our wealth. Both taxation and inflation constitute theft.

One final consequence of this whole system is the boom-bust cycles that are created through this financial magic show. Just as the amount of dollars increases through fractional reserve banking, so too does it vanish when banks hoard money. By recalling debts and not lending money back out, banks are dramatically reducing the money supply in America. Just as inputting new money into the system leads to a growth of over ten times the amount initially injected, hoarding reduces the money supply by the same ten-times proportion. When this happens—and it does so when the banks need cash—it fuels the fire of a declining economy.

Why the Banks Want the Fed

Fortunately for the cartelists, a solution to this vexing problem lay at hand. Monopoly could be put over in the name of opposition to monopoly! In that way, using the rhetoric beloved by Americans, the form of the political economy could be maintained, while the content could be totally reversed.

—MURRAY N. ROTHBARD[5]

We speak of America as a free market and a haven for capitalism. While it might be viewed that way in comparison to other countries in the world, nothing could be farther from the truth in the banking industry, and the men on

Jekyll Island knew that. It is rarely spoken about today, but the system of the Federal Reserve was carefully crafted by big–business leaders and politicians working together during the Progressive Era. Two of these politicians were Theodore Roosevelt and Woodrow Wilson. Speaking to Congress in 1913, Wilson pleaded for the creation of a central bank, stating, "It is perfectly clear that it is our duty to supply the new banking and currency system the country needs, and it will need it immediately more than it has ever needed it before."[6]

One-quarter of the world's wealth was represented in 1910 on Jekyll Island. These men, who understood everything we have discussed in the foregoing pages of this chapter, were not meeting to discuss how the government could get *out* of their way. Quite the opposite. The men were meeting for the explicit purpose of getting the government *in* their way.

The big banks on Wall Street did not reject the formation of the Federal Reserve. The Federal Reserve is a central banking system that exists for the profit of the big banks and the convenience of the government of this country. Without the Federal Reserve, this country would have a much fairer banking system that is open to free-market competition benefitting people who had money to save rather than benefitting Wall Street.

At the dawn of the twentieth century, Wall Street was losing power in the banking industry. Powerhouses like J. P. Morgan and the Rockefellers were losing significant market share to the new banks arising in the West. By 1913, 71 percent of the banks in the country were non-national and held 57 percent of all assets in the banking industry.[7] Wall Street was bleeding power and money. Wall Street needed the government to help it to devise a way to capture the market once more and put an end to these smaller banks.

To answer their quandaries, they devised the Federal Reserve. It is a rights-violating, property-stealing, unconstitutional cartel that is sponsored by the government, which is the only thing which makes it legal. The stated purpose of anti-trust statutes such as the Sherman Act, the Clayton Act, and the Federal Trade Commission Act is to place limitations on how companies can do business so that the free-market economy is protected. These laws imposed civil and criminal sanctions on anyone trying to end-run the free market.

The big banks on Wall Street, however, had been trying to do this for some time. To effectuate this cartel, bankers would serve on "competitors'" boards, they would have significant holdings of their "competitors," and they had largely agreed not to compete with one another. Thus, Wall Street in the early 1900s was really one giant bank, with different divisions. While these banks were quite effective at conducting a banking cartel, it was far from certain that they could survive certain market failures. Then the Panic of 1907 happened.

The Panic of 1907 was set off by many factors, but most important in terms of this discussion was the run on the banks, and the men at Jekyll Island understood this. As discussed earlier, in a system of fractional reserve banking the banks hold in reserve only a small fraction of their deposits and lend the rest. Thus, when depositors lost faith in the banks in 1907, they demanded their money from the banks. Due to these heavy bank runs, the Wall Street cartel barely survived the panic.

This was to be the spark of inspiration that led the banks to realize their current organization was not a guarantee of continued existence. For perpetual dominance in the financial industry they needed the government. As happened so often during this era, the banks welcomed regulation and traded some power and profits in the short term for what would ultimately become a massive engine for profit.

In response to the Panic of 1907, President Theodore Roosevelt signed into law the bill creating the National Monetary Commission in 1908, which was led by Senator Nelson Aldrich. This commission accomplished nothing and wasted $300,000 of public funds doing it. However, this type of government support gave Aldrich and his cronies the impetus and funding that took them to Jekyll Island.

The trick for the bankers and Wall Street was that they could not openly support the creation of a central bank. These bankers needed the public to believe that the movement toward a more "elastic" system of banking was coming from the "people." Therefore, they created a fake grassroots movement. This movement was strategically centered in the Midwest, the heart of America. Rather than just bankers, they also recruited businessmen, economists, intellectuals, and academics to provide much-needed legitimacy to their cause. This push for a grassroots movement was realized after cunning political maneuvering by Hugh Henry Hanna, president of the Atlas Engine Works of Indianapolis. His enthusiastic encouragement for the midwestern states to take charge of the reform movement started publicly with the Indianapolis Monetary Convention in 1897.

Although this convention was meant to bring grassroots legitimacy to the monetary reform movement, the executive committee empowered to act for the convention that was created could not have been further from grassroots. This committee consisted of a number of corporate and financial leaders. One was Henry C. Payne, president of the Morgan-controlled Wisconsin Telephone Company. Payne also had a strong relationship with Theodore Roosevelt. Roosevelt appointed Payne postmaster general of the United States when he became president after McKinley's assassination.

Another powerful member of the committee, also a Morgan man, was George Foster Peabody. Peabody was appointed secretary of the Treasury during Wilson's administration. All the members of the committee had similar ties to banking, corporations and trusts, and powerful government officials. As we can see, Theodore Roosevelt and Woodrow Wilson had close ties with many of the bankers and businessmen involved in the creation of the Federal Reserve. Many of these men just happened to be appointed to high-level positions in the federal government by these two presidents.

Although the initial committee was able to convince President McKinley to urge Congress to appoint a monetary commission, this proposal died in the Senate. Unwilling to accept defeat, the Indianapolis Monetary Convention appointed new members to another Indianapolis Monetary Commission. This commission consisted of attorneys, bankers, railroad directors, businessmen, cotton manufacturers, and academics. With $50,000 raised by their rich and powerful supporters, this commission worked to sell the public on the necessity of monetary reform.

This effort included putting together a questionnaire compiled of "expert" recommendations, all of which happened to support the need for banking reform, which would just happen to benefit Wall Street, bankers, and corporate America. This report was published in academic journals and newspapers. As was typical of the Progressives, they were attempting to use their control of academics and the media to convince the public that monetary reform was not only necessary, but was also an idea that began with the people. Luckily for the Progressives, the academics were eager to become involved in this scheme, for "[t]hese intellectuals needed the State to license, restrict, and cartelize their occupations, so as to raise the incomes for the fortunate people already in these fields."[8]

This initial round of public relations campaigns led to a second Indianapolis Monetary Convention in 1898, which produced a final report from the convention that explicitly called for a central bank. Despite the mobilization of the banking reform movement, it would be several years before a central bank would officially be established. However, as we can see, the seeds were planted within the banking community, which worked together with politicians and big business for years prior to the creation of the Federal Reserve.

In 1906, Jacob H. Schiff, head of the investment bank of Kuhn, Loeb & Company, spoke to the New York Chamber of Commerce and suggested that a committee on finance was needed to draw up a plan for a new banking system. This commission consisted of two Rockefeller men, two Morgan men, and one man from Kuhn, Loeb. Their suggestion: A central bank under the control of the government. After all of this political maneuvering, and after the Panic of 1907, bankers and business leaders finally had the motivation, support, and momentum to launch a central bank. The men who gathered at Jekyll Island were not a random group, but the result of all this conspiring.

Thus, Congress enacted the Federal Reserve Act of 1913. Politicians have their own reasons for wanting the Federal Reserve, but for banks it essentially comes down to the existence of a lender of last resort. Many have hailed this feature from time to time as a means for providing stability to our markets, but it is merely a means to effectuate a cartel. When the big banks are about to fail, the Federal Reserve flushes them full of cash, inflating the money supply and allowing the banks to pay back their loans with our stolen wealth. By inflating the money supply, the banks can pay back their loans with cheaper dollars than before, and we as the taxpayers finance this action through the hidden tax of inflation.

Additionally, banks want inflation because it lets them maintain their business. Before the Federal Reserve came into existence, 70 percent of corporate financing was generated internally and without the banks.[9] This meant that corporations were largely free from needing banks, and through lost business and opportunities, the banks were suffering.

However, if the banks, through fractional reserve banking and the Federal Reserve, can inflate the money supply according to their own policies, then they can induce businesses to take loans from the banks at low interest rates. Therefore, once the Federal Reserve was established, it was more beneficial for businesses to borrow money from the banks than it was for the corporations to generate the funding internally. Thus, the banks, through the Federal Reserve, were able to capture business that they were otherwise losing in the early 1900s.

The Federal Reserve also sets the rules so that all the banks can conduct business according to the same basic terms. When running a cartel, there is inevitably a problem of cheating. If everyone works together, then everyone makes maximum profits. However, if a partner in the cartel decides to cheat on the cartel, even a little bit, that partner stands to make more money than his fellow members of the cartel.

Thus, cartels always break down eventually, *unless they are made lawful*. By making a cartel lawful, it is then regulated. In so doing, the governmental regulators serve as the enforcer of the cartel agreement. For banking, this is accomplished through the Federal Reserve. By setting the reserve ratio, interest rates, and other factors, the Federal Reserve is the policing agent for the cartel. Essentially, this quasi-governmental agency is forcing all the banks to compete on the same terms, which is exactly why the Federal Reserve was conceived.

The banks needed regulated "competition" because they had repeatedly witnessed the specter of currency drains. A currency drain occurs when the demand for money exceeds the reserves a bank holds, but this occurs *between banks*, not due to a bank run. In 1910, a currency drain was the most common reason for a bank to declare bankruptcy.[10] Most banks would lend out 90 percent of their deposits in the form of loans and generate profits from the interest. Yet some adopted a practice called loaning up, which really meant driving down their reserves. In this practice some loaned as much as 99 percent of deposits, leaving only 1 percent in reserve.[11]

When people write checks to one another, the banks then settle the exchange of assets between themselves to honor the checks. This is typically not an issue so long as the banks have close to the same demand made of each other. Yet when a bank loans up, it will typically have more checks written against it than it receives because so much of the deposits have been loaned out to customers.

Too many people writing checks can quickly mean the bankruptcy of a bank by draining the entire reserve the bank has kept. Therefore, the banking industry needed the Federal Reserve to counteract currency drains. So long as all the banks were *forced* to have a minimum reserve, they all could loan up to that level without any increased liability due to a currency drain. This is the major policing action that the Federal Reserve serves for the cartel. By the Fed establishing the rules by which all banks must conduct business, they all stand to make the maximum amount of profit without becoming liable to a currency drain.

Thus, it stands that the banks only want to "compete" so long as they can compete on the same terms as all other banks. Highlighting this truth is the famous quotation by John D. Rockefeller, who said, "Competition is a sin."[12] Of course, to Rockefeller the sin was other industry players being able to compete in the marketplace and therefore enticing business, as had been occurring before the Federal Reserve was established.

The result of this entire scheme is higher profit for the big banks. When everyone competes on the same terms, the banks do not need to worry about cheating on one another. Thus, they can maximize their profits and not worry about anyone cheating on the cartel. These banks can also enter into incredibly risky bets. Since the Federal Reserve is the lender of last resort, there is always someone to foot the bill. However, as we have seen, the Federal Reserve, as the lender of last resort, generates money through government debt, which is in reality a tax on you and me.

When the Federal Reserve is in charge of setting all this policy in the first place, and since it is not beholden to Congress, and since it cannot be audited, the banks can lean heavily on the policy makers at the Federal Reserve to get sweetheart deals.

The Revolutionary War brought the return of fiat money in America. Between 1775 and 1779 the money supply expanded 5,000 percent.[13] The new currencies issued were paper Continentals, and the phrase "not worth a Continental" arises from this period. The inflation was so wildly out of control that George Washington wrote, "[A] wagon load of money will scarcely purchase a wagon load of provisions."[14] The Founding Fathers discovered firsthand the disastrous effects of fiat money on an economy. Thus, in the Constitution they gave only the federal government the power to "coin Money, regulate the Value thereof, and of foreign Coin, and fix the Standard of Weights and Measures."[15] This phrase for most of our early history meant literally *coining* money, meaning the ability to make *coins* from gold and silver. However, the advent of the Civil War and the immense power wielded by Abraham Lincoln would change everything.

A series of cases before the Supreme Court known as the *Legal Tender Cases* gave rise to the constitutionality of fiat money in America. The Union during the Civil War had almost no money. If all the coin in the entire Union were transferred to the government, that money would support the Union only three months.[16] Thus, the Union needed a source of funding where none existed.

During Abraham Lincoln's administration, the government began to issue greenbacks. These notes were initially redeemable for gold. Once it became apparent that the government would never be able to pay that debt, the bills were stamped with the phrase "This Note Is Legal Tender." This change meant that now the bills *must* be accepted as payment of debt. Samuel P. Chase was the secretary of the Treasury then, and he supported this move. Yet later, as Chief Justice of the Supreme Court, he would rule that the money was unconstitutional.[17]

In 1860, Mrs. Hepburn and Mr. Griswold had entered into a contract in which Mrs. Hepburn agreed to pay Mr. Griswold $11,250. At the time, *money* was gold on deposit. Subsequently, the government began issuing greenbacks. The greenbacks, as discussed above, were then made lawful money. However, at the time of forming their contract, neither Hepburn nor Griswold could have contemplated payment in greenbacks, as they did not exist. The issue came to court because Mr. Griswold refused to accept payment of the contract in greenbacks. Greenbacks were worth significantly less than the same dollar amount in either gold or silver. Mr. Griswold sued Mrs. Hepburn for breach of contract, contending that she had not tendered payment.

In the Supreme Court's opinion, Chief Justice Chase noted a few first principles which guided his decision. He noted that paper money is never on par with coin unless it is redeemable for coin, that increasing the quantity of notes decreases the purchasing power of each note, and that no force of law could change these two basic economic principles. He wrote for the Court that the power to "coin money" is constitutional but that it is not a grant of power to create fiat money as the government had done.

The government argued that the power to coin money was a grant of power, but that through the Necessary and Proper Clause, it also had the ability to issue greenbacks and deem them lawful money. The Necessary and Proper Clause has been understood to recognize implied powers in the Constitution.[18] Where the Constitution explicitly states a power of Congress, the Necessary and Proper Clause is understood to grant those powers to Congress which are necessary and proper to implement that explicit power. Yet Chief Justice Chase held that paper money is not "necessary and proper" to effectuate any grant of power the government has in the Constitution, including the power to coin money, regulate the value thereof, declare war, borrow money, or regulate commerce, and he warned that if it were held as such, then almost all limitations on the government would be removed.

He ended his opinion by saying that in times of war, policies and laws are made in the emergency of the times, but after a return to peace, this law cannot stand because it is unconstitutional.

One year later, after President Grant appointed two new justices and one justice from the previous year retired, the new majority on the Court turned this reasoning upside down. In two cases decided by the Supreme Court that year (*Knox v. Lee* and *Parker v. Davis*, both decided in 1871),[19] the Court ruled that Congress has the power to make paper notes legal tender that citizens must accept in payment of debt.[20] Since then we have been dealing in paper money.

In justifying these opinions, the Court ruled that the powers granted in the Constitution, when looked at in the aggregate, are a grant of power beyond those powers that are expressly granted or impliedly granted. This distinction is important because up until this point the Court understood powers to be either expressed or implied. However, the Court here recognized the existence of powers that are not expressed and cannot rationally or credibly be said to be necessary and proper and are therefore not implied powers. This means that the Court recognized powers that have no foundation in the Constitution.

Fourteen years after the initial rulings, after paper money had depreciated, been redeemed, and withdrawn, the Court ruled that the government can reissue previously redeemed currency and that such paper money being legal tender must be accepted for payment.[21] Ever since that time we have been using paper money. Unlike today, the paper money used then was still at least partially backed by gold or silver. It would take until 1971 to abandon this commodity backing completely.

Thus, the stage was set for the Federal Reserve to come into existence. It was only a matter of time until central banking was again proposed in America.* Once the government realized the potential of central banking within a system of fiat money and fractional reserve banking, it proved to be a temptation too sweet to resist.

Woodrow Wilson wrote in a letter to Ralph Pulitzer in 1913,

> The influences which are working against it [the creation of a central bank] . . . are very subtle and very powerful, and this is our opportunity to prove that we [have] the knowledge and the ability to set the business of the country free from the forces which have too long controlled it.[22]

Wilson really wanted to have the system of currency and banking under the control of the federal government, with big-business leaders at the helm behind the scenes. There is no way that this new system would set anything "free."

Big Government needs tremendous amounts of money. However, the normal mode of financing Big Government, taxation, is incredibly unpopular. Politicians have partnered with the banks through the Federal Reserve to inflate the money supply and, in so doing, steal our wealth. This is vexing considering one of the Federal Reserve's mandates is to control inflation. Yet we have seen the purchasing power of the dollar destroyed.

Since the establishment of the Federal Reserve, the purchasing power of the dollar has fallen by 90 percent.[23] With inflation of the money supply the purchasing power of every individual dollar is driven down. The government increases the money supply through the Mandrake Mechanism as discussed earlier, as well as through other tools the Federal Reserve has at its disposal. Therefore, by inflating the money, the government can extract wealth from you and me to spend on whatever it pleases.

If one doubts this, consider the fact that since the Federal Reserve came into existence, inflation has increased by 1,000 percent. Even Alan Greenspan, who would later become the Federal Reserve chairman, wrote in 1966:

---

* The current Federal Reserve constitutes the government's fourth attempt at a central bank; this includes the Bank of North America established in Philadelphia before our independence was complete.

[T]he earnings saved by the productive members of the society lose value in terms of goods. When the economy's books are finally balanced, one finds that this loss in value represents the goods purchased by the government for welfare and other purposes. . . . In the absence of the gold standard, there is no way to protect savings from *confiscation* through inflation. . . . This is the shabby secret of the welfare statists' tirades against gold. Deficit spending is simply a scheme for the "hidden" *confiscation of wealth*.[24]

These words were true then and are true today. It is their author whose credibility has been destroyed.

The Rascals at Jekyll Island

American politics, from the turn of the twentieth century until World War II, can far better be comprehended by studying the interrelationship of major financial groupings than by studying the superficial and often sham struggles between Democrats and Republicans.

—MURRAY N. ROTHBARD[25]

Woodrow Wilson was elected to put the Federal Reserve into law. President Taft would not support the Federal Reserve; therefore, the banks needed to force him out of office. Despite Wilson's and Roosevelt's huge egos, these men were nothing but puppets to the financial elite. Using their money and influence, big bankers were able to fix the presidential election of 1912 in order finally to get the banking reform bill passed; the bill for which they had worked so hard. This election made it clear that the Progressives were neither Republicans nor Democrats. The Progressive Party advocated for statism and centralization of power in the federal government and formed an alliance between big business and the federal government to accomplish these goals.

Wilson had heavy connections with Wall Street insiders. Cleveland H. Dodge and Cyrus McCormick, directors of National City Bank, financially propped up Wilson. The two men made a point of advancing his career from his time at Princeton. Their support is the means by which Woodrow Wilson was able to leap from a relatively unknown academic, to the president of Princeton, to the governor of New Jersey, to the President of the United States in only ten years.

More important to the banks was not Wilson the man, but rather his views on the marketplace. He believed that the days of open competition were gone and that planned economies were the future. In order to drive out President Taft and put Wilson into office, J. P. Morgan's deputies, in conjunction with the other major Wall Street firms, convinced Teddy Roosevelt to run for the Republican ticket. When Roosevelt did not win the Republican Party's nomination, they convinced him to run on the Progressive Party ticket, knowing full well that Roosevelt's running for another party would split the Republican voting bloc and create a clear path to the White House for Woodrow Wilson. They were correct. The election of 1912 was completely contrived by the banking elites, specifically J. P. Morgan. This election was just the final part of a plan that started with the Indianapolis Monetary Convention in 1896.

Bankers wrote the bill, they supported the presidential candidate whom they wanted, and they got Wilson elected to office. He signed the Federal Reserve Act into law on December 23rd 1913 and immediately used the new bank to pump money into Europe to fund World War I. Ultimately, two things were achieved: Money for the bankers and power for the government. There is evidence that even Wilson himself knew that the passing of the Federal Reserve Act was a huge mistake. He is quoted as saying, "I have unwittingly ruined my country."[26] And although he clearly knew that he made a mistake, Wilson was lying when he used the word *unwittingly* because he knew exactly what he was doing.

Conclusion

Our economic liberty is inherently tied together with our civil liberties. It is inconsistent to proclaim that America is the land of the free while we fail to recognize economic liberties and instead have a government that steals our wealth by inflating the currency. The solution is simple; we must put an end to the Federal Reserve, at least in its current form. We must stop printing fake money with the grand illusion that we are generating wealth. We must demand of our politicians the recognition of their wayward policies.

When men and women have no real economic consequence to funding wars and subjecting the world to our policies, what is to stop the same men and women from diverting our society onto a path that we do not want to take? The power of the purse is the power of policy. Governments must have some ability to control money, as we have granted ours in the Constitution.

Yet our government has far exceeded its authority, and the Supreme Court has been complicit in the exchange. If we are to be a truly free nation, we deserve a currency that has real value, and we must be able to reap the fruits of our labor. Inflation is a hidden tax and a means for the political elite to extract our wealth for their own projects. The Federal Reserve allows them to do this. If we end the Fed, we regain our liberties.

All this accumulation of power to control money paralleled an accumulation of power that would destroy federalism. The Progressives who could by now regulate cash needed to subjugate the states.

Chapter 5

Destruction of Federalism

The Seventeenth Amendment

It is not by the consolidation or concentration of powers, but by their distribution that good government is effected.

—Thomas Jefferson[1]

In 1913, thanks to a fierce nationwide campaign led by the Progressive Party, the Seventeenth Amendment to the United States Constitution was ratified. This amendment took away the states' voice in the federal government by taking the power to elect senators away from the state governments. Concentration of power in the federal government was a goal of the Progressives, specifically Presidents Theodore Roosevelt and Woodrow Wilson.

Roosevelt and Wilson knew that the direct election of senators was an ideal way to concentrate power in the federal government, and therefore, they advocated strongly for this reform. As Theodore Roosevelt wrote, "[T]here is a constantly growing feeling also in favor of the election of United States senators by direct popular vote. . . . I believe the weight of conviction is on the side of those who elect the senators by popular vote."[2]

In 1912, Woodrow Wilson called for the direct election of senators in a campaign speech, stating,

> Returning to the original principles upon which we profess to stand, have the people of the United States not the right to see to it that every seat in the United States Senate represents the unbought influences of America? Does

the direct election of senators touch anything except the private control of seats in the Senate?[3]

The passing of the Seventeenth Amendment was an important aspect of the goal of concentration of power, because it destroyed the balance of powers between the states, the people, and the federal government that the Constitution had originally set out; and it prevented the states as states from blocking federal encroachments of their sovereignty.

The true nature of what the Progressives hoped to accomplish is made evident by Woodrow Wilson himself. He would speak of himself as a man acting in the interest of the people he represented, as though he was merely a benevolent servant rather than a power-hungry authoritarian academic who wanted to bend the country and the Constitution to his will. In the article "The People Need No Guardian" published in *The New Freedom*, Wilson proclaimed that the Founders were "willing to act for the people, but . . . not willing to act *through* the people. Now we propose to act for ourselves." As well, he would criticize Alexander Hamilton, who relied heavily on constitutional forms, otherwise termed *structures*, rather than rely on pure democracy and the people. Wilson would say of Hamilton that he was a "great man, but, in my judgment, not a great American."[4]

This point is further clarified when considering Wilson's view of the Constitution itself. He and his Progressive colleagues spoke of the Constitution as a *living* document and one that *evolves* with time rather than being the bedrock of immutable values. They believed that the Constitution should be interpreted as a "Darwinian" as opposed to a "Newtonian" instrument, meaning it evolved with the times rather than upheld established norms. Wilson argued that "living political constitutions must be Darwinian in structure and in practice. Society is a living organism and must obey the laws of Life . . . it must develop."[5] Such a belief erodes the very foundation and principles which the Constitution embodies. But that is exactly what the Progressives sought to do; and that is what they did.

When the Constitution is thought of in this manner, the meaning of the Constitution becomes whatever those who run the government say it is. Woodrow Wilson believed in this ideology. Here is Jonah Goldberg summarizing Wilson's views:

[A] more authentic form of leadership was needed: a great man who could serve both as the natural expression of the people's will and as a guide and master checking their darker impulses. The leader needed to be like a brain, which both regulates the body and depends on it for protection. To this end, the masses had to be subservient to the will of the leader. In his unintentionally chilling 1890 essay, *Leaders of Men*, Wilson explained that the "true leader" uses the masses like "tools." He must not traffic in subtleties and nuance, as literary men do. Rather, he must speak to stir their passions, not their intellects. In short, he must be a skillful demagogue.[6]

Wilson continued, in his own words, in "Leaders of Men," to say that the masses

must get their ideas very absolutely put, and are much readier to receive a half truth which they can promptly understand than a whole truth which has too many sides to be seen all at once. The competent leader of men cares little for the internal niceties of other people's characters: he cares much—everything—for the external uses to which they may be put. . . . He supplies the power; others supply only the materials upon which that power operates . . . it is the power which dictates, dominates; the materials yield. Men are as clay in the hands of the consummate leader.[7]

Still, Wilson would go further and express his belief not of individualism and freedom but of the need for collectivism as he demonstrated time and again during his presidency. In the same essay he said,

[W]hile we are followers of Jefferson, there is one principle of Jefferson's which no longer can obtain in the practical politics of America. You know that it was Jefferson who said that the best government is that which does as little governing as possible. . . . *But that time is passed. America is not now and cannot in the future be a place for unrestricted individual enterprise.*[8]

Because many Progressives shared Wilson's views, the direct election of senators by the people of each state was not a new idea when the Seventeenth Amendment was sent to the states for ratification. The idea was first debated at the Constitutional Convention but voted down by a proportion of ten to one. The government that the Founding Fathers would establish was to be a constitutional federation of states. Therefore, the states needed to have a seat at the federal table. Through state legislatures selecting their U.S. senators, the states as states would be materially and consequentially involved in the federal government.

Direct election of senators was first introduced in 1826 by New York representative Henry Randolph Storr. However, the idea never gained serious traction until the early 1900s. Two senators were convicted on corruption charges in 1906, providing the needed spark for William Randolph Hearst to launch his campaign against the sovereignty of the states.

Hearst, then a representative from New York, had acquired *Cosmopolitan* magazine in 1905. To boost circulation of the magazine, he commissioned the popular novelist David Graham Phillips to write a series of investigative articles on corruption in the U.S. Senate. This work, published in *Cosmopolitan*, was entitled "Treason of the Senate."

Due to extreme sensationalism, known as *muckraking*, the magazine's circulation doubled in only two months. The Progressive Party had all the support it needed to push through the Seventeenth Amendment thanks largely to the magazine's igniting populist outrage at the supposed scandals in the Senate.

By 1913, the Progressives had successfully created a system where senators were directly elected by the people of their state. In doing so, states were removed from the federal table, and power was concentrated in Washington, D.C. The Progressives, specifically President Theodore Roosevelt and President Woodrow Wilson, are to blame for this disruption in the carefully crafted balance of powers that our Founding Fathers created.

The Senate had experienced its share of troubles since the founding of the country, but those troubles did not require a constitutional amendment to rectify. One such problem that plagued the Senate around the enactment of the Seventeenth Amendment was deadlocks in the state legislatures. When a state legislature could not agree on whom to send to Congress as its senator, then no senator would be sent. Such situations happened periodically. The most egregious example is that of Delaware. During three Congresses Delaware sent only one senator, and from 1901 through 1903, Delaware had no representation at all in the Senate.

These deadlocks were greatly exacerbated by the enactment of a law in 1866 governing the election of senators. Before 1866, when the election of a senator was contested, the Senate had the duty to resolve the conflict because under Article I, Section 5, of the Constitution, "Each House shall be the Judge of the Elections, Returns and Qualifications of its own Members." In 1866, the election of a New Jersey senator, John Stockton, came into question. It was this year that the Senate decided to enact a uniform system for all state legislatures to follow so that deadlocks and questions about election validity would be remedied. This law was to have the opposite effect.

The 1866 law established that each house of a state legislature independently must take a voice vote and on the next day convene in a joint assembly. If one person had been named senator by a *majority* of *each* house, then that person was the senator elected. If not,

> the joint assembly shall then proceed to choose, by a [voice vote] of each
> member present a person for the purpose aforesaid, and the person having
> a majority of all the votes of the said joint assembly, a majority of all the
> members elected to both houses being present and voting, shall be declared
> duly elected.[9]

This measure led to even greater problems, though. Through voice voting, an obstructionist minority could determine exactly how many members, and more important *which* members, needed to be swayed in order to thwart the election of a particular senator. Thus, deadlocks ensued in ever increasing numbers. From 1885 to 1912 there were seventy-one deadlocks in the state legislatures.[10]

Along with exaggerated tales of senator corruption, the inability of the state legislatures to select senators was used as the impetus for reform. Yet all that needed correcting was the 1866 law. Before that time, a majority of all the members of the state legislature was not needed to select a senator; therefore, it was easier to select a senator.

Additionally, when deadlocks occurred, it became more frequent to grease the wheels of senatorial politics with bribes. Before the 1866 law came into existence, there was only one case of bribery in the history of the Senate.

From 1866 through 1900 there were nine cases. There were an additional five cases from 1900 through 1912.[11] The correlation between deadlocks and bribery was clear. Despite the popular uprising crafted after the publishing of "Treason of the Senate" and the belief in rampant corruption in the Senate, corruption had been proven in only .013 percent of all elections to the Senate in the history of the United States. Given the correlation between the 1866 law and the rising number of deadlocks and corruption charges, it would make the most sense simply to amend the 1866 law, not the Constitution. Yet the Progressives wanted to change the Constitution, for it would centralize power in Washington, D.C., and remove the institutional and constitutional check that the states had on the federal government.

In the quest for reform, the Progressives ultimately were able to push through a constitutional amendment. However, it took a long road to get there. In 1907, Oregon was the first state effectively to craft a statute that allowed the direct election of its senators by the voters. Other states followed Oregon's lead, and before the Seventeenth Amendment was ratified, as many as twenty-nine states had enacted similar legislation. Twenty-seven of the required thirty-one states would petition for another Constitutional Convention to amend the Constitution if Congress declined or refused to propose an amendment for the direct election of senators.

The Senate had struck down every bill it was sent seeking to amend the Constitution for direct election of senators until this point. Yet faced with the incredible threats posed by opening up another Constitutional Convention, the senators finally succumbed to the populist desires. This is how the Seventeenth Amendment came to pass, through the states threatening to convince a few more to join their fight and possibly upending our entire constitutional system through another Constitutional Convention. The entire structure of the Constitution would in fact be upended, and this would be done singularly through the Seventeenth Amendment.

Progressives such as Woodrow Wilson and Theodore Roosevelt had no respect for the Constitution. This amendment did not give more power to the people, as the Progressives promised, but simply took power away from the states and concentrated it in the federal government. This amendment also did nothing to eliminate corruption. Corruption in the Senate is even worse today, as C. H. Hoebeke wrote:

Exorbitant expenditures, alliances with well-financed lobby groups . . . [have] continued to characterize Senate campaigns. . . . In fact, such tendencies have grown increasingly problematic. Insofar as the Senate also has participated in lavishing vast sums on federal projects of dubious value to the general welfare, and producing encyclopedic volumes of legislation that never will be read or understood by the great mass of Americans, it can hardly be the case that popular elections have strengthened the upper chamber's resistance to the advances of special interests.[12]

The Progressives Want Power

The story of the Seventeenth Amendment is the story of the most destructive movement to our Constitution we have ever known in this country. The Progressives, led by Roosevelt and Wilson, were determined to tear down the walls of federalism and bicameralism in the quest for "democracy." Yet democracy was hardly the goal which these men and their allies in hegemony sought to attain. Cleverly veiling their power-thirsty rhetoric in the guise of democracy and power for the people, these men pushed an amendment that would grow the federal government massively, while destroying the power of the states, in an effort to control the population.

To Wilson, and to the Progressives, the government rules everything, and as the heads of government, the Progressives would rule everything. They desired power and control of the entire nation. In their minds it was not up to individuals to chart their own paths through life and make their own decisions. It was the government's role, as Wilson so eloquently stated, through the president to *tell* the people how to live their lives. They were to be but "clay in the hands" of Woodrow Wilson.

However, Woodrow Wilson, Theodore Roosevelt, and the other Progressives ran into one sizeable problem with their ideology: The Constitution. The very structures which Alexander Hamilton and the other framers put in place, most important of which was the election of senators by the state legislatures, disallowed such an authoritarian system of government. Therefore, the only way to effectuate Progressive policies was to amend the Constitution and destroy its "absolute safeguard" against federal tyranny, thus, becoming the tyrants. Alexander Hamilton was not a great American, but Woodrow Wilson was an evil one.

The Constitution Is in the Way

The original form of the Constitution was carefully crafted by the Founding Fathers as a means to protect individual liberties. These liberties could come under attack from a minority, a majority, a state, or the federal government. They could be attacked by the executive branch, the legislative branch, or even the courts. The system itself must be a means of protecting liberty, for we cannot rely on the goodwill of politicians to protect the cause of liberty. As James Madison noted,

> [I]f men were angels, no government would be necessary. If angels were to govern men, neither external nor internal controls on government [i.e., a constitution] would be necessary. In framing a government which is to be administered by men over men, the great difficulty lies in this: you must first enable the government to control the governed; and in the next place oblige it to control itself. A dependence on the people is, no doubt, the primary control on the government; but experience has taught mankind the necessity of auxiliary precautions.[13]

Important constitutional forms were put in place to create not just a system of checks and balances, but also a system with constitutional walls erected against tyranny. The indirect election of senators, by state legislatures choosing them rather than the people voting them into office, existed to protect the sovereignty of the states and thus everyone's individual liberties as well as the minority against the majority.

Embodied in the idea of indirectly electing our senators are two important constitutional principles which we have lost with the adoption of the Seventeenth Amendment. Both federalism and bicameralism were important means to protect and defend liberty from tyrants like Wilson and Roosevelt. Yet these two men and their colleagues toppled those two great principles and replaced them with the tyranny of the majority and the unrivaled domination of the federal government.

Federalism

The idea of federalism is that of having coexisting sovereignties where both interact with one another and govern in their own particular sphere of power. Thus, the states governed state matters, and the federal government governed only those national matters as set forth in the Constitution; matters called federal. In order to protect federalism, constitutional forms were set in place by our Founding Fathers, most important of which was indirect election of senators.

As initially adopted, the Constitution granted a majority of the states the unfettered ability to check the federal government through the Senate. Although this was clearly set out in the Constitution, Wilson and the Progressives took it upon themselves to change the relationship between the federal government and the states. Wilson stated,

> The question of the relation of the States to the Federal Government is the cardinal question of our constitutional system. At every turn of our national development, we have been brought face to face with it, and no definition either of statesmen or of judges has ever quieted or decided it.[14]

By enacting the Seventeenth Amendment, Wilson clearly felt that it was his job to decide this issue by taking away the states' representation in the federal government and thus their sovereignty.

The idea behind the division of powers was to have three different representative bodies, each representing a constituency at the federal table. The Senate embodied the states as sovereigns. The House of Representatives represented the people as the people. The president represented the nation as a whole. The Founders saw to it that the states as sovereigns had equivalent power to the people as people.

The states, through their senators, had the ability to block every affirmative act of Congress. Through the requirement to pass a bill in both houses of Congress,[15] the Senate can stop a bill from becoming law even if the House of Representatives passes it. Through the Advise and Consent Clause,[16] the Senate must approve presidential appointees and judges, and ratify treaties. Finally, through the ability to try impeachments,[17] the Senate has the ability to hear the prosecution of a president if he oversteps his constitutional authority. The Senate, in reality meaning the states, had the power to stop the federal government from assuming too much power and did so for most of our early history.

Moreover, because the senators were beholden to the states that sent them to Congress, the senators were placed in a uniquely protected and simultaneously vulnerable position. They were protected from having to align with national special interest groups, the media, or their political party since their tenure in office stemmed *only* from pleasing the state legislature that had selected them. Therefore, if the senator pleased the state legislature, he was likely to remain in and be returned to office. Yet this also made the senators vulnerable because their votes would receive great scrutiny by other professional politicians desiring power for themselves in the state legislature. Ambitions of the states would curb ambitions of the federal government through the control the states could exert on their senators.

As well, being responsible solely to the state legislature meant that senators did not have to campaign and they did not have to worry about popular opinion. These two freedoms from the current political process were important. First, not having to campaign meant that a senator could concentrate his time on the legislation at hand and not on pleasing voters. This encouraged honest and deep deliberation at all times in the Senate. Second, not having to respond to the popular opinion meant that the senators did not have to bend to popular demand, as did the House of Representatives. This feature is immensely important because it meant that senators could quell upheaval created by a popular torrent. Cooler minds could prevail in the Senate and stop destructive legislation from passing in the heat of the moment.

However, a system where the states could check the actions of the federal government did not align with the beliefs of the Progressive Party. Roosevelt and Wilson took it upon themselves to expand greatly the power of the federal government. Under their administrations, the federal government gained power at the expense of the states and the people. As Roosevelt stated in 1911, the Progressives needed to "fearlessly champion a system of increased Governmental control, paying no heed to the cries of worthy people who denounce this as Socialistic."[18] The enactment of the Seventeenth Amendment was one of the most important triumphs among countless desperate attempts to claim as much power for themselves and the federal government as possible.

One only needs to consider whether under the system the Founders created the Patriot Act, Obamacare, or TARP would have passed in order to understand the power that states wielded in our earlier history. Today, thanks to Roosevelt and Wilson, we cannot even imagine what it would be like to have a system of government where the states' power equals that of the federal government; a system that the Founding Fathers intended us to have.

Bicameralism

The second constitutional form that was destroyed by the Seventeenth Amendment was bicameralism. While it is true that we still have two houses of Congress, we no longer have bicameralism in its intended form.

During the Constitutional Convention many proposals were put forth concerning the structure of the federal legislature. Famously, one of our Founding Fathers, Roger Sherman* of Connecticut, introduced what is now known as the Great Compromise, or the Connecticut Compromise, which allowed the large and small states to come to an agreement on the form of the federal legislature. The idea was simple. The House of Representatives, with each state receiving a proportionate number of representatives based on its population, would be elected by the people of the state and would therefore favor the large states. The Senate, with each state receiving an equal number of senators, would be chosen by the state legislatures and thus put the small states on par with the large states, respecting the sovereignty of all states. The consensus around structure allowed conversations at the convention to continue and ultimately our federal government to be formed.

---

*   Sherman was the only person who signed all four great state papers of the United States— the Continental Association, the Declaration of Independence, the Articles of Confederation, and the Constitution.

Splitting the legislature, aside from bringing about compromise among the states, was important because, as James Madison wrote in *Federalist* No. 51, "[i]n republican government, the legislative authority necessarily predominates." However, he continued,

> The remedy for this inconveniency is to divide the legislature into different branches; and to render them, by different modes of election and different principles of action, as little connected with each other as the nature of their common functions and their common dependence on the society will admit.

Further, Sherman, in affirming the view that the Senate was meant to be the states' check on the federal government, stated in a letter to John Adams that "[t]he senators, being . . . dependent on [state legislatures] for reelection, will be vigilant in supporting their rights against infringement by the legislative or executive of the United States."[19]

Support for this original reasoning was also declared by President Ronald Reagan in his first inaugural address where he stated,

> It is my intention to curb the size and influence of the Federal establishment and to demand recognition of the distinction between the powers granted to the Federal Government and those reserved to the States or to the people. All of us need to be reminded that the Federal Government did not create the States; the States created the Federal Government.

By recalling that the states created the federal government, President Reagan was emphasizing the role that the states should have at the federal table. This emphasis is particularly poignant when considering that President Reagan's intention to "curb the size and influence of the Federal establishment" is intrinsically linked to the powers "reserved to the States or to the people."

All this is important because of its implications for bicameralism. Bicameralism was the process by which a bill had to pass both houses of Congress to be sent to the president and become law. However, it was not only this process but what the process represented that was profound. Both houses of Congress approving a bill would mean that not only were the people's representatives in support of the bill, but the states were in support of the bill. Thus, a bill could become law only when there was a consensus between the federalism concerns of the states and the demands of the people.

In our current system, bicameralism exists only in that there are two houses of popularly elected representatives. As well, the minority of this country no longer has any checks on Congress other than the goodwill of the politicians. No structure in the legislative branch exists to stop the tyranny of the majority.

Our Current System

Our current system is a mere shadow of what it once was. The indirect election of senators was one of the most fundamental underpinnings of the Constitution, and almost one hundred years ago it was swept away, ushering in an era of unbelievable government growth and the attendant loss of liberty and property.

The principle of federalism, although gaining support in the Supreme Court over recent history, is no longer a serious constitutional principle. True, it was basic to the idea of even forming the Union, but it has since been abrogated by the Seventeenth Amendment. Now that the states have no place at the federal table, there is no longer any principle that the states and the federal government must work together in a system of federalism. Put simply, the federal government is all-powerful, and states have been effectively commandeered by the federal government.

Without the power of the states to vote in the Senate, the division of powers between the states and the federal government no longer exists. When the vestiges of our federal structure prohibit the federal government from enacting intrusive laws, the federal government simply bribes the states, forcing them to enact those laws in exchange for money.

A good example is the 1987 case of *South Dakota v. Dole*, where the State of South Dakota challenged the constitutionality of the National Minimum Drinking Age Act. This Act directed the secretary of the Treasury of the United States to withhold federal highway funds from states "in which the purchase or public possession . . . of any alcoholic beverage by a person who is less than twenty-one years of age is lawful." South Dakota contended that the Twenty-first Amendment to the Constitution prohibited Congress from legislating a national minimum drinking age; therefore, to withhold federal highway funds unless the drinking age is raised to twenty-one is an unconstitutional use of Congress's spending power.

The Spending Clause[20] gives Congress the power to "lay and collect Taxes, Duties, Imposts and Excises, to pay the Debts and provide for the common Defence and general Welfare of the United States." Thus, in order to "provide for the . . . general Welfare," Congress would withhold federal highway funds unless a state raised its minimum drinking age to twenty-one. This law was said to provide for the general welfare because "the lack of uniformity in the State's drinking ages created 'an incentive to drink and drive' because 'young persons [commute] to border States where the drinking age is lower.'"[21]

Ultimately, the Court held that "[e]ven if Congress might lack the power to impose a national minimum drinking age directly . . . that encouragement to state action found in [The National Minimum Drinking Age Act] is a valid use of the spending power."[22] In so doing the Court did not directly decide if the Twenty-first Amendment banned Congress from passing a national minimum drinking age. However, the Court did declare that the "'independent constitutional bar' limitation on the spending power is not, as [South Dakota] suggests, a prohibition on the indirect achievement of objectives which Congress is not empowered to achieve directly."

Rather, a constitutional bar to Congress conditioning funding laws it otherwise could not pass applies to "the unexceptional proposition that the power may not be used to induce the States to engage in activities that would *themselves* be unconstitutional."[23] Therefore, this case solidified the ability of Congress to pressure individual states into enacting its federal policy *even if the Congress itself cannot write such a law.* As an aside, which president signed this state sovereignty–assaulting legislation into law? Might it have been he who promised in his first inaugural address to curb the federal government's encroachments upon state sovereignty? It was Ronald Reagan.

While the minimum drinking age was quickly raised to twenty-one in most states with little opposition, it still stands that Congress wields enormous power over the states that would otherwise have required acquiescence of the states in the first place through the Senate. No one can know whether the states enacted the laws simply to keep their federal funding or whether they truly agreed with the legislation. Yet if the states were still represented in the Senate, such coercive powers as conditional grants of federal money would be unnecessary to effectuate laws and even impossible politically, as a threatening senator could be re-called home.

Yet this power over the states was the Progressives' goal. Senator Henry Cabot Lodge, a Republican from Massachusetts, expressed the desire to subdue the states through the passage of the Seventeenth Amendment. In the Sixty-first Congress he said,

> Self-preservation is the first law of governments as it is of nature and it seems to me that no matter how we should decide the question of the methods by which senators should be elected, the preservation of the power of the *United States* to control those elections, if need be, is essential to the [federal] Government's safe and continued existence.[24]

This is almost inconceivable considering the history of our country up until that point. The entire reason for the Senate and for indirect election was that it *could* arrest the government if the states so desired. If the federal government were attempting to encroach on the States' rights or individual liberties, it was perfectly foreseeable that the Senate would, as well as constitutionally and rightfully could, *stop* the federal government.

Self-preservation for an animal is natural, yet the federal government is not a body that can decide for itself that it is to exist at the detriment of the states and the people of this nation simply to protect itself. Some may say that since the amendment was passed, it was proper for the federal government to decide such matters. However, the amendment itself is unconstitutional, for it unraveled the very fabric of our Constitution. It did not simply remove a process; it removed the dominant framework and the entire theory behind our federation. Without indirect election of senators by the states there is no federalism.

Some men were brave enough to fight the Progressives. Senator Elihu Root gave a terrific speech about the evils of the Seventeenth Amendment should it be enacted. He said,

> Let me tell the gentlemen who are solicitous for the preservation of the sovereignty of their States that there is but one way in which they can preserve

that sovereignty, and that is by repudiating absolutely and forever the fundamental doctrine on which this resolution proceeds.[25]

Depriving state legislatures of the power to select senators would deprive them "of power, of dignity, of consequence," and the states would become "less and less competent, less and less worthy of trust, and less and less efficient in the performance of their duties. You can never develop competent and trusted bodies of public servants by expressing distrust of them, by taking [constitutionally granted] power away from them." He would continue to say that by adopting the Seventeenth Amendment, we would be doomed to "the cycle of concentration of power at the center [federal government] while the States dwindle into insignificance."[26]

Senator Root knew all too well exactly what was at stake, and his prediction has come true. We have witnessed the rapid expansion of not only the size but also the power of the federal government.

Representative Franklin Bartlett explained why the expansion would take place when, in 1894, he was speaking out against the direct election of senators. He stated,

[T]he Framers of the Constitution, were they present in this House today, would inevitably regard this resolution [the direct election of senators proposed in 1894] as a most direct blow at the doctrine of "State's" rights and at the integrity of the State sovereignties; for if you once deprive a State as a collective organism of all share in the General Government, you annihilate its federative importance.[27]

Thus, by enacting the Seventeenth Amendment, our country was denying the theory of federation that our Constitution was founded upon and giving all of such power to one authority, the federal government. In so doing the Progressives were able to concentrate most of the power in America in Washington, D.C., where they could wield that awesome power as they wished.

What is more shocking is that these two speeches were two of only three made in the entire volume of debate in Congress from 1826, when the first resolution for direct election of senators was introduced, until 1912, when the amendment was sent to the states.

Today

In the month of March most people are looking forward to the spring and enjoying the outdoors. Baseball's spring training is under way, and the fog of winter is lifting. Yet spring is not always so simple.

In the spring of 2012, Congress is getting ready to ram through legislation that neither the people of the United States nor the state legislatures want. However, beholden to their political party bosses, the congressmen and senators are conducting a delicate dance of managing public opinion and staying in office, all while cramming through legislation that no one wants.

But how can this be? How can a piece of legislation that is so unpopular be forced through? Politicians keep talking about their "political mandate" from the last election, but no one quite understands what that means in the face of such an unpopular bill.

States begin enacting laws that will be in direct conflict to this legislation. By creating these laws these states, if the bill becomes law, will be able to challenge the law in federal court. Clearly, these states are opposed to the bill, and they are making sure they have at least some manner of recourse in the courts.

The bill passes, and soon twenty-seven states are suing over the legislation.

This is not some fictitious story, though; it is the story of how Obamacare became law, and it is the story of the Progressives from almost one hundred years before, led by both Woodrow Wilson and Theodore Roosevelt. These Nanny Staters and their comrades were able to amend the Constitution and remove the states from the federal table. In so doing, they were able to empower the federal government to do what it wishes with little recourse from either the public or the states. Once enacted, the Seventeenth Amendment destroyed our idea of a federal constitutional republic and made the federal government a superpower in America.

Conclusion

What the Progressive Era has given us is a majoritarian rule with one massive government under a system reflecting only a shadow of our once great Constitution. The federal government is able to grow as it wishes and enact any law it desires. Woodrow Wilson, when he was president-elect and still governor of New Jersey, urged the New Jersey legislature to ratify the Seventeenth Amendment. Yet it is Alexander Hamilton whom Wilson branded a "great man, but . . . not a great American." For all of Alexander Hamilton's faults, he could not have conceived of such an abhorrent assault on freedom and our Constitution as the Progressives conjured up under the auspices of democracy all the while mimicking Lincoln's war-time and iconic phrase that the federal government is "of the people, by the people, for the people." It is not. It is of, by, and for *the Constitution*.

So we know the Progressives wanted power for the people, but they really wanted it for the "right" people. Next we shall look at the racist roots of Theodore and Woodrow.

Chapter 6

The "Lesser Races"

Racism and Eugenics

Someday we will realize that the prime duty of a good citizen of the right type is to leave his blood behind him in the world and that we have no business to perpetuate citizens of the wrong type.

—Theodore Roosevelt[1]

It's a normal afternoon in Atlanta, Georgia, but this afternoon is anything but normal for you. While strolling down the street leisurely, you run into an old childhood acquaintance, Mary. She's late for a meeting and does not have more than a moment to acknowledge your existence before dashing off to conquer the world of finance. She is stressed and does not appear to have slept well in quite some time. Yet you cannot help but wish that you had somewhere to run, a place where people depended on you, and a place where you felt important. Instead you are on your way to Planned Parenthood for another abortion.

At least you do not have to cover the full cost of the abortion because it is funded partially by the federal government. You think this to yourself because you have not had a job in months and have never been able to find steady employment. You feel like you are not made for the working world, but at least in the United States of America there is welfare to help support you.

So what would have been child number three is about to lose his or her life this afternoon. You think that you are out of options; there is just no way to raise and support a child in this world.

You are not aware that this is exactly what the Progressive Era politicians wanted. These mostly men and few women set up systems and administrations that were inspired by insidious racism and had one goal in mind: To control the "lesser races." Of course a member of a lesser race in their time meant little more than someone who was anything but a white Anglo-Saxon Protestant. If someone was unlucky enough to be Irish, Italian, Catholic, Slavic, Jewish, or black, or any other ethnicity, race, or religion, that person had the joy of incurring the wrath of "great" leaders like Theodore Roosevelt and Woodrow Wilson. These two historical tyrants despised black Americans more than any others. Unfortunately for you, their policies still apply today.

The Progressive Era had various policies designed to rid the world of, or at least control the population of, lesser races. (I obviously use the phrase "lesser races" with condemnation. It was the phrase of choice for the Progressives.) Some of these policies were meant to discourage a particular culture, to discourage childbirth for certain races, or even to change the way children are educated so that lesser races' small-mindedness would be replaced by the flourishing of Anglo-Saxon thinking.

Some of these policies were meant to murder children outright or even to sterilize the "unfit" so that their bloodlines would become extinct. Unfortunately for you in this scenario, welfare programs, minimum-wage laws, compulsory education, legalized abortion, contraception, and all the other benevolent-sounding programs have conspired to place you back at Planned Parenthood time and time again.

The policies and programs would take years to develop, but the intellectual arguments that led to such horrific administrations and systems actually took hold during the Progressive Era. Purely dominated by a misguided belief in the power of a master race, the Progressives set out to control the world because it was their God-given right; it was, to use a phrase the Progressives liked, "the white man's burden." The difference between Nazi Germany and American Progressivism when it comes to race is the pains with which politicians had to try and bend or remold the Constitution to implement such awful policies. The Germans were able to adopt these policies wholesale and to an extreme level. Ultimately, the Progressives sought the same general goal as the Nazis—a pure white race—but preferred to use subtler means to achieve their goals.

As we have seen, the two most important figures in the Progressive Era are Theodore Roosevelt and Woodrow Wilson; two American presidents who were uniform not only on their views of the role of the executive and America's place on the global stage, but also on race.

These two presidents ascribed to the popular theories of the day on the purity of Anglo-Saxons from Britain and the white man's burden. Such backward, baseless, and unnatural ideologies as these men held led to despicable laws and agencies designed to control the population and alter the reproductive habits of Americans.

Racist Twins

Theodore Roosevelt was a racist president. Before becoming president in 1902 he wrote an article in 1894 titled "National Life and Character." This article was a critique on a book written by Charles H. Pearson, which had recently been published, titled *National Life and Character: A Forecast*. This article reveals the level of racism embodied by Theodore Roosevelt.

According to Roosevelt, the white Anglo-Saxon Protestants were the epitome of humanity and, as such, rightly ruled the world. In order to understand where these beliefs came from, we must trace the intellectual theories of the day to which he and many elite members of American society were exposed.

Aryan tribes were thought to have risen in the Caucasus Mountains between modern-day Europe and Asia, and to have spread through the globe from that initial location. This is why today white people are termed *Caucasian*. Aryans who went north, south, or east purportedly lost the purity of their seed by mating with the natives, creating a new hybrid race of people that was part white and part native. It was thought that the initial infusion of white blood into these races was beneficial and elevated these groups of lesser people.

However, over time the amount of white blood would be so reduced that the end result was not a raising of the lower race but a lowering of the higher race. Yet, according to Roosevelt's theory, the Aryans who traveled west took great measures, through mass genocide of native peoples, to maintain the purity of their race.

From the Caucasus Mountains, the pure Aryans spread west to what is now Germany. Here they became the Teutons and were believed to have experimented with democracy. Thus began the long march of the Aryan descendants through history, which culminated in the founding of America's constitutional democracy. Woodrow Wilson would write in his scholarly work *The State: Elements of Historical and Practical Politics,*

> For purposes of widest comparison in tracing the development of government it would of course be desirable to include in a study of early society not only those Aryan and Semitic races which have played the chief parts in the history of the European world, but also every primitive tribe, whether Hottentot or Iroquois, Finn or Turk, of whose institutions and development we know anything at all. Such a world-wide survey would be necessary to any induction which should claim to trace government in all its forms to a common archetype. But, practically, no such sweeping together of incongruous savage usage and tradition is needed to construct a safe text from which to study the governments that have grown and come to full flower in the political world to which we belong. . . . *The main stocks of modern European forms of government are Aryan.* The institutional history of Semitic or Turanian peoples is hardly part of the history of European governments: it is only analogous to it in many of the earlier stages of development.[2]

Thus, the Wilsonian argument goes, European governments from which we derive were Aryan in origins. The great nation of America is an Aryan nation, according to Woodrow Wilson.

From Germany the Aryan bloodline came to Britain when the Teutons became the Anglo-Saxons. Finally, from Britain the Anglo-Saxons crossed the Atlantic Ocean and came to America. Wilson and Roosevelt believed that it was necessary to have followed the sun west to maintain purity. Only those who followed the sun would not be mongrelized by the native peoples, they thought.

With this bizarre theory in mind, Roosevelt wrote the article "National Life and Character" which exhibits his domestic and worldviews on the "lower races."

It was his contention that constitutional democracy derived from the

Teutons and culminated in the founding of America. Australia, too, would become a great nation. Together, these two major nations would secure for the white man, of Aryan descent, the privileges and honors of being the dominant race. America and Australia were important safeguards against lower races, in Roosevelt's mind, because in Africa, for example, there will be "white States, although even these States will surely contain large colored populations, always threatening to swamp the whites."[3]

Additionally, again in Africa, white men would not be able to colonize the tropics effectively "because of the ease with which [the Spaniard] drops to a lower ethnic level."[4] In summation of this thought, Theodore Roosevelt said, "Nineteenth century democracy needs no more complete vindication for its existence than the fact that it has kept for the white race the best portions of the new world's surface, temperate America and Australia."[5]

With these theories firmly engrained, Roosevelt set in motion his imperialistic conquests for America. Through the Spanish-American War, America won the Philippines, Guam, Puerto Rico, and Cuba. These territories, though, were occupied by lesser races, and according to Roosevelt, they did not deserve the same government as we had under our Constitution.

Many thought at the time of the Spanish-American War and its aftermath that the "Constitution follows the flag." Stated differently, wherever the federal government goes, so goes the Supreme Law of the Land that created, defined, and restrained the federal government, whether Memphis or Manila, Baltimore or Baghdad, Kennebunkport or Kabul. Under this theory the constitutional guarantees of law and the prohibitions on the government would apply equally to the territories which were ceded to America from Spain, as they do in the mainland of America.

Such a view is consistent with the Founders' ideology and view on the origin of our rights. The Founders ascribed to the theory of Natural Law, which holds that rights are derived not from government but by our very humanity and ultimately from the Creator of humanity, God. All humans desire freedom and have a right to be free. In understanding that this desire for freedom stems from our human nature, St. Thomas Aquinas directly contends that God is perfectly free, and since we are created in His image and likeness, our right to freedom is a divine right, not one from government. Freedom is our nature.

Thus, to the Founders it was "self-evident, that *all Men* are *created equal, that they are endowed by their Creator with certain unalienable Rights,* that among these are Life, Liberty, and the Pursuit of Happiness."[6] The Founders believed in these rights so much that "for the support of this Declaration [of Independence], *with a firm Reliance on the Protection of divine Providence,* we mutually pledge to each other our Lives, our Fortunes, and our sacred Honor."[7]

The Constitution was created to protect those "unalienable Rights." Since these "unalienable Rights" are God-given rights of all men, the Constitution must follow the flag. Thus, wherever the United States government goes, the Constitution restrains its interference with those rights.

The *Insular Cases* began in 1901 and dealt with the governance of newly acquired territories. For more than one hundred years before this time, the Northwest Ordinance had governed the addition of new lands to America. The Northwest Ordinance created the Northwest Territory west of the Ohio River and governed the relationship the United States would have with the territory and the persons living there. Under the Northwest Ordinance, Congress established territorial governments, and once certain population triggers were met, sections of the territory could apply for statehood. Thus, the federal government exercised territorial control over sections of land that were not then part of the United States, but these parcels of land were on a direct path to statehood. Yet the *Insular Cases* created the judicial theory of territorial incorporation.

Under this doctrine, if a territory is incorporated into the United States, the territory may be destined for statehood, and its occupants shall be treated as Americans are. However, if the territory is not yet incorporated into the United States, rights and guarantees which are not considered fundamental do not necessarily apply. A fundamental right is "one of the basic civil rights of man."[8] The Court in *Balzac v. Porto Rico* in 1922 summarized this, stating,

> The Constitution, however, contains grants of power, and limitations which in the nature of things are not always and everywhere applicable and the real issue in the Insular Cases was not whether the Constitution extended to the Philippines or Porto Rico when we went there, but which ones of its provisions were applicable by way of limitation upon

the exercise of executive and legislative power in dealing with new conditions and requirements. The guaranties of certain fundamental personal rights declared in the Constitution, as, for instance, that no person could be deprived of life, liberty, or property without due process of law, had from the beginning full application in the Philippines and Porto Rico.[9]

The Court, in the *Insular Cases*, established a distinction between particular constitutional rights and protections which it was free to interpret as "fundamental." So long as the Court determined that a right or protection was not "fundamental," the U.S. government did not need to concern itself with the provision. Through the creation of this distinction, America was able to become an imperialistic power and circumvent the Constitution.

In 1901, the Court in *Downes v. Bidwell* first decided that the Constitution did not apply in full force to territories that were not an "integral part" of the United States. The case was brought by Samuel Downes, who owned S. B. Downes & Company. The company imported oranges into New York from Puerto Rico and was forced to pay import duties on the oranges. Downes sued George R. Bidwell, who was then the U.S. customs inspector for New York. Downes contended that Puerto Rico, being a territory of the United States, was protected from this duty because under Article I, Section 8, of the Constitution "all Duties, Imposts, and Excises shall be uniform throughout the United States," and the duty on oranges did not exist elsewhere in the United States.

The Court states that the true issue in the case was

whether the particular tax in question was levied in such form as to cause it to be repugnant to the Constitution. This is to be resolved by answering the inquiry, Had Porto Rico, at the time of the passage of the act in question, been incorporated into and become an integral part of the United States?[10]

The Court resolved this question in holding that Puerto Rico had not been incorporated into the United States and was not an integral part of the United States. Therefore, many guaranties of the Constitution would not apply. After this case the U.S. government was capable of colonizing a foreign land while not adhering to or administering the Constitution, except according to those rights and protections that the Court determines are "fundamental."

However, the Court made this decision in a five to four split. Justice Horace Gray, who had voted with the majority, then retired. Theodore Roosevelt needed to know that American power over these areas would remain unchecked; therefore, his judicial appointee needed to share such views. Massachusetts senator Henry Cabot Lodge was influential in convincing Theodore Roosevelt to pick Oliver Wendell Holmes Jr. as his judicial appointee. In a series of letters between Roosevelt and Senator Lodge, his political advisor and best friend, the qualifications and political views of Justice Oliver Wendell Holmes were discussed.

In support of Holmes, Lodge wrote Roosevelt that he was "absolutely for Holmes unless he should be adverse on Porto Rican cases, which I am informed he is not."[11] The "Porto Rican cases" to which the men refer are the 1901 decisions of the *Insular Cases* and in particular the decision in *Downes v. Bidwell*. Additionally, Justice Gray, who was in the majority in *Downes* and who was retiring, agreed with Lodge that Holmes was an appropriate choice given the criteria.

Roosevelt and Holmes personally met in Oyster Bay on June 25th 1901 to discuss his appointment. It was in that meeting that Roosevelt finally decided to appoint Holmes. Upon hearing of the successful meeting, Lodge wrote to Roosevelt, "I felt sure that you would [be satisfied] for he is our kind right through."[12]

With the appointment of Justice Oliver Wendell Holmes Jr., Theodore Roosevelt was assured that his appointee would vote against this theory that the Constitution follows the flag; and Holmes repeatedly did so, securing American imperialism.

The marked incompatibility between these theories developed by the Court and the Natural Law and the plain meaning of the words of the Constitution becomes apparent when considering that, through the *Insular Cases*, the rights of the people living in Puerto Rico, Guam, and the Philippines were not those guaranteed by the whole Constitution for Americans living in the states but were instead a piecemeal set of rights applied to their unincorporated territories.

The *Insular Cases* were decided between 1901 and 1905 and created an entirely extra-constitutional judicial fiat which allowed our republican form of constitutional government to act as a monarch over lands that were either conquered or gifted through treaty. The idea that these territories can be governed without the government recognizing even the most basic protections of our Constitution is an untenable result largely grounded in the racial theories of the times; racial theories ardently promulgated by Wilson and Roosevelt.

When America was expanding to these territories, many policy makers were forthright about their racial views. Senator Albert Beveridge, a Republican from Indiana, exclaimed,

> God has not been preparing the English-speaking and Teutonic peoples for a thousand years for nothing but vain and idle self-contemplation and self-admiration. No! . . . He has made us adept in government that we may administer government among the savage servile peoples.[13]

Senator Beveridge was also the keynote speaker at the Progressive Party's convention, which nominated Roosevelt for president in 1912. No surprise here.

Roosevelt would comment on Puerto Rico, saying,

> We have not been frightened or misled into giving to the people of [Puerto Rico] a form of government unsuitable to them. While providing that the people should govern themselves as far as possible we have not hesitated . . . to keep the power of shaping their destiny.[14]

In relation to the Philippines he said, "[W]e have acted up to the highest standard that has yet been set at marking the proper way in which a powerful and advanced nation should treat a weaker people."[15]

Yet it is entirely unclear how America treats these colonies over time. Puerto Rico is still not a state, while Hawaii was granted that status in 1959. The Philippines are now an independent nation. Through the *Insular Cases* and later cases, such things as indictment by a grand jury, a trial by jury, and women's suffrage in the Nineteenth Amendment have been held inapplicable to these territories because they were not considered "fundamental rights."

This is completely against the tradition of our Constitution. The Founding Fathers sought to protect fundamental rights and enshrine those rights in our Constitution.

Somehow, Roosevelt, Wilson, Congress, and the Supreme Court have been able to pervert the ideas in our Constitution and turn America into an imperial power not unlike that against which we revolted when we fought the Revolutionary War.

Most troubling are the racial underpinnings of the *Insular Cases* and the entire federal government working to turn off the Constitution when it wished. The Court in *Downes v. Bidwell*, discussed previously, summed it up when stating:

> It is obvious that in the annexation of outlying and distant possessions grave questions will arise from the differences of race, habits, laws and customs of the people, and from the differences of soil, climate and production, which may require action on the part of Congress that would be quite unnecessary in the annexation of contiguous territory inhabited only by people of the same race or by scattered bodies of native Indians.[16]

People today criticize these decisions as being unconstitutional and standing on faulty logic. At the time, as discussed above, there was general acceptance of a racial theory that put white men above all other races. Thus, as Roosevelt said many times, it was the white man's burden to rule over the lower races. Constitutional democracy was a method of government that white men had supposedly been experimenting with for thousands of years, tracing back to the Teutons. Accordingly, these lower races, Roosevelt believed, such as inhabitants of Puerto Rico, were thought not to have the capacity for self-government. The idea of a liberal democracy, as we have in America, and colonization of other people were thought to be consistent with one another.

But we know today that such theories are wholly inconsistent. A constitutional democracy cannot proclaim freedom for its people while colonizing foreign lands. The decisions in these *Insular Cases*, while repugnant and unconstitutional when first decided, are even more offensive to our idea of constitutional democracy than ever before. These cases are still subsisting law today, despite the racism which served as their bedrock.

Roosevelt's racial policies had dramatic effects on the world that far surpassed the colonization of Puerto Rico, Guam, and the Philippines. He executed secret treaties with foreign nations without any consent of Congress, and they were animated by racism.

In 1905, Roosevelt negotiated the end of the Russo-Japanese War through the Portsmouth Peace Treaty. He even won the Nobel Peace Prize for his efforts. However, Roosevelt fooled more than the Nobel Committee as he was secretly executing a treaty with Japan in order to conquer China. Roosevelt believed that the Chinese were a declining race. As a weak people, the Chinese should make way for a stronger nation to occupy their land.

Roosevelt believed America and Britain should be those stronger nations to take over areas of China. The Japanese were to take over Korea, and America and Britain would take over northern China. The two nations would walk over the Asian continent hand in hand when the time came for China finally to fall.

Roosevelt was wrong in his assessment of the Japanese. He believed that they were an ascending race and would willingly take only Korea as payment for American involvement, and that they had the ability, for the first time, to take on some of the white man's burden.

When World War II was raging, the Japanese attacked Pearl Harbor in furtherance of their desire to expand into Asia. The attack on Pearl Harbor was not so that the Japanese could fight the United States; it was to stop America from intervening in Japanese expansion. The Japanese decided it would be better for Asians to rule Asia than for America to rule Asia. The attack on Pearl Harbor was to destroy America's Pacific Fleet, thus securing the Japanese ability to wage war in the Pacific and Asia without American interference.

Theodore Roosevelt's distant cousin, Franklin Delano Roosevelt, would enter World War II in order to rectify this failed foreign policy and additionally battle the Nazis. FDR repeatedly announced that he would not send American men into any foreign war, but that was exactly what he wanted. However, 88 percent of Americans opposed intervention. Therefore, FDR, believing it was in America's interest to enter World War II, devised a plan along with the navy's top brass to goad Japan into striking the first blow, thereby rallying the public behind America's entry to World War II. By doing so, FDR assured himself the ability to wage war against Japan, but more important, against Germany.

On October 7th 1940, fourteen months to the day before the attacks on Pearl Harbor, Lieutenant Commander Arthur McCollum of the Office of Naval Intelligence submitted a memorandum known as the McCollum memo to his superiors. This was ten days after the governments of Germany, Italy, and Japan signed the Tripartite Pact allying themselves to one another.

The Pact provided the connection between Germany and Japan that FDR needed to engage in the European war. If the Japanese attacked, and they were allies with Germany, certainly war with Japan and therefore Germany would be sanctioned. The memo outlined possible responses to Japanese aggression and an eight-point plan designed to provoke Japanese attack. Franklin Delano Roosevelt implemented this eight-point plan.

The plan must have been on FDR's mind when he first learned that Pearl Harbor was the Japanese target in *January* 1941, eleven months before the attack on Pearl Harbor. In November 1941, America adopted the "Vacant Sea" policy, which cleared the North Pacific of Allied shipping, both military and commercial, to clear a path for the Japanese. Now that Japan had an unobstructed path to Hawaii, the Pacific Fleet was called back to port, and FDR warned Rear Admiral Husband E. Kimmel, commander of the fleet in Hawaii, of a *possible*, even though FDR knew it was *imminent*, Japanese attack, but stressed that the "United States policy calls for Japan to commit the first overt act."[17]

On December 7th 1941, the culmination of both Theodore Roosevelt's racial foreign policy and FDR's desire for war against Germany combined to facilitate the Japanese attack on Pearl Harbor, resulting in 2,403 American deaths.*

The Progressives Decide Who Deserves to Live

Theodore Roosevelt was also an ardent believer in racial suicide. He believed that industrial capitalism was structured such that lower races, who were

---

*   I have written about this in more depth in my 2010 book, *Lies thee Government Told You*.

able to live at such a low and intolerable level of existence, would drive out the higher-race workers because they would be willing to work for less and outbreed the higher race. According to racial suicide theory, the higher race is literally bred out of existence by the lower races. Such a misguided and destructive belief would be the impetus of the eugenics movement.

Eugenics is a term coined by a British statistician, Francis Galton, and brought to America by Charles Davenport. The word comes from the Greek word for "well born" or "of good stock." Its proponents sought to eliminate the lower "unfit" classes of persons from the human population. It could be practiced in a number of ways, all utilized by the Progressives during the time of Theodore Roosevelt and Woodrow Wilson.

Positive eugenics is the practice of encouraging the higher-race citizens to breed more and thereby secure their spot in society and the world. Theodore Roosevelt subscribed to this idea. In 1905, as president, Roosevelt gave a speech to the National Congress of Mothers in Washington, D.C., where he urged women to "perform the first and greatest duty of womanhood" which is to bear "healthy children . . . numerous enough so that the race shall increase and not decrease."[18] In the same speech he said,

> A race that practiced such a doctrine—that is, a race that practiced race suicide—would thereby conclusively show that it was unfit to exist, and that it had better give place to people who had not forgotten the primary laws of their being.[19]

As well, in his 1894 article, "National Life and Character," discussed earlier, Roosevelt argued that "with much of the competition between the races reducing itself to the warfare of the cradle, no race has any chance to win a great place unless it consists of good breeders as well as good fighters."[20]

Negative eugenics, on the other hand, is the practice of *inhibiting* lower races from procreating. This took the form mainly of sterilization through eugenics statutes. One of the most infamous Supreme Court cases of all time upheld the constitutionality of forced sterilization on an eighteen-year-old girl who was considered to be "feeble minded."

Buck v. Bell was decided in 1927 and was written by Justice Oliver Wendell Holmes Jr., the same justice who wrote for the Court in favor of denying persons in American territories full constitutional protection in the *Insular Cases*. The ability to sterilize persons was recognized as a state's right during this time, so the Court was not deciding federal law directly implemented during the Roosevelt or Wilson administration. However, the membership of the Court was a careful product of their ideas.

Carrie Buck, through her guardian, appealed a decision by the superintendent of Virginia's State Colony for Epileptics and Feeble Minded to sterilize her so that she could not have additional children. Virginia law allowed her to appeal the decision to the Virginia courts. This case reached the Supreme Court of the United States after the Supreme Court of Appeals of the State of Virginia affirmed a decision by the Circuit Court of Amherst County to perform the sterilization. Ms. Buck was to have a salpingectomy; her fallopian tubes were to be cut.

She was an American citizen and a resident of Virginia at the time of the suit. Indiana had given America its first sterilization law in 1907, but Virginia had crafted a well-drawn piece of legislation applicable here. The Court quickly dismissed the procedural due process claims under the Fourteenth Amendment. Simply put, the Court ruled that there were sufficient procedural safeguards in place to allow Ms. Buck to appeal the decision to sterilize her.

The greater challenge was on what is called *substantive due process* under the Fourteenth Amendment. Ms. Buck challenged the law on the premise that under no circumstances can forced sterilization be justified. The essence of substantive due process is "fairness," and Ms. Buck argued that it was plainly unfair for the government to destroy her reproductive organs against her will.

In one of the most reprehensible judicial rejections of the Natural Law and the right to live, the Court quickly dismissed this claim, explaining that Carrie Buck was determined to be "the probable potential parent of a socially inadequate offspring, likewise afflicted, that she may be sexually sterilized."[21]

Justice Holmes would continue to say that "[i]t is better for all the world, if instead of waiting to execute degenerate offspring for crime, or to let them starve for their imbecility, society can prevent those who are manifestly unfit from continuing their kind."[22] This statement could have been written by Adolf Hitler.

Yet further, considering the fact that Carrie's mother was "feeble-minded," as was Carrie's daughter, Justice Holmes famously concluded the opinion, stating that *"[t]hree generations of imbeciles are enough."*[23] Only Justice Butler, the lone Catholic on the bench, dissented in this opinion.

Theodore Roosevelt certainly held the same repugnant ideology, as evidenced by his letter to Charles Davenport, the man who brought eugenics to America. There Roosevelt would write, "Society has no business to permit degenerates to reproduce," and

[i]t is really extraordinary that our people refuse to apply to human beings such elementary knowledge as every successful farmer is obliged to apply to his own stock breeding. Any group of farmers who permitted their best stock not to breed, and let all the increase come from the worst stock, would be treated as fit for an asylum.[24]

Woodrow Wilson's Hatred

Things would get worse. This time, rather than imagine yourself walking to Planned Parenthood, imagine your current life. Whether you are a policeman or an accountant, imagine you work for the government. Your people have been discriminated against in the past, but things are getting better, and you have a stable life. The problem is, in the space of one election, everything that so many people have worked so hard to achieve is about to be destroyed.

You are fired from your job for no apparent reason. Those of your friends who are lucky enough to keep their jobs are segregated from all of their co-workers. The people committing these heinous deeds are the same individuals who run the federal government.

Woodrow Wilson's racism and hatred toward people who were different became evident before he was elected president. While he was governor of New Jersey, Wilson signed legislation creating the Board of Examiners of Feebleminded, Epileptics, and Other Defectives. Under this law New Jersey had the power to determine when "procreation is inadvisable" for the "defectives" and others who were referenced under the legislation. Even with that deplorable track record, Wilson was still elected to the highest office in the United States.

When Woodrow Wilson came into office, he brought with him not only the same racial ideas that Theodore Roosevelt held concerning the hierarchy of races, but also a severe hatred for black Americans. He exacted revenge for the woes of the Civil War and brought Jim Crow to Washington. He feared what would happen to his native South should it be "ruled by an inferior race."[25] This notion and his fear of black Americans were the inspiration for many of Wilson's racial policies designed to keep black Americans subdued in society. Once enacted, this state sponsorship of racism would run well into the 1960s in Washington.

Woodrow Wilson was the most racist president of the twentieth century. His administration and the policies he put in place served to undo much of what had been done during Reconstruction.

He was quick to act on his racial impulses once he entered the White House. Wilson re-segregated the navy. He allowed his cabinet members to segregate their various departments, and most of the black figures in the government were fired. Woodrow Wilson would support these moves because for him "[s]egregation is not humiliating but a benefit" and "distinctly to the advantage of the colored people themselves."[26] America, he believed, was lucky to have such a benevolent racist at the helm of the federal government!

In his academic works, Wilson clearly evidenced his extreme racism. As discussed previously, he wrote of the superiority and long history the Aryans had with democracy. He believed in the racial theory of the time which made America the epitome of human development.

His work would help to inspire D. W. Griffith's *Birth of a Nation*. This movie is unapologetically racist in its depiction of the Ku Klux Klan as saviors rescuing the South after the Civil War. This silent movie was controversial even for its time when it debuted in 1915. It was a rallying cry for what would become the second Ku Klux Klan, and it arguably inspired an entire generation of bigotry.

The movie was based largely on the novel *Clansman* by Thomas Dixon. However, even in this silent movie, Woodrow Wilson's legacy would shine as D. W. Griffith quoted the president on one of his slides. The slide read, "The white men were roused by a mere instinct of self-preservation . . . until at last there had sprung into existence a great Ku Klux Klan, a veritable empire of the South, to protect the Southern country."[27] So sayeth President Thomas Woodrow Wilson.

Later, the president would confirm his beliefs once again. He would say of the movie, "It is like writing history with lightning, my only regret is that it is all so true."[28]

Indeed, Booker T. Washington commented on the state of affairs in Washington under Wilson, saying that he had "recently spent several days in Washington, and [he had] never seen the colored people so discouraged and bitter as they are at the present time."[29] Wilson was an enemy of change, growth, and equal rights for all, and his attitudes were readily apparent to everyone who was not blinded by the Progressives' rhetoric.

Today

Today, it is generally known that the Nazis in Germany committed awful atrocities on their own people and the people they conquered because of a racial belief that the descendants of the Aryans who maintained the purity of their seed were destined to rule the world. Less known is that much of the same ideology was shared by such men as Wilson and Roosevelt. While the Germans established a party and took over their government to implement their radical policies on a massive scale, the Progressives preferred a softer approach. Republicans and Democrats alike agreed on the racial theories of their day. The two parties were one party in that respect.

Whereas Nazis blatantly forced mass death camps on people, the Progressives talked of the need to rid the world of diseases and use science to cure the ailments of the human condition. Through sterilizations they claimed they could stop plagues like epilepsy and feeble-mindedness. Through abortions they could control the population of particular races of people and maintain a check on their numbers so as not to commit race suicide. Through minimum-wage laws they thrust the "unemployable" out of the labor force.

Once people are on welfare, family planning becomes the government's burden because children become expenditures of the state. In reality this was just another way to control how many children the undesirables conceived and brought forth. These policies are still strong and increasing in acceptance once more.

The landmark Supreme Court decision of *Roe v. Wade* (1973) is the judicial culmination of Rooseveltian and Wilsonian eugenics. This case solidified the constitutional right of a woman to destroy the baby in her womb in the United States.

While many hail this case as furtherance of a woman's right to do with her body what she desires, it is almost never spoken of in terms of its effects. In America from 1973 through 2008 nearly fifty-five million children were aborted, which is approximately four thousand abortions per day.[30] An even more telling statistic is who is being aborted. In 1994 while comprising approximately 12.5 percent of the population, black Americans had 34.7 percent of all abortions![31]

Margaret Sanger would be proud. She founded the American Birth Control League, which was the predecessor of Planned Parenthood. She was a champion of the women's liberation movement. Yet while promising women that through contraception and abortion they would be liberated from the woman's bondage of pregnancy, she did not publicly state her real intentions.

In 1939 Sanger founded the Negro Project which issued a report stating that "[t]he mass of significant Negroes, still breed carelessly and disastrously, with the result that the increase among Negroes . . . is [in] that portion of the population least intelligent and fit."[32] Further, she would write to a colleague, "We do not want the word to get out that we want to exterminate the Negro population."[33]

This attitude is still alive. *Freakonomics* author Steven Levitt wrote in that book, "Legalized abortion led to less unwantedness; unwantedness leads to high crime; legalized abortion, therefore, led to less crime."[34]

Hidden under the veil of this logic is the reality that the black population commits crime disproportionate to the rest of the population. Therefore, Levitt is really arguing for disproportionately aborting black Americans, as we know has been the case since *Roe v. Wade*, because it reduces crime.

Conclusion

The policies and beliefs of Theodore Roosevelt and Woodrow Wilson live on in America today. Although the two men did not generate these theories all alone, they did ascribe to these fanatical views on the world and on races. This type of thinking, at least in the language that these two presidents spoke, has been long retired, but the heart of the belief is still there.

Simply put, the government's philosophy from and since Roosevelt and Wilson has been that there are some who should live and prosper and others who should be controlled and eliminated. Which person are you? Which persons were they? Who is to decide? It is time that America reconciles the policies and laws under which we currently function and the intellectual history that led to them while eliminating these destructive structures erected by Theodore Roosevelt, Woodrow Wilson, and their Progressive Era supporters.

Any government that could reduce the numbers of undesirables in society could certainly commandeer them to do its dirty work. We turn next to the draft.

Chapter 7

Service or Slavery?

Conscription

In the course of his [General Westmoreland's] testimony, he made the statement that he did not want to command an army of mercenaries. I stopped him and said, "General, would you rather command an army of slaves?" He drew himself up and said, "I don't like to hear our patriotic draftees referred to as slaves." I replied, "I don't like to hear our patriotic volunteers referred to as mercenaries." But then I went on to say, "If they are mercenaries, then I, sir, am a mercenary professor, and you, sir, are a mercenary general; we are served by mercenary physicians, we use a mercenary lawyer, and we get our meat from a mercenary butcher." That was the last that we heard from the general about mercenaries.

—Milton Friedman[1]

The country is engaged in a fruitless war being fought nearly halfway around the globe. You are not even sure that you believe the story of how we were dragged into this war or why we are fighting. Maybe it is to prevent a dictator from conquering and enslaving innocents. Maybe it is to rectify some tragic wrong committed against our country like that of Pearl Harbor. Or maybe it is simply to fight a war for interests which you, the ordinary American, will have no way to know of for decades, if ever.

Yet to fight this war the president and his men need bodies to use as cannon fodder. Unlike wars that draw national support and people who feel a moral compulsion to fight, this war is different. There seems to be no great drive or reason for engaging the enemy. You are not even sure what the enemy did to justify the full weight of the American military tearing through its borders.

The people, unwilling to fight for a cause which they do not understand, are then used as instruments of the state and of the president's imperialistic policy. What the country cannot get voluntarily, it will get through compulsion. Thus, a draft is commenced to force able-bodied men into military service against their will.

To keep up the appearance of allowing some choice in the matter, the government allows people to claim that they are conscientious objectors and, therefore, cannot be drafted. However, such objectors are put to work in an industrial sector that needs workers for the war effort, or else they are jailed.

Is economic enslavement really so different from military conscription? Is military conscription so different from involuntary servitude; from slavery? The master needs bodies for his cotton, the president needs bodies for his war, and those bodies can be put to work by the force of law and against their will.

Riots rage in the streets. Sons are pulled from the clutches of their parents' arms, brothers are estranged from one another, and lovers are lost, all to the cruel blood thirst of war.

This scenario is a depiction neither of some horrible Stalinist state nor of some Roman conquest. This is the story of America. Abraham Lincoln established the precedent for conscription into military service in this country; he was the first to do so under the Constitution. Woodrow Wilson, however, exploited and mastered it.

Today, through subtler means, the same involuntary servitude forces many into the storm of bullets and barrage of bombs. Whether it be the theaters of war during World War I, the jungles of Vietnam, or the deserts of the Middle East, America fuels its desire for conquest and war through involuntary service, and the groundwork for how to do this was laid by Woodrow Wilson.

Woodrow Wilson and World War I

The draft existed at various times throughout our history, but since the adoption of the Constitution, only Abraham Lincoln instituted the draft before Woodrow Wilson, and Wilson greatly expanded its reach.

To fight the Civil War, Lincoln instituted two forms of the draft. The states conducted the first attempt at a draft. When a state could not meet its quota for soldiers, that state would institute a draft to make up the remainder. However, these means proved ineffective, and Lincoln instituted a national draft by the federal government pursuant to the Enrollment Act of 1863[2] passed by Congress. He was the first president to carry out a draft since the adoption of our Constitution, although he was not the first to try.

During the War of 1812 against the British, President James Madison and his secretary of war, James Monroe, attempted to create a national draft of forty thousand men. Strong opposition mounted, as evidenced in a speech by Senator Daniel Webster from Massachusetts on the Senate floor where he stated,

> The administration asserts the right to fill the ranks of the regular army by compulsion. . . . Is this, sir, consistent with the character of a free government? Is this civil liberty? Is this the real character of our *Constitution*? No, sir, indeed it is not. . . . Where is it written in the Constitution, in what article or section is it contained, that you may take children from their parents, and parents from their children, and compel them to fight the battles of any war, in which the folly or the wickedness of government may engage it? Under what concealment has this power lain hidden, which now for the first time comes forth, with a tremendous and baleful aspect, to trample down and destroy the dearest rights of personal liberty?[3]

Ultimately, the War of 1812 was resolved before the matter was to be decided.

Despite Lincoln's instituting and enforcing a national draft, the number of men who were subject to it was not nearly as great as under Wilson during World War I. Of the more than two million men in the Union army, 6 percent were drafted: approximately 46,000 conscripts and 118,000 substitutes.[4] Although many records are incomplete, it is estimated that about 750,000 to 1,000,000 men served in the Confederate army. The Confederate Congress adopted conscription in 1862, drafting more than 80,000 men.[5] It would take Woodrow Wilson to bring the draft level to staggering heights.

American involvement in World War I began in 1917, and on June 15th of that year, so did the draft and the Selective Service. With the enactment of the Selective Service Act of 1917, all eligible men ages twenty-one through thirty-one were required to register for conscription, and those who did not were punished and jailed. Three million men were drafted into World War I overall, including black Americans, who were drafted on equal terms, yet segregated into different units to avoid what Wilson called "friction."

It was not long until men began to challenge the draft in various ways, including refusing to register or speaking out in opposition to it. One of these challenges would go before the Supreme Court, which ruled that the draft was constitutional.

In the 1918 case *Arver v. United States*, six men challenged the constitutionality of the draft by refusing to register. Upon failing to register, the men were convicted, and the appeals ensued.

In holding that the draft is constitutional, the Supreme Court ruled that the Congress held the power to create the draft because the draft was "necessary and proper" to wage war. Article 1, Section 8, of the Constitution gives the Congress the power "To declare War . . . To raise and support Armies . . . To make Rules for the Government and Regulation of the land and naval Forces," as well as to "make all Laws which shall be necessary and proper for carrying into Execution the foregoing Powers." Thus, the Court held that the Congress, in its ability to declare war, raise and support armies, and make rules and regulations governing those armies, can implement a national draft.

Furthermore, when the six men asserted that the power is a grant of the ability to raise armies but not through means of involuntary induction, the Court stated that this "challenges the existence of all power, for a government power which has no sanction to it and which therefore can only be exercised provided the citizen consents to its exertion is in no substantial sense a power." Thus, the Court stated a general principle that one does not need to consent to a law for that law to be lawful. Yet the men in this case further contended that while this may be true generally, it certainly cannot be held to be so in their case because the idea of conscription into military service is "repugnant to a free government and in conflict with all the great guarantees of the Constitution as to individual liberty."

This is the same sentiment that Senator Webster expressed during the

War of 1812. Nevertheless, the Court quickly dismissed this idea when stating that the "proposition is so devoid of foundation that it leaves not even a shadow of ground upon which to base the conclusion."

The defendants also challenged the draft on the theory that it was prohibited by the Thirteenth Amendment which states, in relevant part, that "[n]either slavery nor involuntary servitude, except as a punishment for crime whereof the party shall have been duly convicted, shall exist within the United States, or any place subject to their *jurisdiction*." The Court completely dismissed this notion as ludicrous and plainly absurd on its face, stating,

> Finally, as we are unable to conceive upon what theory the exaction by government from the citizen of the performance of his supreme and noble duty of contributing to the defense of the rights and honor of the nation as the result of a war declared by the great representative body of the people can be said to be the imposition of involuntary servitude in violation of the prohibitions of the Thirteenth Amendment, we are constrained to the conclusion that the contention to that effect is refuted by its mere statement.[6]

Senator Daniel Webster would certainly have agreed with the men in this case based on his position, which he held even before the Thirteenth Amendment was enacted. More recently, Congressman Ron Paul summed up the argument about enslavement well when he stated,

> A conscripted, unhappy soldier is better off [i]n the long run than the slaves of old since the "enslavement" is only temporary. But in the short run the draft may well turn out to be more deadly and degrading, as one is forced to commit life and limb to a less than worthy cause. . . . Slaves were safer in that their owners had an economic interest in protecting their lives. Endangering the lives of our soldiers is acceptable policy, and that's why they are needed.[7]

The *Arver* case establishes the government's power to subject a man to the torments of war involuntarily.

The draft in 1917 did make some exceptions to military service for men who did not want to fight the war. The Quakers, Amish, and members of the

Church of Brethren were outright exempted due to their religious beliefs. Certain men, such as miners and chemists, were exempted because their occupations were essential to the war effort. No specific occupations were listed in the Act, presumably to allow the government more discretion in deciding which occupations would be exempt.

Still others who objected to military service were put either in noncombat roles or in civilian service. Men who were conscientious objectors and absolutely refused to take part in the war effort were jailed and subjected to harsh treatment. Some two thousand conscientious objectors during World War I were jailed at facilities such as Fort Lewis, Washington; Alcatraz Island in San Francisco Bay; and Fort Leavenworth, Kansas. At these facilities conscientious objectors were subjected to small rations, solitary confinement, and physical abuse. Two draftees died from this harsh physical abuse.

Those who were opposed to the draft were jailed for their speech and writings as well. In 1919, in the famous case of *Schenck v. United States*, the Supreme Court upheld the conviction of a draft opponent for writing and distributing leaflets encouraging others to oppose the draft and assert, what he believed to be, their constitutional rights. This case was decided one year after the Supreme Court, in *Arver v. United States*, flatly rejected the notion that the Thirteenth Amendment applied against the draft. Nonetheless, Charles T. Schenck was jailed for printing and distributing his leaflets protesting the draft because these actions violated the Espionage Act of 1917.

How Can Speech Be Dangerous?

Charles T. Schenck was the general secretary of the Socialist Party and in charge of the party headquarters. He was convicted of creating and distributing approximately fifteen thousand leaflets concerning the draft. Despite the First Amendment clearly stating that "Congress shall make no law . . . abridging the freedom of speech, or of the press," the Court determined that Schenck's rhetoric was dangerous and therefore was a violation of the Espionage Act. In stating what kind of language these leaflets contained which was so dangerous, Justice Holmes wrote that the leaflet, upon its first printed side recited the first section of the Thirteenth Amendment, said that the idea embodied in it was violated by the conscription act and that a conscript is little better than a convict. In impassioned language it intimated that conscription was despotism in its worst form and a monstrous wrong against humanity in the interest of Wall Street's chosen few. It said, "Do not submit to intimidation," but in form at least confined itself to peaceful measures such as a petition for the repeal of the act. The other and later printed side of the sheet was headed "Assert Your Rights." It stated reasons for alleging that any one violated the Constitution when he refused to recognize "your right to assert your opposition to the draft," and went on, "If you do not assert and support your rights, you are helping to dent or disparage rights which it is the solemn duty of all citizens and residents of the United States to retain."[8]

Surely this language is not dangerous, is it? Here the author is doing little more than encouraging men and women of the country to petition their representatives peacefully to repeal a statute which this author believes is unconstitutional and a form of slavery. The author states the Thirteenth Amendment in support of his argument. Am I to be jailed for penning this chapter? Thankfully, the law concerning such speech has been enlightened somewhat over the past century, but had I been writing in 1917 when the draft began, surely I would have been prosecuted and jailed under the Espionage Act, as were so many people for expressing intellectual beliefs about a system that forces young people to serve as slaves and to die for the government.

In upholding the conviction of Schenck, the Court reasoned, he must have intended to have an effect on the draft, and therefore he was guilty of violating the Espionage Act. Surely he did intend to have an effect; it was unfortunate for him, though, that Woodrow Wilson was the president because at that time if Wilson disagreed with one's opinion, one could be sent to jail.

After stating that the language used may well be constitutional in many other instances, the Court expressed that it was the circumstances in which the words were written that mattered in this case. Justice Holmes then famously stated that

[t]he most stringent protection of free speech would not protect a man in falsely shouting fire in a theater and causing a panic. . . . The question in

every case is whether the words used are used in such circumstances and are of such a nature as to create *a clear and present danger* that they will bring about the substantive *evils* that the Congress has a right to prevent.

In upholding Schenck's conviction, Justice Holmes and the Supreme Court agreed that otherwise constitutional speech is evil because it is political dissent during a time of war. Never mind the First Amendment to the Constitution. If Woodrow Wilson did not like what you said, it was criminal, according to Justice Holmes. Here, intellectual debate concerning the constitutionality of conscription itself, which inducted three million young men, was apparently sufferable by imprisonment. Ultimately, Schenck spent six months in jail for this "crime."

In a similar case decided in 1919, *Debs v. United States*, Eugene V. Debs, a leader in the Socialist Party, was jailed for delivering a speech because the "opposition was so expressed that its natural and intended effect would be to obstruct recruiting." After the *Schenck* case, the Court quickly dismissed any claim that the Espionage Act, under which Debs was convicted, was an unconstitutional abridgment of the rights protected by the First Amendment. Debs was convicted and sentenced to ten years in jail for a *single speech*. However, he ran for president in the 1920 election and received nearly one million votes, which at the time was 3.4 percent of the popular vote. A man earning 3.4 percent of the popular vote for president from a jail cell is evidence of the magnitude of dissent that was present in the country concerning the draft. Surely President Wilson was lying when he stated the draft is "in no sense a conscription of the unwilling; it is, rather, selection from a nation which has volunteered in mass."[9]

Woodrow Wilson did almost everything possible to quell opposition and force men into fighting his war. Wilson not only signed legislation that would send men like Schenck and Debs to jail for political dissent, for pure speech, but also fiercely guarded the ports of America. He needed to guard the ports in order to capture any men who tried to flee the country rather than choose between service in the military or jail. If such actions are not indicative of a system of indentured servitude or slavery, then such a system does not exist.

More correctly stated, the system of indentured servitude does exist. The issue at hand is the ability of the *government*, not its citizens, to force slavery upon another person. As discussed above, the first national draft occurred during Lincoln's presidency. The idea of his time was stated squarely in a *New York Times* article from 1863:

> When it is once understood that our national authority has the right under the Constitution, to *every dollar and every right arm* in the country *for its protection*, and that the great people recognize and stand by that right, thenceforward, for all time to come, this Republic will command a respect, both at home and abroad, far beyond any ever accorded to it before.[10]

The Civil War and Abraham Lincoln set the precedent expressed in this article that the government has the right to "every dollar and every right arm." Only Lincoln, with a straight face, could use slaves to fight the institution of slavery. However, after the Civil War, the Thirteenth Amendment to the Constitution was adopted. As discussed previously, the Supreme Court dismissed any notion that the Thirteenth Amendment applied against the draft, making the draft unconstitutional. The theory of Woodrow Wilson's era was that the Thirteenth Amendment did not apply to the government and that, when in war, the government could force individuals into the military or into a specific labor market.

Work or Fight!

This theory was made evident by the "Work or Fight!" campaign. The campaign essentially meant that an individual could either be drafted or forced to work at a state-approved job. Bernard Baruch, the head of the War Industries Board during Woodrow Wilson's presidency, summed up the program, stating,

> No matter what the grounds for your deferment may be, unless you are faithfully, continuously and usefully employed in a capacity and for an enterprise determined by the Government to be essential to the prosecution of the war, your deferment will be cancelled and you will immediately be called for service with the colors.

So, with the threat of being sent to war, conscripts were forced into a labor position of which the government approved. Central planning of the economy, therefore, was now achievable through coercion and threat of enlistment in the armed forces.

When trying to reconcile this blatant form of slavery of our own citizens, Baruch believed that although "[e]nforced and involuntary service for a private master is and has been clearly and repeatedly defined by our Supreme Court as slavery inhibited by the Thirteenth Amendment," this notion "does not say, however, that men not under military discipline are free agents in war. The Government cannot say, 'Work here, Work there,' or 'Work for Mr. A.' But it can say—as it did say in 1918: 'Work or Fight!'"[11]

Justification for conscription in Woodrow Wilson's era was military collectivism and the supreme power of the state. If the government can violate the Thirteenth Amendment with impunity when it forces its citizens into battle or into approved labor markets against their will, and if "every dollar and every right arm" are subject to the will of the state, it naturally follows that, as Baruch stated, "in war, [the country's] entire resources of men, money and things should suddenly become a compact instrument of destruction. . . . [T]he entire population must suddenly cease to be a congeries of individuals, each following a self-appointed course, and become a vast unitary mechanism."

After World War I

Conscription officially ended in 1919 after World War I was over. The activities of the Selective Service System were curtailed upon the armistice in November 1919 ending World War I. All local, district, and medical advisory boards were closed on March 31st 1919. The last state headquarters were shut down on May 21st 1919, and the provost marshal general was relieved of duty on July 15th 1919; thus, finally putting to sleep the draft system of World War I. However, the same justifications and precedent would be used to establish another draft under President Franklin Delano Roosevelt.

Despite publicly stating that America would not enter World War II, President Roosevelt presided over the first peacetime draft in our nation's history. The Selective Training and Service Act of 1940, which reestablished the draft and the Selective Service System, borrowed largely from the system that Woodrow Wilson created during World War I.

Overall, ten million men were inducted into the military through the draft during World War II. As well, more than six thousand conscientious objectors were jailed for their refusal to take part in the war effort as directed.

The draft and opposition continued in much the same way during the Cold War. However, during the Cold War the government realized the awesome power of Wilson's draft. Whereas Wilson used the draft as a blunt instrument to force citizens into the armed forces or as a means to bring about central planning of the economy through forced labor, the Cold War administrations realized that the Selective Service System could be used with much more finesse to accomplish the same objectives. Rather than *force* massive numbers of men into the military, the government realized that it had the power to *coerce* them.

During this time four million of the eleven million men eligible for the draft entered the military voluntarily. By giving volunteers preferential placements and less dangerous postings, the government scared millions of men into the military; if they did not volunteer, they were sure to be placed on the battlefield. From 1964 to 1970, the percentage of recruits who entered the military to avoid being placed on the battlefield, rather than some safer assignment, rose from 34 percent to 50 percent, respectively.

Through the same reasoning, the government was also able to regulate society through deferments. Special deferments were granted for recruits who were engaged in an occupation that the government found beneficial. For example, undergraduate education, technical or religious training, skilled labor, teaching, and research were occupations that one could enter and by doing so earn a deferment from the draft. Through deferments during the Cold War, the government was able to channel people into endeavors of its choosing.

Once again the idea from Woodrow Wilson's administration—that the citizen serves at the pleasure of the state—was held by the federal government during World War II and the Cold War. The only difference is how various administrations decided to effectuate that policy. The draft ended with the conclusion of the Vietnam War, but the same policies are still at work today.

The Draft in Our Day

In our time the draft looms over every man once he turns eighteen years old. Within thirty days of being granted the right to vote, we are reminded of the awesome sense of duty that the government claims we owe it. Although the draft is currently not active, it can be instituted at any time, and the government has all the information and structure it needs to restart it.

The penalties for not registering were steep until 1986, when the government stopped prosecuting these offenses. Before that time, the penalty was a fine of up to $250,000 or five years in jail, or both. Now the government, once again, is using a finesse approach. In order to receive government benefits, federal employment, or financial aid, as well as federal grants and loans for education, a young person has to register with the Selective Service System. If he does not do so by twenty-six years of age, he is no longer able to register and can be permanently barred from federal employment and other benefits. Despite not having a draft, we force those who need college loans or government assistance to register for the draft should it be re-instituted.

Stop-Loss

David W. Qualls sued the government over its stop-loss program in 2005.[12] Stop-loss is the process by which the military, under order of the president, retains individuals in military service despite the expiration of their time of active duty or their term of service. Stop-loss is a statutorily authorized way to keep members of the armed forces under obligation to serve past the time to which they agreed.

Qualls was a member of the army for eight years, from 1986 through 1994. In July of 2003 he decided to re-enlist in the Army National Guard, which provides a reserve stock of soldiers in the event the government needs, or simply wants, to go to war.

Qualls signed a contract for his services for one year.[13] Shortly after enlisting in the program, he was called to active duty. Subsequently, under the stop-loss statute, the government extended his term of service to twenty-nine years, even though he believed he was only signing up to "Try One" year as an Army National Guardsman!

When he took his case to court, the court ruled that he was not entitled to relief because the terms of his contract made it clear that his term of service may be extended involuntarily.

Although he did not keep his original contract, Qualls maintained that his contract did not contain the provision explaining the stop-loss statute, and the army was unable to produce any version of his contract in its records which contained this section. The court still held that Qualls was subject to stop-loss and his twenty-nine-year end-of-term-of-service date because Qualls was unable to produce his original copy.

This case illustrates that stop-loss can be used as a form of indentured servitude. Here, stop-loss took a one-year enlistment contract and turned it into twenty-nine years, based on language no one could find.

The stop-loss program is basically a draft that uses men and women who have already enlisted. The stop-loss program exists primarily to secure a means by which to *keep* people in military service against their wills, rather than having to induct people *into* the military service against their wills.

Conclusion

The draft is a form of slavery and therefore tyranny. The roots of the current Selective Service System and stop-loss were planted in 1917 by Woodrow Wilson. We are told it is our patriotic duty to fight when we are commanded, yet Representative Ron Paul was correct in asserting that "liberty cannot be preserved by tyranny."[14]

The same Progressives who really believed that the government owns our bodies also believed that they could tell us when, where, and how to work; and that they could use the government to regulate the workplace.

Next we look at the destruction of freedom of contract.

Chapter 8

The Government Tries to Pick Winners

Labor Law and the Regulation of the Workplace

> Rights to property include something more than mere ownership and the privilege of receiving a limited return from its use. The right to control, to manage, and to dispose of it, the right to put it at risk in business, and by legitimate skill and enterprise to make gains beyond fixed rates of interest, the right to hire employees, to bargain freely with them about the rate of wages, and from their labors to make lawful gains—these are among the essential rights of property.
>
> —Supreme Court Justice Mahlon Pitney[1]

Michelle Berry privately owns a small day-care service in Flint, Michigan. In 2009, she was forced to join the Child Care Providers Together Michigan union. The Michigan Department of Human Services suddenly began taking union dues out of the child-care subsidies it sends her.[2] Without her consent or knowledge, Berry had become a government employee and a public sector union member.

The most puzzling aspect of her new status is that as a private business owner, Berry does not have a government employer. In the spirit of the Progressive Era, this did not stop the union from organizing or the government from taking her money. They used their imagination to create a union that all child-care providers in Michigan were forced to join.

Because some of Berry's low-income clients receive government subsidies, she was considered to be a government employee. A government agency was then created out of thin air called the Michigan Home Based Child Care Council, which acted as a government "employer" of privately owned child-care centers.[3]

All of this political maneuvering turned Berry into a faux government employee, with a faux government employer, and a faux government agency to bargain with. Instead of helping Berry, the union and the government worked together to take money from the subsidies she should have received and give it to Child Care Providers Together union. Berry had no desire or need to join a union.

Berry's story is recent, but its seeds were planted during the Progressive Era, which marked the beginning of unprecedented regulation of labor and the workplace. Prior to Progressive Era reforms, deciding where, when, and how many hours to work was left up to the individual. Employers and employees were given the freedom to negotiate hours and wages. Parents were able to decide when their children were allowed to work. Workers were not coerced by unions into striking, boycotting, and only accepting certain wages. Thanks to the influence of the Progressive Era, these decisions are now regulated by the federal government.

Progressives such as President Theodore Roosevelt and President Woodrow Wilson are known for being pro-labor and pro-union. They are praised as heroes of the working class. However, they were actually attempting to expand the power of the federal government while simultaneously getting involved in private matters that they believed common workers could not handle. The relationship between the federal government and unions provided unions with legal immunity while they used coercive tactics such as boycotts, threats, and even violence in order to force businesses to submit to them and workers to join them.

This unconstitutional legacy of the Progressive Era is still evident today, as you can see from Michelle Berry's day-care example at the beginning of this chapter. This type of forced unionization happens all over the country, at the behest of the government and labor leaders. The freedom to associate that is guaranteed by the Constitution allows for the formation of unions, but it follows that individuals also have the freedom *not* to associate with unions. However, Progressives such as Wilson and Roosevelt had little interest or respect for the Constitution or individual rights.

The Rise of Unions; the Demise of Freedom of Choice

Those who tell you of trade-unions bent on raising wages by moral suasion alone are like people who tell you of tigers that live on oranges.

—HENRY GEORGE, 1891[4]

A goal of Progressive Era reformers such as Wilson and Roosevelt was to give unions a voice in the federal government and to pass legislation that was favorable to unions. Although fundamental rights–based perspectives dictate that people should have the freedom *not* to associate with unions, just as they should have the freedom *to* associate with unions, the Progressives did not share this view. Among unions, "the silent corollary was that everyone— union member or not—must 'strike' too, that is, withhold his or her labor, willing or not, and refuse employment at pay less than that demanded by the workers."[5] This complete seizure of individual rights went perfectly with Progressive ideology that often advocated for the public good at the expense of the individual.

Although unions used coercive tactics such as threats and violence to force individuals and businesses to unionize, eventually the courts condoned these actions. However, before Progressives were able to force through unfair legislation that exempted unions, they were subject to anti-trust laws. For example, in the 1908 case *Loewe v. Lawlor*,[6] the Supreme Court held that the Sherman Antitrust Act, which generally and basically prohibits contracts or combinations in restraint of interstate trade, except for the cartels the government created, did apply to unions, because they can be combinations in restraint of interstate trade or commerce under the meaning defined by the Sherman Antitrust Act of 1890.

It was clear in this decision that Congress had not intended for unions to be exempt from this statute. In this case, the United Hatters Union of North America was targeting non-union hat manufacturer Danbury Hatters. The owner of Danbury Hatters, Dietrich Loewe, refused to unionize. The Hatters Union attempted to organize a nationwide boycott of Loewe's products in retaliation. These types of coercive tactics were used to restrain trade and targeted businesses for simply exercising their right not to associate with certain groups. However, this decision caused union leaders to demand favorable legislation to come to their rescue, and it eventually did. During Woodrow Wilson's presidency, the Clayton Antitrust Act was passed to weaken the Sherman Antitrust Act by exempting union activity from its reach.

Additionally, the U.S. Department of Labor was created on March 4th 1913, Wilson's inauguration day. The quest to gain an official federal government department to represent the interests of labor was led by labor leaders such as Samuel Gompers, president of the American Federation of Labor (AFL).

In 1903, the American Federation of Labor persuaded the Democratic Party to adopt a platform advocating for a cabinet-level Department of Labor. President Taft was then bullied by labor leaders until he reluctantly signed the bill. He had even pleaded with Samuel Gompers for a compromise. Taft asked to take out a provision in the bill that the Department of Justice could not use its funds to prosecute organizations in defense of labor. The AFL refused Taft's request, yet Taft signed the bill anyway. He stated, "I sign this bill with considerable hesitation. . . . I forbear, however, to veto this bill, because my motive in doing so would be misunderstood."[7] This bill, signed on Wilson's inauguration day, would set the tone for the rest of Wilson's presidency, as well as the progression of pro-union laws that would characterize the Progressive Era.

It was not until the early 1900s, when the collectivism movement and the Progressive Era began, that national trade unions became popular and pervasive throughout America.[8] For example, President Theodore Roosevelt intervened for the first time in a miners' strike on the side of labor in 1902. Although he had no legal right to intervene in a strike that threatened coal production in Pennsylvania,[9] Roosevelt never let a little thing such as the Constitution get in the way when he wanted to use his power to get involved in something.

In Progressive Party materials bragging about Roosevelt's labor record, he is portrayed as courageous for daring to stand on the side of labor in the mine strike, even though he was told the problem was merely one of "supply and demand."[10] These "heroics" ignore the fact that, as even his own attorney general warned him, he had absolutely no right to intervene.[11] This marked the beginning of a significant change in the role of the president and set a precedent that called for intervention into private commercial disputes that were traditionally outside the scope of the federal government.

Roosevelt's intervention in a disagreement between business and labor was a precursor to President Truman's intervention in a steelworkers' strike during the Korean War in 1952. The steel industry's rejection of the regulations set out by the Wage Stabilization Board, which had been established to regulate the economy during the war, led to this steelworkers' strike. Rather than invoke legislation or ask approval from Congress, Truman gave himself emergency powers during a time of war and attempted *to seize* the steel production facilities so that they would come under government control.

The Supreme Court decided the president's behavior was an unconstitutional use of executive power to seize private property in the case of *Youngstown Sheet & Tube Co. v. Sawyer* in 1952.[12] The strike continued after the issuance of this opinion, until Truman once again intervened and threatened to use the Selective Service Act so as *to draft* striking workers into the army and gain control over the steel mills. This case represents Theodore Roosevelt's legacy of using any means possible to overcome the structure of the government that was so carefully crafted by our Founding Fathers.

The Demise of Freedom of Contract

"Progressive" actions were not limited to Congress, as the courts took part in ushering out the concept that the Constitution protected *individual* rights and replacing it with a collectivist notion of "public interest."

—WILLIAM L. ANDERSON[13]

During the Progressive Era, Progressive reformers began to enact legislation at the state and federal levels that was supposedly in the interest of laborers. These reforms were touted as protecting workers, for example, by setting minimum-wage and maximum-hours provisions. However, these paternalistic reforms actually took away the freedom of workers to negotiate their own contracts. The Progressives' justification for this unconstitutional seizure of liberty was that the average worker had unequal power in bargaining with large companies. Yet big businesses actually favored these laws because they drove smaller competitors out of business. The Progressives had their own reasons for enacting these laws, such as governmental expansion.

During this time of increasing governmental regulation, the courts attempted to uphold traditional notions of constitutionality and freedom. Progressives and modern historians and legal scholars have heavily criticized the Supreme Court for its attempt to uphold economic liberties through the "freedom of contract" doctrine during what legal historians call the Lochner Era.

The case of *Lochner v. New York* in 1905[14] is criticized in history books and legal texts as one of the most egregious examples of judicial interference in legislative matters. That is why today the Lochner Era and the case itself are often referred to with disdain and have become synonymous with the idea of the judicial branch taking the side of big business. However, this legacy is based on the Progressives' inaccurate portrayal of the situation. The twisted rhetoric of the Progressives and their progeny somehow managed to inject into the national psyche that the economic rights of business owners and workers, their natural rights to trade goods and services and money, and the natural economic laws of supply and demand did not exist or deserve protection.

The theory of freedom of contract and economic liberty was originally set out in 1872 in the infamous *Slaughterhouse Cases*. The *Slaughterhouse Cases* were three separate cases that were argued and reported together. In this decision, the Supreme Court severely narrowed the protections of the Thirteenth and Fourteenth Amendments by allowing a state-run monopoly in the slaughtering business in Louisiana, against the objection of privately owned slaughterhouses.

Dissenting from the majority's decision in these cases, Justice Field stated, "It is to me a matter of profound regret that [the statute's] validity is recognized by a majority of this court, for by it the right of free labor, one of the most sacred and imprescriptible rights of man, is violated."[15] Although this was merely a dissent, this idea of the right to pursue a lawful occupation free from the confines of a government-sponsored monopoly eventually gave way to the "liberty of contract" doctrine.

The liberty of contract doctrine was upheld for the first time in *Allgeyer v.*

Louisiana in 1897.[16] There the Supreme Court unanimously held that Louisiana could not use its "police powers" to prohibit E. Allgeyer and Company from buying insurance from an out-of-state insurance provider. The Court held that there is a right to freedom of contract inherent in the Due Process Clause of the Fourteenth Amendment, which allows individuals or businesses to engage in contracts out of their own free will, regardless of what the state thinks is in their best interest. The word *liberty* as used in the Fourteenth Amendment does not merely mean "free from physical restraint"; it also means "to live and work where he will, to earn his livelihood by any lawful calling, to pursue any livelihood or avocation, and for that purpose to enter into all contracts which may be proper, necessary, and essential to his carrying out to a successful conclusion the purposes above mentioned."[17]

In addition to *Allgeyer*, the liberty of contract doctrine comes from a natural rights theory which "means, in this context, the idea that individuals possess pre-political rights that antedate positive law and that can be discovered through human reason."[18] It is clear that the decisions involving an employment contract should be left to the contracting persons, not the government.

The tension between the regulation of working conditions and freedom of contract came to a head in *Lochner v. New York* in 1905. *Lochner* reached the Supreme Court from New York, where Progressives and labor leaders had relentlessly campaigned for legislation designating maximum hours for bake shop workers.

In order to get this legislation passed, one thing labor leaders employed was the help of muckraking journalists. Since public health and safety regulations can be considered valid justifications for the use of a state's police power, unions such as the Journeymen Bakers of New York decided to call attention to the health and safety conditions in New York bakeries. This effort led to a piece in the *New York Press* exposing the unsanitary workplace environments in bakeries. Although a May 1896 investigation by the Brooklyn Commissioner of Health found that the stories had been "greatly exaggerated and most of [them] absolutely false,"[19] these efforts were successful.

New York's Bakeshop Act was enacted in 1895. In addition to provisions regulating the health and safety in bakeries, it included provisions limiting the hours of workers to not more than ten hours per day or sixty hours per week. This law provided criminal penalties and had no flexibility to accommodate or excuse overtime or emergency situations, or even the wishes of bakers to work more and earn more.

This legislation drove small immigrant-owned bake shops out of business. A state factory inspector noted, "It is almost impossible to secure or keep in proper cleanly condition the Jewish and Italian bakeshops. Cleanliness and tidiness are entirely foreign to these people, and their bakeshops are like their sweatshops, for like causes produce like effects."[20] In his brief for the *Lochner* case, New York's attorney general actually admitted that the laws targeted immigrants: "There have come to [New York] great numbers of foreigners with habits which must be changed."[21]

One of these small immigrant bakery owners whose habits the white Anglo-Saxon Protestant government elite wanted to change was Joseph Lochner, an immigrant from Bavaria. Lochner came to America at the age of twenty in 1882. He worked at a bakery for eight years in Utica, New York, before opening his own bakery there in 1894. According to the *Utica Herald*, Lochner's bakery started off small and then grew profitable. Thanks to the "neatness and the excellence of its products it soon won an enviable reputation among local consumers."[22]

In 1895, the local bakers union withdrew the union label from his products and initiated a boycott of Lochner's bakery after he was charged with violating the Bakeshop Act. Lochner had allowed one of his employees to sleep above the bakery because he had nowhere else to live. This employee, Aman Schmitter, stated, "I cannot live with my folks, and do not want to live in a boarding house."[23] Even though Schmitter was not continuously working in the bakery, the government counted the time he *lived* there as if he had been *working* there; and so his *residence* there caused him to exceed the maximum hours of work provision.

History shows that Lochner and Schmitter had a close relationship. Lochner was providing a home for one of his immigrant employees who would otherwise be forced to live in a crowded and unsanitary boarding house. Schmitter's request to the government for an exemption to the Act was denied.

The small bakeries in New York needed a vehicle to challenge the Bakeshop Act, and Lochner's situation was the perfect case. Although unsuccessful in the lower courts, Lochner's case eventually made it to the Supreme Court. The Court held that the Bakeshop Act was an inappropriate use of the state's police powers and violated the "liberty of contract" doctrine. This case established liberty of contract as a fundamental right stemming from our humanity and thus protected by the Fourteenth Amendment's Due Process Clause. The Court stated, "The employee may desire to earn the extra money which would arise from his working more than the prescribed time, but this statute forbids the employer from permitting the employee to earn it."[24]

The freedom of workers to make economic decisions and negotiate their own contracts is a basic right. The fact that the government was attempting to make this decision for them is not only degrading and offensive; it interfered with their rights.

In *Lochner*, the Supreme Court was not attempting to harm workers and impose its supposed laissez-faire political viewpoint into its judicial interpretation. The Progressives used "rich" business owners as scapegoats to incite the middle and lower classes to support these economic regulations. However, the historical evidence shows that these claims were exaggerated by politicians and muckraking journalists, and only hurt small-business owners. *Lochner* was not a case of a big business exerting unequal bargaining power over a poor laborer. Yet Presidents Theodore Roosevelt and Woodrow Wilson would spend a great deal of their time and energy attempting to get this decision and others like it overruled because they wanted to gain more power for themselves and the federal government over all of commerce.

Do Children Have the Right to Work?

Throughout the Progressive Era, in cases such as *Lochner*, the courts attempted to stay true to the Constitution in the midst of sweeping attempts at reform. One goal of Progressive Era reformers, specifically Theodore Roosevelt and Woodrow Wilson, was to eradicate child labor through the passage of federal initiatives, so the federal government, and not parents, could control the lives of children in America. Despite the obvious problems with child labor, especially for very young children, the Progressives also hoped that the eradication of child labor, combined with compulsory education laws, would get children out of the care of their immigrant parents and into state-owned schools. Although education laws were still the constitutional purview of the States, federal child labor laws were a way to get around this constitutional complication.

For example, the Keating-Owen Act of 1916, for which Wilson lobbied, punished businesses that employed children in the production of goods that moved in interstate commerce. This piece of legislation was invalidated in the 1918 Supreme Court case of *Hammer v. Dagenhart*.[25] There, the Court decided that the Act, which prevented interstate commerce in the products of child labor, was not a matter for Congress to regulate. It was held that the matter of child labor in local businesses was a purely local matter that was beyond the scope of Congress's power to regulate. Additionally, under the Tenth Amendment these types of regulations were reserved to the States.

This was a time when the Court did not condone Congress's use of the Commerce Clause to justify all legislation that was not within its designated powers. The Court held that "the grant of power to Congress over the subject of interstate commerce was to enable it to regulate such commerce, and not to give it authority to control the States in their exercise of the police power over local trade and manufacture."[26]

As this case suggests, during the Progressive Era, Theodore Roosevelt and Woodrow Wilson often had trouble passing labor-friendly legislation because it was not constitutional, and legislation that was passed was continuously shot down by the courts. This remained true well into Franklin D. Roosevelt's presidency, until he threatened to add justices to the Court, and that threat forced the Court to reexamine its jurisprudence and torture its well-established interpretations of the Constitution.

Although the Keating-Owen Act was clearly in violation of congressional power in the Commerce Clause and impeded on States' rights, Wilson did not care. He wanted to end child labor and force children into public schools, and he wanted to claim that power for the federal government.

Additionally, although this law was declared unconstitutional, the initial passage of this type of legislation did have effects on businesses and state laws, as the number of working children between the ages of ten and fifteen declined by almost 50 percent between the years 1910 and 1920. By 1929, every state had a provision banning children under fourteen years old from working. Thirty-six states had laws that prohibited factory workers under the age of sixteen from working at night or for more than eight hours a day.

Thanks to Progressive Era reforms, child labor has been increasingly and heavily regulated on a federal level. The zeal for these regulations comes from both Democrats and Republicans and often paints the picture of young children being forced into deadly manual labor. However, these regulations may actually be more harmful to young people than helpful, especially considering vast improvements in modern working conditions.[27]

For young teens, heavy regulation takes away opportunities for them to gain valuable work experience. These laws also take away the right of the parents to make decisions regarding their children's balance of work and school. There is undoubtedly a high value in education, and much to be learned in schools. There is also value in learning skills through work. Children learn and gain work ethics, contacts, and real-world experience, which can transition into successful careers. In public schools, the state is able to guide children's learning and impress upon them values that are products of what the state wants students to learn. Through heavy regulation of child labor, the state is able to gain more control over a child's educational experience and take away the role of the parents in determining the best path for their individual child.

Minimum wages, another Progressive Era legacy, make it unlikely that young teens will get certain entry-level jobs. When employers are forced to pay certain minimum amounts, they will hire overqualified people for entry-level jobs, taking away entry-level positions from students who have not had the opportunity for prior experience. This is especially true when the economy is suffering and jobs are limited for everyone, regardless of qualifications. This is evidenced today, as teens face an unemployment rate *at least* 15 percent higher than adults.[28] Let me ask you, President Wilson: Is it preferable for a high school graduate to earn less than the minimum wage or to have no job and nothing to do?

Roosevelt in 1912

Despite setting the ball in motion for pro-union and pro-labor sentiments, Theodore Roosevelt was once again running for president by the time of the presidential election of 1912, and he had a new strategy to enable him to accomplish even more labor reform. In its 1912 campaign literature, the Progressive Party listed Roosevelt's many "accomplishments" in the way of labor reform throughout his political career. One brochure went on to note what Roosevelt planned to accomplish after the election of 1912 since he was no longer associated with the Republican Party. Among these goals were abolition of child labor, minimum wage for women, abolition of night shifts for women, and eight-hour workdays.[29] Despite these seemingly pro-female reform goals, these goals are actually based on Roosevelt's belief that women are the frailer sex; that they require more protection from the federal government than males. Where is that in the Constitution?

He also specifically encouraged workers to "organize." His campaign literature advocated that just in case

the law is declared unconstitutional, as are so many laws which are friendly to labor. With the recall of judicial decisions, a partial or unfair judge hasn't the last word. There is an appeal from the judge to the people. The people who live under the law will decide in the last instance about the constitutionality of the law.[30]

Roosevelt was planning to undermine the system of government set out in the Constitution by allowing judicial and legislative decisions to be "overruled" by popular mandates because he knew that many of the reforms he advocated were not within the power of the federal government. He was all for the tyranny of the majority. He loved it.

After abandoning all pretense of belonging to the Republican Party, Theodore Roosevelt ran for reelection in 1912 in an unabashed campaign to change the entire structure of the government for the benefit of the Progressive Party. Although clearly the Progressives were aware that their labor-friendly platform and proposed legislation were unconstitutional, they had a plan. Their plan was to have the people "vote" to change the decisions of the federal courts regarding the constitutionality of these laws. This was a blatant attempt to neuter the judicial branch and give power to the people led by their president (or king?).

Although Roosevelt was unsuccessful in the election of 1912, this process of overruling judicial decisions through popular mandates has been instituted on the state level in California. In 1911 these procedures were added to the California State Constitution under a Progressive governor, Hiram Johnson.

The procedures gave voters in California the power to recall state-elected officers, enact state laws and constitutional amendments by initiative, and repeal state laws by referendum.[31] This allowed for the type of direct democracy that Roosevelt advocated in 1912. The implementation of a system of direct democracy in California during the Progressive Era was allegedly to combat the influence of special interests, such as the railroad industry, on politics. However, the Progressive agenda, like Roosevelt's agenda, was to allow Progressives a more direct relationship to the citizenry that they were brainwashing.

These procedures have been used with varying success in California, but can be seen today as having potentially dangerous effects. As recently as 2008, voters in California passed a constitutional amendment prohibiting same-sex marriage. Known as Proposition 8, this amendment overruled the California Supreme Court's decision in *In re Marriage Cases* in 2008 that same-sex couples have a legal right to marriage under the California State Constitution.[32] The Court's decision was based on the truism that marriage is a fundamental liberty that should not be denied based on sexual orientation. However, thanks to Progressive Era reformers, this basic human right was snatched away.

As is typical of Progressive reforms, although this system was touted as a way to give more power to the people, it has actually ended up denying many people their fundamental liberties.

The New Deal and Beyond

Despite the best efforts of Theodore Roosevelt and Woodrow Wilson, the end of Lochner Era freedom of contract and protection of individual economic rights was not completely realized for many years. Pro-labor reforms were not finally and fully realized until the presidency of Franklin D. Roosevelt and his fascist and Socialist New Deal legislation. Even for Franklin D. Roosevelt, this was not an easy feat. He found himself, just as Theodore Roosevelt and Woodrow Wilson before him, fighting with the Supreme Court over the constitutionality of his proposed and enacted legislations. According to Professor William L. Anderson, "Not only did the New Deal transform U.S. governmental structures as we know them, it also left an economic and legal legacy that to this day is both influential and controversial."[33]

In order to combat the Great Depression, President Franklin D. Roosevelt attempted to enact various new laws such as the National Industrial Recovery Act (NIRA) and the Agricultural Adjustment Act (AAA), which sought to give the federal government more control over the national economy by forcing prices up and reducing output.[34] A group of Supreme Court justices who opposed FDR's first attempt at a New Deal were portrayed, similar to the way the justices in *Lochner* were, as standing in the way of reform that would save the economy and help the average citizen. FDR, however, would not let these justices or their fidelity to the Constitution stand in the way of Big Government.

After the retirement of older justices and appointment of new justices, the Lochner Era unofficially ended with the case *West Coast Hotel Co. v. Parrish*,[35] in 1937, which represented a significant departure from past decisions. This case upheld a minimum-wage law and marked the beginning of the end for the freedom of contract. This decision also led to a slew of new pro-labor decisions and legislation and marked a change in the interpretation of the Commerce Clause.

For example, the Supreme Court in *NLRB v. Jones & Laughlin Steel Corp.*[36] ruled in 1937 in favor of the National Labor Relations Act of 1935,[37] which stated that labor-management disputes fell under the Commerce Clause and therefore could be federally regulated. This decision represents the transition from Theodore Roosevelt simply taking it upon himself to intervene in labor disputes. Through coercion and threats, Franklin D. Roosevelt was able to make this type of intervention into private disputes "legally" a job for the federal government.

From this point on, the Constitution no longer protected an individual's economic rights, and the Supreme Court could justify almost any legislation by using the Commerce Clause. For example, in the 1942 case of *Wickard v. Filburn*[38] and the 2005 case of *Gonzales v. Raich*[39] the Supreme Court used the Commerce Clause to justify congressional regulation of wheat for personal use and medical marijuana for personal use. Neither of these products was intended even to enter the local stream of commerce, let alone into interstate commerce.

Conclusion

Reform of labor laws was an important goal of the Progressive Era reformers such as Theodore Roosevelt and Woodrow Wilson. It is easy to put a positive spin on these reforms; however, the Progressives were once again playing on the emotions of the people in order to gain control over their lives. Since the labor reforms set in motion during the Progressive Era were realized, the federal government is now able to decide which types of contracts people may enter into, how much they must be paid, when they may work and at what age, and may force businesses to negotiate with unions. The Lochner Era, which has been heavily criticized, was actually a time when the Supreme Court was giving deference to individual freedom of choice and fundamental rights. However, thanks to Theodore Roosevelt and Woodrow Wilson, the government may now take control of all our economic and property decisions, at the expense of our liberty.

But regulating the workplace was not enough for the do-gooders. They needed a way to regulate the structure of corporations so that the government could be wealthier and more powerful than any hardworking business owner. Their answer was anti-trust. *Anti* the trusts they hated and feared. We go there next.

Chapter 9

The Government's New Straw Man

Anti-trust

If private profits are to be legitimized, private fortunes made honorable, these great forces which play upon the modern field must, both individually and collectively, be accommodated to a common purpose.

—Woodrow Wilson[1]

The people have but one instrument which they can effectively use against the colossal combinations of business—and that instrument is the government of the United States.

—Theodore Roosevelt[2]

The Real Story Behind the "Robber Barons"

Class-warfare politics—where successful businessmen and women are treated as the enemies of working folks—is everywhere today. It is ugly, but it is not a new tactic. With the help of muckraking journalists, politicians during the Progressive Era managed to portray certain business leaders of the time as greedy and corrupt. And it was the beginning of significant governmental anti-trust regulation.

One of these supposed robber barons was James J. Hill. Hill's father died when James was fourteen years old. Hill immediately quit school and began to work at a grocery store in order to support his mother. He worked his way up through various industries, taking care of his mother while simultaneously saving his money in order to start his own enterprise. Hill developed his business acumen through his various jobs in the farming, shipping, steamship, fur-trading, and railroad industries. He specifically developed a talent for railroad construction.

His hard work and dedication paid off when he built the Great Northern Railroad, which was one of the most profitable and well-constructed railroads of all time.[3] At the time of his death in 1916, Hill was worth approximately fifty-three million dollars.

Hill was an example of a market entrepreneur, or a businessman whose success did not depend on any governmental handouts or subsidies.[4] His success is attributable to his own ability to overcome adversity and achieve the American dream.

Another of these robber barons was John D. Rockefeller, the son of a peddler, whose early jobs included work as an assistant bookkeeper and a produce clerk.[5] Rockefeller started his first company, Clark and Rockefeller, at the age of nineteen. Rockefeller was successful because he "paid meticulous attention to every detail of his business, constantly striving to cut his costs, improve his product, and expand his line of products."[6] Like Hill, Rockefeller started small and worked his way up through hard work and a penchant for business relations. Rockefeller's Standard Oil Company prospered quickly because of its efficiency in cutting costs and eliminating waste. Today, it is called ExxonMobil.

Despite their humble roots, self-sacrifice, and enormous financial success without government assistance, these men were often vilified during the Progressive Era. Politicians such as Wilson and Roosevelt took it upon themselves to tear down their privately created companies and bring them under governmental regulation.

Anti-trust During the Progressive Era

The Progressive Era is known for increased anti-trust enforcement and litigation. Prior to the Progressive Era, the Sherman Antitrust Act was actually being used against labor unions that thwarted interstate commerce, not the big businesses that enhanced it. However, this all changed during the presidencies of Theodore Roosevelt and Woodrow Wilson.

Roosevelt was affectionately known as the "trustbuster" for bringing more than forty anti-trust lawsuits during his years in office. By the time he ran for president in 1912, Roosevelt advocated that the government should be able to choose between "good trusts" and "bad trusts." This idea was similar to the fascist regimes in Europe that were attempting to consolidate power by regulating corporations.

Although Roosevelt did not win this election, his idea was not far from the reality that existed during the Progressive Era and continues today. The government's role in creating and sustaining monopolies is often overlooked. However, it was governmental interference in the forms of subsidies, tax abatements, land grants, and mergers that allowed many monopolies to prosper in the first place.

For example, during World War I, under Woodrow Wilson, much of the economy was regulated by the federal government, creating state-run monopolies that the government said were justified by the war. Even today, government bailouts and subsidies continue the relationship between the federal government and the big corporations that politicians publicly deride for their anti-competitive business practices. The government does not want to destroy all businesses; it just wants to pick and choose the winners and losers in the market.

One frequently overlooked fact due to the muckraking journalism that portrayed the "horrors" of these big corporations was how the business practices of these companies were actually helping, rather than harming, consumers. An efficient corporation has the ability to reduce costs and prices while increasing the quality of a product. Competitors may be "forced" to decrease prices and increase the quality of their products, but this would be to the benefit of the consumer.

Although some businessmen of the time were genuinely crooks, some large companies were dominating the market because they were using effective and successful business techniques that were driving down prices, creating quality products, and winning the business of vast numbers of consumers. Dismantling these corporations increased governmental control of the market, destroyed private property, and increased unemployment.

Theodore Roosevelt: The Trustbuster

The power for the federal government to regulate interstate commerce comes from Article 1, Section 8, of the Constitution, or the Commerce Clause. The Commerce Clause grants Congress the power to "regulate Commerce with foreign Nations, and among the several States, and with the Indian Tribes." The Supreme Court in *Charles River Bridge v. Warren Bridge*,[7] in 1837, defined the right of the federal government to police property rights and to limit them is in the public interest as implied in the Commerce Clause. In this case, the Massachusetts legislature incorporated the Charles River Bridge Company in 1785 to build a bridge which would collect tolls. In 1828, the legislature created the Warren Bridge Company to build a free bridge in the same area. The Charles River Bridge Company argued that this new bridge took away its tolls and traffic, and violated the initial contract. The Court ruled on the side of the State, holding that the interest of the community in creating new channels of travel and trade outweighed the private interest of the Charles River Bridge Company. This case established the lamentable principle that with respect to interstate commerce, rights of ownership are subordinate to rights of the community.[8]

The Supreme Court affirmed this theory in the 1877 case of *Munn v. Illinois*,[9] which established that private property that involves the public must submit to being controlled by the public for the common good. In 1871, the Illinois legislature responded to pressure from a farmers' association called the National Grange and set maximum rates that private companies could charge for grain storage. The private Chicago firm Munn and Scott was charged with violating this law by charging less than its competitors. The Supreme Court held that a state may regulate these private practices, since grain storage involves the public interest. Justice Waite, writing for the Court, stated, "When property is affected with a public interest, it ceases to be *juris privati* only."[10] He obviously spent more time reading *Das Kapital* than *The Wealth of Nations* or even the U.S. Constitution.

Increasing government regulation of private ownership for the good of the public interest is the basis for anti-trust legislation. However, these early cases show that the Supreme Court was significantly overreaching in allowing states to interfere with private property rights. The Court established this extremely vague "public interest" justification which would be used throughout American history to justify unprecedented amounts of governmental regulation and thus destruction of private property.

Anti-trust regulation also prohibits the free exchange of private property and hinders the ability of people to enter into agreements out of their own free will. The horrors portrayed to the public during the Progressive Era were pervasive and persuasive enough that few questioned the motives or desirability of anti-trust laws.

Adding fuel to the fire were actual crooks who took advantage of the free-market system, often with aid from the government. It is clear, as the chairman of the Ludwig von Mises Institute, Llewellyn H. Rockwell Jr., states, anti-trust laws are "a political weapon that accomplishes no social good and imposes much social harm."[11]

Roosevelt was attempting to take down big business as a political tool to further his own political agenda. He believed that no corporation should be as powerful as the government. Roosevelt also wanted to concentrate power in the executive and therefore thought of himself as a competitor of the large corporations. Anti-trust enforcement also furthered his agenda of social reform. By dismantling trusts, regardless of their legitimacy, he was able to take down the wealthy. At the time, countless reforms, including a federal income tax, were enacted by targeting the upper class.

Roosevelt became widely known for his enforcement and strengthening of anti-trust laws such as the Sherman Antitrust Act. The Act was passed in 1890[12] and formed the basis for prosecution of trusts and monopolies that the government argued restrained interstate trade or commerce. However, this Act was rarely utilized to prosecute businesses until Roosevelt's administration. As he stated in 1902 in a speech at Providence, Rhode Island: "The great corporations which we have grown to speak of rather loosely as trusts are the creatures of the State, and the State not only has the right to control them, but it is duty bound to control them wherever the need of such control is shown."[13]

Enforcement of the Sherman Act prior to Roosevelt's efforts was scarce: "Early Supreme Court cases did not treat bigness per se as illegal under the new antitrust law."[14] This is illustrated in the 1895 Supreme Court case of *United States v. E. C. Knight Company*,[15] where the Court held that the Sherman Act did not apply to manufacturers. This case was brought after the *American*

Sugar Refining Company acquired the E. C. Knight Company in 1892. The American Sugar Company gained control of several other companies as well, which gave it control over a significant portion of the American sugar manufacturing industry. This acquisition combined sugar manufacturing companies that had been in competition with each other. It was alleged that this transaction violated the Sherman Antitrust Act. However, the American Sugar Company only gained control over the production and manufacture of the sugar, which was efficient because it allowed these companies to share resources while still being able to operate independently.

The Court held that American Sugar's manufacturing monopoly only indirectly affected trade and commerce, and thus did not violate the Sherman Act. The Court ruled that Congress did not intend "to make criminal the acts of persons in the acquisition and control of property which the states of their residence or creation sanctioned or permitted."[16] Historical evidence validates this decision. American Sugar's domination of the market slipped from almost 98 percent in 1893 to about 25 percent in 1927. This was due to competitive market forces, not governmental interference.[17] This example shows that when left alone, the market can regulate itself.

This decision was overturned in the landmark Supreme Court case of *Northern Securities Co. v. United States*[18] in 1904. In 1901, James J. Hill, the grocery clerk turned railroad owner and president of the Great Northern Railway, attempted to take over the Chicago, Burlington and Quincy Railroad (CB&Q) with the financial support of J. P. Morgan, who owned the Northern Pacific Railway. However, Hill and Morgan ended up competing with Edward Henry Harriman, president of the Union Pacific Railroad and the Southern Pacific Railroad, for ownership of the CB&Q. Hill and Morgan were ultimately successful in acquiring a majority of stock in the CB&Q and created a holding company to manage all three railroads. Although President William McKinley did not want to pursue anti-trust litigation in this case, after his assassination in 1901, Roosevelt ascended to the presidency and was eager to begin his legacy as the trustbuster.

The holding company that had been established, the Northern Securities Company, was now owned by two former competitors in interstate railroads. The Court determined that this fact alone was enough to restrain trade and commerce, in violation of the Sherman Act.

This case also significantly changed the common law definition of *restraint of trade*.[19] Under common law, an illegal restraint did not exist unless outsiders were somehow excluded from competition. This standard significantly changed during the Progressive Era. The new standard held that when two companies combined, they automatically could not compete with each other and therefore would constitute a restraint of trade. As Justice John Marshall Harlan stated in the opinion, "[T]he mere existence of such a combination and the power acquired by the holding company as its trustee constitute a menace to, and a restraint upon, that freedom of commerce."[20]

The decision in *Northern Securities Co.* was not unanimous, but instead warranted two separate dissents, one written by Chief Justice White and the other by Justice Holmes. Justice Holmes surprisingly not only put forth the argument regarding the departure from common law, but also attacked the far-reaching effects of this decision. He stated that if such a "remote result of the exercise of an ordinary incident of property and personal freedom is enough to make that exercise unlawful, there is hardly any transaction . . . that may not be made a crime by the finding of a jury or court."[21] However, this type of restraint upon the use of personal property and the exercise of commercial freedom by intense governmental regulation characterizes Roosevelt's anti-trust efforts.

The decision in *Northern Securities Co.* dismantled the company that James J. Hill had built from the ground up. Comparatively, the other railroads that competed with Hill were subsidized or funded by the government. They were the true crooks. According to Loyola economics professor Thomas DiLorenzo, "[T]he key to his [the market entrepreneur's] success as a capitalist is his ability to please the consumer, for in a capitalist society the consumer ultimately calls the economic shots."[22]

The market entrepreneur competes against the political entrepreneur, who succeeds by attempting to use money and power to influence politicians to grant him business subsidies or favorable legislation. As Hill once wrote regarding his competitors who received governmental aid, "The government should not furnish capital to these companies, in addition to their enormous land subsidies, to enable them to conduct their business in competition with enterprises that have received no aid from the public treasury."[23] The Union Pacific and Central Pacific railroads were created by the Pacific Railroad

Act of 1862 to connect Omaha, Nebraska, and Sacramento, California. The Lincoln administration pulled off this stunt aimed at keeping Nebraska and California neutral during the Civil War.

The companies that the feds funded took blatant advantage of the taxpayers' money every step of the way.[24] For example, because they were paid by the mile, they often built tracks that were longer than necessary or out of the way. They had no incentive to find the shortest route possible in order to save money, because the project was funded by the government. Political entrepreneurs took advantage of taxpayers and genuinely harmed consumers. On the other hand, private companies were prosecuted for using their own money to build their businesses in the most successful way possible. The historical horror story of robber barons never takes into account this important distinction.

The massive numbers of anti-trust cases brought by the Roosevelt administration continued to reach the Supreme Court. In the 1911 case *United States v. American Tobacco Company*, the Supreme Court's decision once again mandated the dissolution of a successful corporation with little proof of economic harm to consumers, increased prices, or predatory tactics. The Roosevelt administration brought this suit, alleging conspiracy to restrain interstate and foreign commerce in tobacco products through the consolidation of several tobacco companies into the American Tobacco Company.

The Supreme Court stated that the American Tobacco Company

> was manufacturing 86 per cent or thereabouts of all the cigarettes produced in the United States, above 26 per cent of all the smoking tobacco, more than 22 per cent of all plug tobacco [a type of chewing tobacco], 51 per cent of all little cigars, 6 per cent each of all snuff and fine cut tobacco, and over 2 per cent of all cigars and cheroots.[25]

This issue reached the Supreme Court from the United States Court of Appeals for the Second Circuit in New York City in a 1908 case called *United States v. American Tobacco Company*.[26] In this lower court opinion, Judge Emile Henry Lacombe actually found that there was no indication that prices had been increased due to American Tobacco's business practices. Nor was there any persuasive evidence that unfair competition or improper practices were being employed by American Tobacco. In his dissent in the Circuit Court opinion, Judge Henry Galbraith Ward stated that American's conduct was not illegal or oppressive but that "they strove, as every businessman strives, to increase their business, and that their great success is a natural growth resulting from industry, intelligence, and economy."[27]

The history of the American Tobacco Company proves the accuracy of the statement by Judge Ward. The formation of the American Tobacco Company represents the efforts of the five largest tobacco firms at the time combining their efforts to create the most efficient company possible. Although American Tobacco bought 250 firms between 1890 and 1907, few were actually competitive with cigarette manufacturers.[28] Merging some of the largest firms and acquiring companies at all stages of tobacco manufacturing made financial sense at the time. Consolidation was the only way to maximize the use of the best and most efficient machinery and to eliminate or reduce expenditures and thus produce a less expensive product.

While the numbers seem daunting, evidence shows that just a year before the American Tobacco Company was dissolved by the courts, there were three hundred independent cigarette manufacturers, three thousand independent plants manufacturing tobacco, and twenty thousand independent firms in the cigar industry. The tobacco industry was easy to get into, and despite consolidation of the top firms, there were still plenty of independent firms to compete.

Additionally, there is little evidence of monopolistic conduct. American Tobacco was often accused of price cutting by entering a market, deliberately decreasing prices to drive other businesses out, and then increasing prices once they were gone. Price-cutting practices were not a general policy and would not have been practical or fiscally sound. There may have been isolated incidents; however, there is no evidence that this was a generalized national policy put into place to drive out all local competitors.

Leaving out any emotional appeals, using predatory pricing to knock out local competition does not make economic sense. As D. T. Armentano, Professor of Economics Emeritus at the University of Hartford, stated, "Predatory practices are expensive, and it is not usually profitable to attempt to eliminate competition through this technique."[29]

American Tobacco was also accused of buying firms just to shut down the facilities. Although American did acquire firms for the brand name, and shut down factories that did not make sense to operate, this was done purely as a business measure. The firms were fairly and generously compensated, and the justification of acquiring brand names was highly relevant at the time. Brand-name identification was a key to cigarette sales.

Another pivotal case carrying on Roosevelt's legacy was the 1911 Supreme Court case of *Standard Oil Company of New Jersey v. United States* in which the Standard Oil Company of New Jersey was dissolved. Beginning in the 1870s, the Standard Oil Company of New Jersey grew in size through its ability to refine oil effectively while cutting the cost to the consumer. Standard Oil was accused of using its size against competitors in ways that were legal but considered to be anti-competitive. The company was charged with under-pricing, getting preferential treatment from railroads, and threatening to cut off suppliers and distributors who cooperated with Standard's competitors.

At the pinnacle of Standard Oil Company's sales in the oil market, the costs and prices of refined oil reached their *lowest* levels in the history of the petroleum industry. However, Roosevelt wanted to dismantle the company in order to further his political agenda. As Professor William Anderson, who has studied the case, has stated, "Standard Oil had become the single domi-nant producer of oil not because it had used coercion, but rather because it was by far the most efficient petroleum firm in the world. . . . Those facts meant nothing to Roosevelt, however, who was looking to further his repu-tation at the expense of U.S. companies."[30]

Although the Standard Oil Company was deemed to be in violation of the Sherman Antitrust Act, the Court did not address any specific eco-nomic harm to consumers that was a consequence of these violations. For example, the Court did not address in the "reasonable conduct" standard whether Standard Oil raised prices or produced inferior products. It also did not address what exactly were the "unusual" business methods that Standard Oil was supposedly employing.

Standard Oil represents another example of the myth of inferior products and higher prices. The price of oil actually went from sixty cents per barrel when Rockefeller and the Standard Oil Company entered the industry to less than six cents per barrel at the turn of the twentieth century. This must be credited to efforts to eliminate waste and increase production, as that was the key to Rockefeller's fortune. Unfortunately, his political influence could only go so far.

Anti-trust Enforcement under Wilson

The increase in judicial enforcement of anti-trust laws during the Roosevelt administration was adopted and enhanced by Woodrow Wilson's administration. During Wilson's administration, the Clayton Antitrust Act[31] was passed to strengthen the Sherman Act by outlining specific types of anti-competitive conduct and exempting labor unions and agricultural organizations from prosecution under the Act.

Also under Wilson, the Federal Trade Commission Act[32] further increased the power of the federal government by creating a new federal agency. This Act created the Federal Trade Commission (FTC) and charged the body with prosecuting "unfair methods of competition in commerce, and unfair or deceptive acts of practices in commerce." In all of these statutes, Congress essentially gave *itself* the power to engage in a deeper level of predatory regulation of businesses that the president *himself* selected as targets.

Wilson's increase of anti-trust enforcement took a drastic turn during World War I. The façade of judicial enforcement gone, the nation's industry was put into the hands of the government. Enhanced governmental regulation of business was foreshadowed by Wilson's brief time as governor of New Jersey.

The New Jersey Case: Wilson's Failed Experiment

Starting around 1847, New Jersey's leaders decided to advocate for granting charters to citizens of other states, an act which was unprecedented at the time, because traditionally businesses only incorporated in their home states.[33] This push culminated with a revision of New Jersey law in 1896 where the State of New Jersey was able to raise revenue by structuring its laws to be more favorable to corporations. This increase in revenue and decrease in taxes continued to rise through 1904. However, even before the full effects of these changes were felt, Governor George Werts, in 1896, stated, "New

Jersey, with no tax for State purposes and practically out of debt is unique among her sister States. No such showing can be made by any other State, nor, I apprehend, by any civilized nation anywhere."[34]

Other states noticed; a member of the 1867 New York Constitutional Convention observed,

> One of the smallest States of the Union, with not more than two-thirds of her area susceptible of being devoted to agriculture, [New Jersey] has placed herself, by the aid of her location and corporations, as a power in the Union. Strip her of what her corporations have made her, the wealth and position she has obtained through them, and where would New Jersey be to-day?[35]

By engaging in an optimal legal structure through enabling statutes, New Jersey was able to get out of debt and become a national force to be reckoned with. Other states were naturally threatened by the position of New Jersey, which was often referred to during this time period as the "Traitor State." John D. Rockefeller incorporated Standard Oil in New Jersey.

Luckily for every other State in the Union, particularly Delaware, Woodrow Wilson would soon be elected governor of New Jersey and destroy this prosperity. Governor Wilson led the New Idea movement to reform corporate laws in New Jersey. In his gubernatorial inaugural address, he complained, "We are much too free with grants of charters to corporations in New Jersey."[36] However, his plans did not come to fruition until he was a lame duck governor and president-elect in February 1912.

At that time, New Jersey finally adopted strict anti-trust statutes known as the Seven Sisters. Provisions in these laws expanded the definition of a trust to make it more inclusive, forbade forming any future holding companies, and even made it a misdemeanor to *promote* a business venture that might end up as a trust. Not surprisingly, this legislation led to a dramatic drop in franchise tax revenue through the end of World War I. Wilson was long gone as the prosperity that New Jersey had enjoyed as the Mother of the Trusts began to collapse under these new, harsher laws.

New Jersey had been considered the Mother of the Trusts because the State had previously attracted and created a favorable legal environment for big businesses. Lawmakers realized that Wilson's reform changing this standard could not easily be undone. Although in 1917 Governor Walter Edge, in his inaugural address, stated, "The apparently drastic provisions of the laws [Seven Sisters] have driven away from New Jersey many corporations formerly operating under Jersey charters and have prevented others from incorporating here," it was too late.[37] Delaware took New Jersey's position as the preferred state in which to incorporate a business and remains in this position today.

Wilson's anti-trust movement at the state level in New Jersey did not work. His reforms only pushed out the corporations that had been flocking to New Jersey and discouraged future incorporation within the State. Yet this did not seem to discourage Wilson from continuing Roosevelt's trust-busting legacy by enhancing the Sherman Antitrust Act with the Clayton Antitrust Act, and encouraging federal governmental control of businesses during World War I. This wartime collectivism gave almost complete power over all industries to federal governmental agencies that were headed by big-business leaders. This was the height of hypocrisy, but it also served as a blueprint for future regulation of business.

World War I and the Blueprint for Government-Regulated Businesses

More than any other single period, World War I was the critical watershed for the American business system. It was a "war collectivism," a totally planned economy run largely by big-business interests through the instrumentality of the central government, which served as the model, the precedent, and the inspiration for state corporate capitalism for the remainder of the twentieth century.

—MURRAY N. ROTHBARD[38]

American entry into World War I was supported by big-business interests. The decision to enter the war prompted an unhealthy relationship between business and government. From the time the war effort began, plans were quickly set into motion, advocated by big business/governmental agencies such as the United States Chamber of Commerce. The goal was to mobilize all American businesses to support the war effort.

An early effort to fuse business and government was the Council of National Defense, which included the influential Advisory Commission that consisted of private industrialists.[39] This commission designed the system of purchasing war supplies, regulating food, and maintaining control and censorship. Although this commission was intended to be a nonpartisan link between business and government, in reality it put the power to regulate the wartime economy into the hands of big-business leaders.

The Wilson administration soon established the War Industries Board, which gained control over all purchasing, pricing, and allocating of resources. The War Industries Board was led by the notorious Progressive Bernard Baruch, who was clearly eager for the opportunity to regulate the economy, as he had presented an idea for war mobilization to President Wilson almost three years before America's entry into the war.[40]

The War Industries Board was partially run by big-business leaders, who were then granted wartime contracts. The corruption to which this fusion between governmental and business interests led could not be more apparent, and yet there was no check on these policies. As is typical of American governments, war can be, has been, and here was used to justify almost any inappropriate seizure of power.

President Woodrow Wilson also appointed Progressive Herbert Hoover to the position of Food Administrator (or as we would call him today, Food Czar). Under his rule, the U.S. government purchased the entire supply of U.S. and Cuban sugar crops. In order to create and sustain federal regulation of food through the Food Act of 1917, prices of sugar and wheat were then set at one price that was arrived at through a series of calculations. This type of market manipulation ensured that while the prices would not go up, they also could not go down. Amidst heavy regulation of the economy, wartime industry was standardized by the Conservation Division of the War Industries Board. This meant that only certain styles, varieties, colors, sizes, or models of certain products could be produced.

Railroads were seized and operated directly by the government under the Railroad War Board, which ordered them to coordinate all railroad operations. This coordination would undoubtedly have been perceived as an illegal combination under any of the nation's anti-trust legislation. Thus the federal government not only selectively prosecuted, selectively enforced, and routinely broke its own laws; it ordered private businesses to break them as well. The government also took over the telephone, telegraph, shipbuilding, and wheat-trading industries.[41]

Government regulation of industry during this time was harmful to small-business owners and independent contractors. The government was regulating prices and markets, and big-business owners, in conjunction with federal agencies, were given the job of awarding contracts. Unlike a privately run business or monopoly, the government could use its power to control propaganda to embarrass or shame any private industrials that were not benefitting from the wartime economy and dared to protest.[42] Consumers were also harmed by price-fixing, as in the sugar and wheat industries, where too much regulation led to high prices and shortages.

Governmental economic relations during this time may have benefitted certain businesses, but they were more harmful to consumers than most of the monopolies that had been attacked by Wilson and Roosevelt during their trust-busting sprees. Progressives hoped that the ideas of cooperation instead of competition that characterized the wartime economy would transfer into peacetime as well. In fact, many aspects of anti-trust regulation set out during Wilson's administration in the form of the wartime regulations sparked ideas and changes that can still be seen today. Franklin D. Roosevelt was the assistant secretary of the navy at this time and counted influential Progressive figures such as Hoover and Baruch among his friends. Many early aspects of FDR's New Deal legislation such as the AAA and the NIRA can be traced to this time period.[43]

Modern Anti-trust Regulation

Today, Wal-Mart stores have become a pervasive part of American life. Similar to the founders of Standard Oil and the Great Northern Railway, founder Sam Walton started small and worked hard. Wal-Mart began as a discount store in Arkansas called Walton's Five and Dime. Wal-Mart steadily built up to become the largest retailer and one of the largest corporations in the world. This is just another example of the American dream: Through hard work, a mom-and-pop store in the heartland of America could eventually become one of the most profitable companies in the world. Wal-Mart's consumers can always expect low prices due to the company's highly effective business model.

Yet Wal-Mart faces constant criticism and accusations that it should be subject to anti-trust regulation.[44] During the Clinton administration, the Wilson-created Federal Trade Commission launched an investigation into Wal-Mart's business practices.[45] In an article outlining the "necessary" anti-trust case against Wal-Mart, Barry C. Lynn stated, "We must restore antitrust law to its central role in protecting the economic rights, properties, and liberties of the American citizen, and first of all use that power to break Wal-Mart into pieces."[46]

However, just as in the Progressive Era, the American consumer does not need to be protected from a business; the consumer needs to be protected from the government. As it is stated in that very same article, "[T]he firm rose to dominance in the same way that many thousands of other companies before it did—through smart innovation, a unique culture, and a focus on serving the customer."[47] It is therefore unclear why customers, who have the power to make their own decisions in the market, need to be protected from Wal-Mart's low prices, vast array of products, and efficient service.

Maryland legislators even went so far as to create a Wal-Mart Law that would have pushed health-care costs onto large companies, targeting Wal-Mart specifically.[48] This measure was struck down in the United States Court of Appeals for the Fourth Circuit in Baltimore. Modern anti-Wal-Mart fervor proves that the Progressive Era sentiment of anger toward big business, just because it is big, still exists today. Anti-trust crusaders attack all large and profitable companies, such as Microsoft and Intel.

President Barack Obama announced that during his administration, there would be increased enforcement of anti-trust laws.[49] His administration rewrote the Department of Justice guidelines in an attempt to reverse the policies of the Bush administration that were perceived to be pro-defendant in anti-trust cases. However, the relationship between big business and the government is as strong as ever. The Obama administration cannot downplay its relationship to big business through the use of bailouts and subsidies by attempting to distract the American people with a tough stance on anti-trust.

Bailouts to Wall Street and the Detroit auto industry have seemingly accomplished little. However, they do continue to strengthen the dysfunctional relationship between the federal government and big business. As Murray Rothbard stated, "[T]he greater the extent of government subsidy in the economy . . . the more the market is prevented from working, and the more inefficient will the market be in catering to consumer wants. Hence, the greater the government subsidy, the lower will be the standard of living of everyone, of all the consumers."[50] Just as it was used during the Progressive Era, modern anti-trust policy only gives the government more control over winners and losers in the market.

Conclusion

The governmental interference into private business that originated during the Progressive Era in the form of anti-trust regulation is clearly unnecessary and actually harmful to consumers. During the presidencies of Theodore Roosevelt and Woodrow Wilson, anti-trust was never a way to protect consumers but a way to bring big and powerful companies under the control of the federal government and leave the government's friends alone.

Privately owned and run businesses have incentives to cut costs and prices and improve quality, all of which is beneficial to consumers. Meanwhile, the government actually promotes monopolistic practices through bailouts, subsidies, cartels, and political favors, using taxpayer money and diminishing accountability. Additionally, there is no check on the activities of the federal government that are anticompetitive or restrain trade, because it is not subject to its own anti-trust laws. This is what Roosevelt and Wilson wanted, and this is what they brought us.

But controlling the structure of corporations only whetted the Progressives' appetite for control of the land. How could they do that?

Next, we'll see their assault on private property in the name of dirt.

Chapter 10

Mismanagement, Waste, and Hypocrisy

Conservation

In the name of conservation Theodore Roosevelt squandered huge amounts of money and degraded much of our natural environment. He launched a federal dam-building program that flooded canyons, disrupted natural water flows, silted up waterways, raised water temperatures, lost huge amounts of water through evaporation, and increased the salinity of irrigated soil so much that very little could grow on it. Roosevelt's national forest policies contributed to overgrazing of grasslands and to forest fires of unprecedented ferocity.

—JIM POWELL[1]

When Jamestown, Virginia, and Plymouth, Massachusetts, were settled, both had a system of common property. "The settlers did not have even a modified interest in the soil . . . everything produced by them went into the store, in which they had no proprietorship." Because the settlers had no financial stake in their work, they would not push themselves to perform at full capacity. The result of this shirking was starvation.

Just as it seemed that the colonies had no chance of surviving, Sir Thomas Dale in Jamestown and William Bradford in Plymouth discovered that, by recognizing the colonists' private property rights, they could save the failing colonies.

> As soon as the settlers were thrown upon their own resources, and each freeman had acquired the right of owning property, the colonists quickly developed what became the distinguishing characteristic of Americans—an

aptitude for all kinds of craftsmanship coupled with an innate genius for experimentation and invention.[2]

In short, with ownership of private property and a market free of government, the colonies began to thrive.

Like Sir Thomas Dale and William Bradford, America's Founding Fathers understood the importance of private property, and they embedded this principle in the foundations of our country. However, it seems that in recent times America is moving away from this principle, and property rights are being overlooked. How is it that the significance of property rights has been so perverted in our modern times?

It all began in 1890 after the director of the census announced that the frontier had closed. When Theodore Roosevelt came into the presidency after the assassination of William McKinley in 1901, he responded to this news by making it his personal goal to prevent the "greedy" corporations from "exploiting" America's remaining resources. He said,

> I acted on the theory that the President could at any time in his discretion withdraw from entry any of the public lands of the United States and reserve the same for forestry, for water-power sites, for irrigation, and other public purposes. Without such action it would have been impossible to stop the activity of the land thieves.[3]

It was Roosevelt's personal belief that the government was not only better at understanding the people's future needs but also better at striking a balance between the people's present and future needs. Never mind that the political environment easily manipulates politicians, while corporations respond to market conditions.

Acting upon his goal, Roosevelt set aside 150 national forests, 4 national game preserves, 51 federal bird reserves, 18 national monuments, and 5 national parks, which amounted to a whopping 230 million acres of land. The 150 national forests alone were the size of France, Belgium, and the Netherlands combined. So began America's turning its back on the significance of private property and replacing this cherished principle with mismanagement, waste, and hypocrisy.

National Monuments

You get in your car to drive home from a long day at work. You realize that the gas gauge is low, so you need to make a stop at the gas station to fill up. As you pull into the station, you sigh; gas prices are up to $3.90 a gallon! You do the math in your head. To fill up your sedan, it will cost you about $60. You sigh again because there is nothing you can do; you already traded in your SUV last month (the $80-plus per fillup you were spending was more than you could afford), and you need to get to work and back home. Oh wait, there is something you can do: Thank Theodore Roosevelt, because the high gas prices you see today are a direct result of the conservation movement he began in 1902. You may be thinking, *How can somebody who was president more than one hundred years ago affect my life today?* The answer lies within the Antiquities Act.

The Antiquities Act, officially called "An Act for the Preservation of American Antiquities," was passed by Congress and signed into law by Roosevelt in 1906. Originally, the Antiquities Act gave the president the power to limit the use of federal lands by an executive order, specifically for the purpose of protecting antiquities, or Native American ruins and artifacts. In this way, the president could quickly protect any Native American burial site from being pillaged by pot hunters, something that would be much more difficult if it was necessary to wait for the slow approval of Congress before taking action.

The Act was supposed to be "confined to the smallest area compatible with proper care and management of the objects to be protected."[4] However, Roosevelt abused this parameter of the Act from its inception. On September 24th 1906, he proclaimed, via his power under the Antiquities Act, Devils Tower in Wyoming as the very first national monument. It was a massive 1,347 acres, hardly the "smallest area compatible with proper care and management" as the Act called for. Unfortunately, this abuse only seemed to escalate as Roosevelt created more national monuments. The Petrified Forest National Monument, which Roosevelt converted into a national monument on December 8th 1906, was an astounding 15,000 acres.

By 1907, seeing this trend of abuse, Congress tried to curb the president's power. Roosevelt reacted by more broadly interpreting the meaning of "'objects . . . of scientific interest,' and the extent of the reservations necessary to protect them."[5] Under his interpretation of the statute, on January 11th 1908, Roosevelt turned 806,400 acres of the Grand Canyon into a national monument. This unfathomable reservation "far exceed[ed] the expectations of even the most avid supporters of the Antiquities Act."[6]

President Franklin D. Roosevelt continued this egregious abuse when he seized land owned by the State of Wyoming and unilaterally converted it to federally owned land not to protect Native American relics or antiquities, but to allow John D. Rockefeller Jr. to enjoy the land as a vacation spot. Rockefeller was worried that the town of Jackson, Wyoming, was becoming too touristy and overdeveloped, so he collaborated with FDR to prevent this from happening. To this end, Rockefeller bought more than 35,000 acres around Jackson Hole and donated them to the federal government. This was the same John D. Rockefeller whose Standard Oil of New Jersey corporation had been broken up by FDR's distant cousin, Theodore.

Then, in 1943, FDR took that land and the Jackson Hole area and converted it into the Jackson Hole National Monument. This was done against the will of people living in and around Jackson Hole, as well as the Wyoming legislators, and it cost Wyoming a considerable amount in local tax revenue. Nevertheless, FDR chose to veto a federal bill that would have de-established the Jackson Hole National Monument.

In 1950, Congress officially de-established the monument, but instead of giving the land back to Wyoming, Congress turned it into the Grand Teton National Park, which was a whopping 310,000 acres. Wyoming insisted that the bill creating the Grand Teton National Park also include a provision that would amend the Antiquities Act in such a way that congressional approval would be required for any future creation or enlargement of national monuments in Wyoming. Fortunately for Wyoming, it prevailed on this account, even though it could not get back the land the federal government had already stolen.

President Carter fell in line behind this pattern of abuse when he used the Antiquities Act in 1980 to seize fifty-six million acres of public lands in Alaska and turn them into a national monument. Congress opposed Carter's actions to such a degree that it quickly passed the Alaska National Interest Land Conservation Act (ANILCA), which converted the national monument into national parks and wildlife reserves, thus enabling many of the land's resources to be used once again. The ANILCA also instated a congressional approval requirement for any land over five thousand acres that the president sought to take from Alaska under the guise of the Antiquities Act.

However, the ANILCA did set aside part of this land as a wildlife refuge, the Arctic National Wildlife Refuge (ANWR), which was meant to remain untouched. The ANWR, which is an expansive 19 million acres, consists of 1.5 million acres that are sitting on top of a vast amount of oil, which Americans are not lawfully permitted to drill into. Instead, Americans are forced to depend on other countries, such as Saudi Arabia, Venezuela, Nigeria, Iraq, and Colombia for oil, improving their economies while Americans are confronted with ever-rising gas prices at home. While this could all change if the federal government would allow us to access these resources, unfortunately for Americans, the Obama administration continues to follow blindly the staunch conservation policies that Roosevelt set in motion.

In 1996, the Antiquities Act was further abused when Bill Clinton proclaimed, via his power under the Act, that 1.7 million acres of land in Utah would be converted into the Grand Staircase-Escalante National Monument. He did this even though he had publicly assured the American people and Utah's state legislators that he would not do so. In fact, Utah legislators so opposed the measure that Clinton notified them and the Utah governor only twenty-four hours in advance, and the ceremony was held in Arizona. As a result of Clinton's actions, the local economy was destroyed, having forced the Andalex Coal Mine to shut down.

It seems that President Obama also has plans to abuse the Antiquities Act. An internal document from President Obama to Ken Salazar, the secretary of the interior, was leaked in 2011. It listed seventeen sites in eleven States totaling thirteen million acres of state-owned land that Obama was thinking of taking through the Antiquities Act.

The Antiquities Act is no longer used for its alleged purpose, and the States are paying the price with millions of acres of their land. States throughout the country are trying to induce Congress to enact federal legislation that would require congressional approval of any land taken from them. Moreover, some States are trying to pass state laws that would allow them to take back, through eminent domain, federal lands that once belonged to them.

Can the Government Make It Rain?

Although the government had been encouraging people a hundred years ago to move out west and farm the land, few of the homesteaders who did go west ended up securing title to their property. It seemed that the conditions there were too arid for successful farming. In some areas the rainfall averaged less than four inches per year.

Theodore Roosevelt, always concerned with the jockeying of power between countries, thought that the West should be settled; otherwise another country might be encouraged to take that land from America. Therefore, as a part of his conservation movement, Roosevelt sought to develop systems of irrigation throughout the West, believing this would bolster settlement there.

Roosevelt chose to do this in spite of the fact that private companies had tried it before him and gone bankrupt, and in spite of the fact that, following the private companies, states had tried, but only managed to hemorrhage money. For example, *The Irrigation Age* reported that the "Arizona Improvement company controlling the largest irrigation system in the Southwest, will pass tomorrow [November 17th 1897] into the hands of a receiver," having gone bankrupt.[7]

To build all of these dams and irrigation systems, Roosevelt signed into law the Reclamation Act, whereby taxes would be collected from easterners and midwesterners and then used to subsidize the irrigation projects out west. The implications of this Act led to strong objections by easterners and mid-westerners. They did not approve of their tax dollars being used for projects that were of no discernable benefit to them. However, more surprising was the fact that westerners did not support Roosevelt's plan either. They disliked the idea of the federal government controlling how their land would be used. Nevertheless, Roosevelt barreled ahead with his plans, unconcerned with the predominant opinion of the American people or with property rights.

In addition to figuring out the financial logistics of the irrigation projects, the Reclamation Act gave the secretary of the interior, Ethan Allan Hitchcock, the authority to create the United States Reclamation Service. The purpose of this Service was to identify possible irrigation projects out west, and between its inception in 1902 and 1907, the Service began approximately thirty projects throughout the West. Ironically, the Reclamation Service was a dam-building government monopoly. In other words, Roosevelt, the trust-buster, had no problem creating a monopoly when it was government run and would accomplish one of his policy objectives.

Much like the corporations and states before him, Roosevelt encountered many serious problems with his irrigation projects, causing waste on a colossal scale. To begin, the government subsidized the cost of the irrigation projects. Due to this, farmers were able to pay lower prices for water than they would have paid otherwise. The incentive for farmers to conserve water dissipated, leading them to use water on less valuable crops than they would have if they were paying the full price for it.

Additionally, the government didn't always make the wisest decisions about where to conduct its projects. In many instances, the government poured money into locations that were only capable of producing the lowest-valued crops, while areas with more potential remained unimproved.

Moreover, the Service sometimes took up projects on land that was not suited to irrigation. In other words, the Service wasted money by investing in projects that would never come to fruition. In other instances, the Service's projects, though well placed, would go awry, causing the land to become waterlogged. The cost of then draining these lands was very expensive.

Furthermore, even when the government was successful in bringing irrigation to the West, many of the farmers knew very little about the irrigation systems they were using. They did not know how to take care of them, and the systems fell into various states of disrepair. Sadly, since many of these farmers had become dependent on the irrigation systems, this, naturally, led to their ruin.

What's more, even projects that were both successfully completed and didn't fall into disrepair often proved to be disastrous for the farmers. These irrigation systems often increased the salinity of the water to such a high level that the water damaged any crop on which it was used.

Unfortunately, because the people believed in the government officials who were conducting the irrigation projects, thousands of people sacrificed their livelihoods to move out west and ended up losing everything.

One example of a disastrous government irrigation project took place in Boise, Idaho. It began in 1904 when the Reclamation Service promised to provide water to the Boise area at half the current cost. Believing this, Idaho politicians got behind this project, which, in turn, encouraged people to buy up the land adjacent to the proposed canal lines. Even the secretary of the interior promised that "agricultural prosperity could be cultivated in the soil of the Boise Valley in Idaho."[8]

Little did they know, this promise was a farce. In 1905, the cost of the entire project was projected to be roughly $1.3 million, and the cost to each farmer for bringing water onto his land would be no more than $10 to $15 an acre. By 1915, however, the estimate for the project was an astounding $8 million, and the cost to farmers for bringing water onto their lands had escalated to $80 per acre. Worst still, by 1918, the price of the project had more than tripled.

There were other problems in addition to rising costs. During the first nine years of the project, water was available sporadically, at best. Then, in 1909, water became consistently available, for a time, but only after the planting season had already passed. In 1911, leaks in the main canal led to a suspension of the project while the repairs were being made. Water was available for only three days a month. By 1912, the canal was fully functioning again, but by that point, the farmers were so far in debt that they could no longer afford to pay for the water in the canals or even to plant seeds in their fields.

In 1912, the farmers, suspicious that the Service was intentionally prolonging the project to get checks from the government, convinced officials from Washington, D.C., to conduct an investigation. When asked by the government, the Service said that the farmers, who arrived before the project was completed, shouldn't be blaming them. Never mind that the Service had actually been encouraging people to move to Boise since the inception of the project. Naturally, the government believed its own monopoly over the Boise farmers.

Having failed to convince government officials of the Service's incompetence, the farmers continued to suffer. They were all very far in debt, and the Service responded harshly to their plight. If the farmers could not make payments for the water, the Service would simply shut down the farmers' access to it, even though they needed this water to survive.

On April 1st 1918, the farmers brought suit against the Service officials in Boise. The farmers claimed that the Service was trying to collect an extra $6 million from them to build reservoirs that were not part of the original project plans. Additionally, the farmers claimed that Service officials had spent $20,000 of the Boise project's fund on a canal that was neither part of the Boise project nor would provide any benefit to it.

Initially, a judge granted a temporary restraining order, preventing Service officials from shutting off the farmers' water supply. However, the Service convinced the judge that the court lacked jurisdiction to hear a case that challenged the authority of the secretary of the interior, and to the dismay of the Boise farmers, the court, agreeing with this, entered judgment in favor of the Service and lifted the temporary restraining order.

Finally, between 1923 and 1924, the government sent a fact-finding commission across the West to look into its reclamation projects, and only then did the government acknowledge that Boise, as well as many of its other projects, was a failure. The commission reported that "the majority of settlers [lived] under uninviting conditions, far below the ordinarily accepted standards of living in our American civilization."[9] In many of these places there were "[s]hacks instead of houses . . . bareness instead of comforts; cold instead of warmth . . . mortgages and foreclosures instead of growing bank accounts; sullen hopelessness instead of genial courage."[10]

Should the Government Own the Land?

At the end of the nineteenth century, there was widespread fear of a timber famine because loggers were cutting down a vast amount of trees at a very rapid rate. In reality, this had no basis in fact, but Roosevelt responded to this concern by incorporating the preservation of the forests into his conservation projects.

In order to create the forest reserves, the government would, on occasion, take privately held land. When it did this, an 1897 law required that the government provide the private landholder with equivalent acreage elsewhere. However, this law failed to specify that the land given in exchange needed to be of equivalent value. As a result, land speculators took advantage of this loophole. They bribed government officials to give them title to worthless land, then they lobbied other government officials to convert the land they had acquired into forest reserves, asking for a more valuable piece of land in exchange.

This is exactly what happened in the case *Hyde v. United States* (1912).[11] Fredrick Hyde and John Benson used their connections with government officials, including Grant Taggert, a forest supervisor, and Benjamin Allen, a forest superintendent, to get advance information on where forest reserves were being created throughout California and Oregon. Using this information, they acquired these lands, often by bribing Woodford Harlan and William Valk, government officials at the General Land Office in Washington, D.C., to push their fraudulent land applications through the General Land Office, thereby giving them title to the land. Once they had title, it was only a matter of time before the government would announce it was going to take that land and convert it into a forest reserve, giving them the opportunity to select more valuable land as a replacement.

Eventually, they were charged with conspiracy to defraud the United States, and they were convicted in a federal court. This decision was affirmed in the Supreme Court of the United States. Although justice may have prevailed in this case, many others got away with defrauding the government after Roosevelt opened the door for this kind of behavior.

Once the forest reserves were created, other problems ensued, among them overuse of the forests. Instead of doing their jobs, forest managers often allowed themselves to be swayed by timber companies' interests and pursued policies that gave these companies subsidies. As a result, the government was basically controlling the prices on the timber market.

Additionally, because the timber companies were using government land instead of their own, they had an incentive to cut down as many trees as they could and do nothing to replenish the forest. Sadly, this was done despite the fact that they had the resources and technology for methods that would conserve trees. However, they saw no point in using their own money to help preserve the forests when other timber companies would simply take from the government what they had saved. This never would have occurred on private property.

Besides the timber companies, ranchers contributed to the overuse of the national forests. Ranchers whose property bordered the forest reserves treated this public land as common property; therefore, each rancher had the incentive to graze his cattle on as much grass as possible while doing nothing whatsoever to ensure that the land could be grazed in the future. As the report noted, "The general lack of control in the use of public grazing lands has resulted naturally and inevitably, in over grazing and the ruin of millions of acres of otherwise valuable grazing territory."[12]

Roosevelt's policies regulating the forest reserves have been the cause of some of this country's largest forest fires. Roosevelt believed in suppressing all forest fires. This included abandoning the use of light burning, a practice used by foresters to eliminate the small trees and brush in order to create a clearing that would act as a firebreak and eliminate dangerous combustibles. There is no longer anything stopping forest fires from ripping through acres of elegant virgin forests.

The situation only got worse when, in line with the Roosevelt philosophy, President Nixon signed the Endangered Species Act into law in 1973. The purpose of this Act was to prevent, via government intervention, any wildlife on the verge of becoming extinct from doing so. As a part of this Act, all activity within government forests was disbanded. Timber companies and ranchers could no longer log and graze on the land. Now, not only had the government put a stop to the light burning practice, but also the forest was no longer being cleared via the logging and grazing activities of the timber companies and ranchers. This was nothing less than a recipe for inferno.

This policy destroyed many jobs in the logging industry. As loggers left, millionaires moved in to build their mansions by these scenic forests out west. Hoping to curb the possibility of forest fires, many of these millionaires sought to make changes to the surrounding area; however, provisions of the Endangered Species Act have prevented them from doing this. Without these changes, forest fires have, of course, inevitably ensued. In an ironic twist, not only do these millionaires' mansions get swallowed up in the conflagrations, but so do all the endangered animals that this Act was meant to protect.

For example, in Riverside County, California, landowners were prevented from clearing firebreaks due to the government's concern for the Stephens' kangaroo rat, which had been listed as an endangered species. Needless to say, devastating fires followed, which not only burned down many of the people's homes but also ravaged the habitat of the rat, which the government claimed it was protecting.

Recently, the government claimed that global warming is the cause of all the horrible fires throughout the past one hundred years. This is not true.

Just think about how many more devastating forest fires there are in the West, where the forests are government owned, than in the South where the forests are privately held.

Fortunately, not everyone is buying into the government's lies. The Wallow Fire in eastern Arizona, which burned from May 29th 2011 to July 8th 2011 and destroyed 408,887 acres of forest, has opened the eyes of this State's people. Reporter Katie Pavlich explains the cause of the fire:

> In some areas of our forests, Ponderosa Pine trees grow at a rate of 300 to 700 trees per acre. The natural amount of trees per acre in Ponderosa Pine forests is between 20 and 50 trees per acre and with an overcrowding of trees, comes more competition for water, prolonging western droughts beyond normal time periods, resulting in more dead trees and more excess fire fuel.[13]

She calls this a "ticking time bomb waiting for a single lightning strike to set it off."[14]

In 2003, it seemed that there might be hope, when President Bush signed the Healthy Forest Initiative into law. This Initiative provided funds for thinning forests and clearing away excess vegetation, thus creating firebreaks and eliminating dangerous combustibles. Unfortunately, environmentalist groups who follow in the philosophy of Roosevelt are constantly dragging the Forest Service into court, preventing it from implementing this Initiative.

The Endangered Species Act has had other negative impacts besides contributing to forest fires. This Act gave the federal government unfathomable latitude to stop the building on or use of any land, even if that land was privately owned, so long as the government identified any endangered wildlife on that land. The result of putting this breadth of power in the hands of the federal government has been hundreds of flawed decisions at the expense of Americans' property rights.

The building of the Tellico Dam, located on the Little Tennessee River, is a fine example. Although the Tellico Dam is currently fully built and operational, trying to build the dam needlessly wasted both state and federal tax money through numerous congressional meetings and debates, as well as a federal lawsuit.

The Tennessee Valley Authority (TVA) began construction of the Tellico Dam in 1966. During the ongoing construction, researchers found the snail darter, a tiny endangered fish, living in the river upstream from the dam. These researchers believed that finishing the dam would destroy the habitat of the snail darter, causing it to become extinct. The Department of the Interior declared the river to be a critical habitat and sued for an injunction to halt construction of the dam. While the trial court found for the TVA, the Court of Appeals reversed and the Supreme Court affirmed, thus granting the injunction, even though construction on the dam began seven years before the Endangered Species Act was passed, millions of dollars had already been spent on the project, and the project was already 95 percent complete. According to the Supreme Court, "[I]t is clear from the Act's legislative history that Congress intended to halt and reverse the trend toward species extinction—*whatever the cost.*"[15]

This decision, which took more than twelve years to reach, became moot when Congress passed an amendment to an unrelated bill that allowed the dam to be completed in spite of the presence of the snail darter. What's more, as it turns out the river where the Tellico Dam was being built was actually not the only habitat of the snail darter. The researchers were mistaken. Talk about a pointless lawsuit that wasted taxpayers' dollars and stole private property; this is it.

What's more, the government's power to place restrictions on any land that houses an endangered species has led to perverse incentives for many landowners, who will purposely prevent a habitat for an endangered species from being developed or, worse still, will intentionally destroy an existing habitat if one is present on the land.

This is also the case in the Pacific Northwest where farmers fear the implementation of land-use restrictions, which are being put into place by the federal government whenever a habitat for the spotted owl is identified: "According to the Fish and Wildlife Services 'this concern or fear has accelerated harvest rotations in an effort to avoid the regrowth of habitat that is usable by owls.'"[16]

Because the identification of an endangered species in a particular area gives the government such a heightened amount of regulatory control over that area, the Act also leads to perverse incentives on the side of the government. In one instance, it was found that government agents had planted false evidence of the existence of the Canadian lynx in the Wenatchee and Gifford Pinchot National Forests in the State of Washington, so that they would be able to exercise the accompanying amount of regulatory control.

Overall, the Endangered Species Act has had minimal success. In the past thirty years, the government has taken fewer than thirty of the more than one thousand animal species on the endangered species list off it. Included within the thirty are species that were only taken off the list because they became extinct. What's more, even in those instances where the government has supposedly restored the population of an endangered species, this is not always the case. Many times, the government's success stories concern animals that were never at risk of going extinct to begin with or whose population re-growth had nothing to do with the efforts of the government.

For example, the American alligator, which was once on the endangered species list, was taken off only after it was discovered that it had actually never been endangered in the first place. Likewise, "several bird species, including the brown pelican and bald eagle, may have been helped by the ban on DDT in 1972, a full year before the ESA was enacted, let alone came into force."[17] Yet the Act is still being credited for this "success."

These consequences are unsurprising when one considers that the government often builds its plans for saving "endangered" species on virtually non-existent information. For example, according to Dr. Michael Coffman (Ph.D. in Forest Science from University of Idaho),

> [T]he plan for the endangered Cave Crayfish cites "Sufficient data to esti-
> mate population size or trends is lacking." If there is not even sufficient
> data to estimate the population size, let alone trends, then how could the
> USFWS even know it was endangered in the first place? How could it write
> a recover plan?[18]

Can the Government Build a River?

By the end of the nineteenth century, the railroads had vastly expanded, and as a result, the waterways were losing much of their business. Towns that had built up around the waterways were hit hard by this turn of events and lobbied the federal government to spend money improving the waterways so that they could compete with the railroads again. Theodore Roosevelt enthusiastically added this to his list of conservation projects, thinking that this would assuage midwesterners who were upset that their tax dollars were going to the western irrigation projects. Never mind that he would be spending a large sum of money to improve an increasingly less popular method of transporting goods.

In addition, Roosevelt decided to take this as an opportunity to do more than just improve the navigation of the waterways, even though the very interest groups who supported the waterway projects objected to these additional measures. Under this decision, Roosevelt pursued multiple-use water projects, which simultaneously focused on hydroelectric power, flood control, navigation, and irrigation. As it turned out, many of these projects conflicted with one another. While hydroelectric power and navigation required a reservoir full of water, flood control required an empty one. Needless to say, this prevented the multiple-use water projects from ever turning into a success and instead they proved to be a waste, once again, of taxpayers' dollars.

Conclusion

Today the 230 million acres of land that Teddy Roosevelt set aside are nothing more than a great example of government mismanagement, hypocrisy, and waste. Theodore Roosevelt's conservation projects, as well as their legacies, show us that the government is a thief, which has turned its back on the most valued principle of our Founding Fathers, which was the sanctity of private property, and the price we pay when we let our government get away with this is nothing less than our freedom.

Wanting to regulate still more personal choices, the Progressives turned their sight on the most disastrous social experiment in American history: Prohibition.

Chapter 11

A Fierce Attack on Personal Freedom

Prohibition

The global war on drugs has failed, with devastating consequences for individuals and societies around the world. Fifty years after the initiation of the UN Single Convention on Narcotic Drugs, and 40 years after President Nixon launched the US government's war on drugs, fundamental reforms in national and global drug control policies are urgently needed.

—Report of the Global Commission on Drug Policy[1]

From America's inception until the beginning of the 1900s, Americans were free to consume whatever they wanted. It was believed that, because consumption affected only one's own body, one was free to put whatever he wanted into it. However, over the past one hundred years, the federal government has diverged from this individualistic approach to a paternalistic one, increasingly expanding its control over what Americans can put into their bodies.

This trend began under Republican president Theodore Roosevelt in 1906 with his signing of the Pure Food and Drug Act, was continued by Democratic president Woodrow Wilson in 1919 with the enactment of the Eighteenth Amendment, prohibiting alcohol in the United States, and has only expanded over time to include the largely unsuccessful, utterly inhumane, and Constitution-assaulting War on Drugs.

The resulting effect is that now even our own bodies have been swept up in the federal government's unstoppable and overreaching grasp. Americans' lost autonomy is not the only harm caused by this power grab.

As a consequence of these regulations, crime has spread, the economy has suffered, and government racism has been condoned. The resulting effect is that American liberty has been assaulted across the board.

Booze or No Booze?

The Progressives' attack on alcohol was especially fierce. This was certainly ironic considering that the United States was actually founded by men who met and drank alcohol in taverns as they planned a revolution. So how is it, then, that America got so far away from this not only well-accepted but also much-beloved pastime of our Founding Fathers?

The answer is the Anti-Saloon League, which was the primary lobbying group behind the Prohibition movement. The League was predominantly made up of members of Protestant churches throughout rural areas and the South, who shared a religious fanaticism and condemnation for the habitual drunkard, as well as xenophobic leanings, often aligning themselves with the Ku Klux Klan.

For these two reasons, the League resented the primarily Catholic immigrants who had taken up residence in their cities and brought with them their culture of alcohol consumption; and they saw Prohibition as a means to address these two "issues." The pastors from these rural and southern churches across the country urged their congregants to vote in support of dry candidates. Overall, the Anti-Saloon League members were a non-partisan group; they simply wanted results on their pet issue, the prohibition of alcohol, both to eradicate the habit itself and to persecute the minorities associated with it.

In order to achieve those results, the group pushed through other legislation in various states and at the federal level. The Anti-Saloon League promoted women's suffrage because they saw women as sympathetic to their cause. Once women gained the right to vote in a state or municipality, the propagandist wing of the Anti-Saloon League, the American Issue Publishing Company, would bombard them with pamphlets explaining how alcohol had primarily negative effects on women. The pamphlets alleged that when men drank, they would come home and beat their wives, come home and rape their wives, or stay out and cheat on their wives. Juxtaposing alcohol with these crimes made it easy to convince women that some form of prohibition was in their best interest. As such, although national women's suffrage in the form of the Nineteenth Amendment was not ratified until after Prohibition, Prohibition was ratified by numerous states in large part due to women's right to vote there.

The Anti-Saloon League also pushed for the direct election of senators. It saw prohibition of alcohol as a popular cause, but also a cause that could not go through on a federal level unless those people who supported it had a direct say in the election of both houses of Congress. In 1913, the Seventeenth Amendment was ratified, and the direct election of senators came to fruition, representing a success for the League on its path to prohibition.

Additionally, the League believed that the direct, un-apportioned federal income tax was essential to passing Prohibition; therefore, it sought a constitutional amendment that would allow this type of tax. The League recognized that Prohibition would be fiscally impermissible without the creation of new taxes, given that, prior to the ratification of the Sixteenth Amendment in 1913, the alcohol excise tax accounted for 40 percent of the federal government's revenue. However, with the passage of the Sixteenth Amendment, the income tax would be the new primary source of government revenue, thus making revenue from alcohol sales unnecessary, or so the argument went.[2] The passage of the Sixteenth Amendment in 1913 represented yet another success for the Anti-Saloon League.

In addition to pushing for favorable restructuring of the government, the League postulated general theories about the benefits of Prohibition to win over the population at large. For example, when the United States entered World War I with Germany as the enemy, the Anti-Saloon League depicted Prohibition as patriotic because many of the manufacturers of spirits were German-Americans. To this end, the Prohibitionists called Milwaukee's beer brewers "the worst of all our German enemies" and called their products "Kaiser brew."[3] The League also sought to identify alcohol with crime; therefore, Prohibition was a means of protecting people.

On January 16th 1919, the ratification of the Eighteenth Amendment was certified. However, this amendment was unique in that there was a delay between when the amendment was ratified and when it was to take effect.

In order to set the Prohibition allowed by the Eighteenth Amendment in motion, Anti-Saloon League member Wayne Wheeler drafted the Volstead Act, which he introduced to Congress later that year. Specifically, this Act set forth which intoxicating beverages would be prohibited, established the governmental regulations that would be put in place for overseeing the manufacture, production, and use of all other non-prohibited alcoholic substances, and sought to ensure that there would be enough alcohol available to use for scientific research, as well as lawful industries, such as the fuel and dye industries, and religious practices.

After having passed both houses of Congress, the bill proceeded to President Wilson, who vetoed it, although largely on technical grounds. Accompanying the veto, Wilson wrote,

> The subject matter treated in this measure deals with two distinct phases of the prohibition legislation. One part of the act under consideration seeks to enforce war-time prohibition. The other provides for the enforcement which was made necessary by the adoption of the Constitutional Amendment. I object to and cannot approve that part of this legislation with reference to war-time prohibition.[4]

Wilson basically vetoed the bill because he felt that the characters of war-time Prohibition and permanent Prohibition were distinct and did not belong in the same bill. Absent from his explanation was an opinion on Prohibition in general.

Wilson had political reasons for vetoing the bill. He knew that many of the dry states were responsible for his reelection, and his Progressive supporters did not want him to forget it. For example, Progressive writer John Palmer Gavit wrote to Wilson that he should not forget that he had "been elected by the vote of 'dry' states."[5] Yet Wilson did not want to alienate the wet voters or political allies, such as Samuel Gompers, president of the American Federation of Labor. Gompers warned Wilson that this bill would only hurt the workingman, who could not afford to keep stocks of hard liquor at home. As a consummate politician, Wilson was able to sidestep the issue of Prohibition, because after his veto on technical grounds, the issue was out of his hands.

When the bill went back to Congress, Wilson's veto was overridden, and on October 29th 1919, the bill went into effect. In doing so, it functioned as the enabling act for the Eighteenth Amendment.

Despite the promises of the Anti-Saloon League and other supporters of Prohibition, the Prohibition of alcohol proved to be disastrous. By making alcohol illegal, everyone who sold or consumed it was now a potential criminal, thus forcing all alcohol-related activity underground and converting what used to be legitimate businesses into criminal enterprises.

Prohibition became the heyday for organized crime in America. Al Capone, Meyer Lansky, Bugsy Siegel, Johnny Torrio, Nucky Johnson, Lucky Luciano, and countless other organized crime bosses rose to wealth and power during this era. Not only that, but crime in general escalated to unforeseen heights, which in turn forced national police funding to increase by 11.4 percent, arrests for drunkenness and disorderly conduct to increase by 41 percent, drunk driving arrests to increase by 81 percent, the number of federal convicts to increase by 561 percent, the federal prison population to increase by 366 percent, and the total federal penal expenditures to increase by more than 1,000 percent.[6] These statistics merely represent criminals who were caught. The truth is that for the most part, violations of Prohibition went un-enforced, and therefore, the reality was far worse than even these drastic statistics suggest.

Rising crime was not the only adverse consequence of Prohibition. Prohibition helped throw the country even further into the Great Depression. Another startling effect of Prohibition was its consequence on Americans' health. Even though Prohibition initially caused the death rate from alcoholism to decrease by 80 percent in 1921, the situation quickly took a turn for the worse.

The criminals who then ran all alcohol production would often water down liquors, thus increasing the volume they could sell and, in turn, the profits they would make. They also added small amounts of harmful chemicals to ensure drinkers would still get a drunken effect despite having consumed watered-down liquors. By 1927 there were almost fifty thousand alcohol-related deaths per year. Countless Americans were also blinded or paralyzed by tainted liquor.[7]

One last effect of Prohibition was that it enabled the federal government to usurp a role that was traditionally held by the family. For 150 years, it was the parents' place to introduce alcohol to their children and teach them how to drink it appropriately. Under Prohibition, parents could no longer legally do this. The consequences were that children often would drink alcohol in secret, often abusing it, and they would continue to do so until the federal government, in a paternalistic fashion, quashed this activity.

Yet there is one noteworthy feature of Prohibition. Even though Prohibition was bad for the nation and its people and, moreover, violated Natural Law, it was put into force through a constitutional amendment ratified by the States, which is the most difficult, but consensus-laden way to make these changes. On the other hand, all other drug-related legislation has been enacted via either a simple bill ratified by both houses of Congress and signed by the president or regulations enacted solely by the FDA, an organization not even elected by the people.

Overall, Prohibition lasted a total of fourteen years. It wasn't until the ratification of the Twenty-first Amendment on December 5th 1933 that Prohibition and the egregious assault on personal liberty that it embodied were finally recognized for what they were and rightfully put to a stop.

Who Owns Your Body?

During the Progressive Era, the government also began to control Americans' use of drugs. The first drug regulations were introduced with the passage of the Pure Food and Drug Act of 1906. Although the Pure Food and Drug Act did not constitute an outright prohibition of any drugs, it did call for each drug to be correctly labeled. Specifically, this label would have to list not only the primary drug in the package, but also any drugs that the primary drug had been laced with to gain its special effect and the correct strengths of each of these drugs.

The next step in regulating drugs took place at the first global Opium Conference, which was held in The Hague, Netherlands, in 1911. At this conference the Roosevelt administration pushed for a global prohibition of drugs, even though the United States did not yet have such restrictions. The government's purpose in pushing for these restrictions was to achieve an equal footing in this area of trade compared to other nations, since these substances were widely produced in nations other than the United States. In other words, because the United States did not have, for example, a vast opium infrastructure and could never compete with China and other nations in the global opium market, it set out to make opium illegal.

Despite its efforts, however, the United States' push at the 1911 conference did not lead to a global prohibition of narcotics. Nevertheless, it did lay the foundation for future attitudes toward drugs that were adopted in the post-World War I era.

In the meantime, the government's next move on drugs occurred with the passage of the Harrison Narcotics Tax Act, which Wilson signed into law on December 14th 1914. This Act used the government's taxation power to police narcotics. Specifically, it made cocaine and opium illegal for distribution and sale by everyone except licensed physicians. Furthermore, the Act required physicians who planned to administer narcotics to register with the federal government and to keep detailed records of any narcotics that they dispensed. Not only that, but each narcotic-prescribing physician was required to pay a one-dollar annual "sin" tax.

A startling feature of the Harrison Act, besides the obvious encroachment on Americans' right to control their bodies, is that its enactment led to the persecution of certain minorities. The Harrison Act primarily focused on controlling the use of opium, which was predominantly consumed by people in the newly conquered Philippines and by Chinese immigrants in the continental United States as a traditional part of their culture. Thus, federal law forced them to abandon an important part of their identity or otherwise face legal consequences.

Another perverse consequence of the Harrison Act was that it forced many users and distributors of opiates underground, thus not only defeating the government's goal of keeping a closer eye on the use of these potentially dangerous substances, but also creating an environment which bred criminal enterprises.

The next step in drug regulations occurred when, as mentioned above, the stance on drugs postulated at the Opium Conference resurfaced following World War I, making its way into Article 295 of the Treaty of Versailles. Because Article 295 was slipped into the Treaty, all the nations that signed it were suddenly required to enact anti-narcotic measures, taking many of these countries, which had predominantly focused on the peace provisions, by surprise.[8] Even though the U.S. Senate never approved the Treaty, and, thus, America was not bound by its drug regulations, Article 295 nevertheless represented a success for the federal government, having finally managed to force the rest of the world to regulate narcotics.

Following this, the federal government's pursuit of drug regulations began to take a more focused approach, specifically singling out one particular drug, marijuana. In the mid-1930s the use of marijuana was on the rise. Initially, President Franklin Delano Roosevelt attempted to pressure the states to adopt the Uniform State Narcotic Drug Act in a fashion similar to how most states had prohibited alcohol before the federal prohibition amendment was ratified.

However, the states proved to be reluctant, leading Congress to enact the Marihuana (*sic*) Tax Act of 1937. This Act placed a nominal tax on anyone who commercially dealt the psychoactive drug, cannabis, as well as the crop fiber, hemp, which was used to make cloth, paper, rope, and other such products. Even though the tax was nominal, the penalty for avoiding it was highly excessive. For avoiding the tax, which equaled roughly one dollar per ounce, a dealer faced five years' imprisonment and a two-thousand-dollar fine.[9]

The government's incentives in passing these restrictions were far from pure. It included hemp within the list of regulated items in response to pressure from individuals with the nation's greatest timber holdings, including William Randolph Hearst and the DuPont family.[10]

These powerful individuals wanted to restrict the production of hemp because the paper that could be created from it would have otherwise directly competed with the paper being made from timber. This was especially the case considering that, because hemp comes from a weed and grows briskly, while the trees used to produce timber grow much more slowly, paper made from hemp would have had a huge production advantage over paper created from timber. By agreeing to regulate hemp, the government chose a winner in the market and helped to create a virtual monopoly over paper production and drive hemp producers (among whom historically were Washington and Jefferson) underground.

Additionally, the singling out of marijuana was grounded in racial considerations. Although not all users of marijuana in the 1930s were illegal Mexican immigrants, the crop originated in Mexico, and its use was common among Mexican immigrants. Thus, the initial marijuana regulation was enacted to give white law enforcement a pretext to arrest darker-skinned Mexicans. Furthermore, this opened the door for an illegal marijuana market, thus encouraging criminal enterprises.

Despite the corrupt underpinnings of the legislation restricting marijuana use, the government continued to build on this precedent instead of tearing it down. In 1961, the government entered into an international treaty, the Single Convention on Narcotic Drugs, which prohibited the production of all narcotic drugs, including among these marijuana, except when used for medicinal purposes.

Marijuana was once again targeted in the Controlled Substances Act of 1970. This Act, which separated the various narcotic and psychoactive drugs into schedules, placed marijuana in schedule 1, the most dangerous and addictive schedule. In doing so, the Act not only rated marijuana as equally dangerous and addictive as cocaine and heroin, but it also stated that marijuana has no accepted medicinal purpose.

In 2001, the Supreme Court stood behind this idea. In *United States v. Oakland Cannabis Buyers' Cooperative*,[11] the Court held that although cannabis had been approved for medicinal use in California, it still had not been approved for any federal medicinal use. Therefore, there was no possible medical necessity exception to the Controlled Substances Act.

Another idea that gained support in the courts was federal superiority over state law regarding the prohibition of marijuana. In 2005, the Supreme Court made a controversial ruling in the case *Gonzales v. Raich*, holding that even homegrown medical marijuana could be prohibited by the federal government, regardless of the fact that California, the state where the defendant resided, permitted such activity.[12] The reasoning was that even an older woman growing marijuana solely for personal use to help with her own extreme pain under the guidance of her physicians adversely affected interstate commerce because her production, despite the fact that it consisted of only six small plants, would disturb the national amount of marijuana on the market, which was supposed to be zero.

It was a precarious decision to say the least, considering that it effectively prohibited all marijuana, even marijuana that had no relation to interstate commerce, despite the fact that Congress had drawn its authority to pass the Controlled Substances Act from the Commerce Clause and otherwise had no constitutional basis for regulating marijuana.

Ironically, however, the legalization of marijuana would provide a huge source of taxable revenue for the government, something that is greatly needed by a government consistently spending outside its means.

Considering this, one might wonder why it has remained a banned substance. Lobbyists from the pharmaceutical companies have campaigned against marijuana because it is just a plant and, as such, cannot be patented like a normal drug. Additionally, it is a very effective painkiller, yet has less severe side effects than many of the drugs produced by these pharmaceutical companies. If marijuana were ever to become legal, these companies would face significant competition. Then there are lobbyists from the Religious Right who do not view consumption of marijuana as a good Christian activity, so they continue to fight hard against its legalization.

Beyond this specific assault on marijuana, President Richard Nixon began a War on Drugs to address America's drug "problem" on a larger, more general scale. The driving instrument of this war was the Drug Enforcement Administration (DEA), a specialized force of thugs hired by the feds and authorized to enforce all drug-related laws and regulations. Besides marijuana, two of the big "enemies" in the War on Drugs were cocaine, in both its pure and its crack forms, and heroin. Much like the prohibition of marijuana, the ban on cocaine and heroin had strong racial undertones, and in fact, during much of the 1980s, the War on Drugs became a race war. Specifically, these drugs were widely viewed as being primarily used by blacks and Hispanics, and thus, DEA raids often targeted these non-white minorities.

Not only was this war racially biased, but during the 1980s President Ronald Reagan authorized several suspect military interventions in the name of the War on Drugs, the consequence of which was that the United States was effectively picking winners in the foreign drug trade.

For example, Panamanian leader Manuel Noriega was a well-known drug trafficker, but because he provided assistance to groups that the United States favored in Panama and was even paid by American intelligence agencies for intelligence on American enemies, the United States allowed him to continue drug trafficking and provided him with hundreds of thousands of dollars per year. Then, in 1989, President George H. W. Bush decided that Noriega should be taken out, and once the United States captured him, he was tried, convicted, and sentenced to forty-five years in an American prison.

Overall, this unofficial war has proved to be one of the greatest governmental mistakes in recent American history, given that the level of drug use and importation into the United States has remained consistent. In fact, in 2011 the UN Global Commission on Drug Policy declared that "the War on Drugs has failed."[13] The truth is that over the past forty years the federal government has wasted countless dollars trying to solve the very drug problem that it created when it decided to regulate drugs back in 1906 with the Pure Food and Drug Act. After all, if the government had just stayed out of drugs altogether, the illegal enterprises it is fighting against never would have been pushed underground in the first place.

In 2012, however, it feels like America is on the edge of a cliff, primed and ready to jump into a new era. Several states have either decriminalized marijuana or approved it for medicinal use, and the Department of Justice has alternatively stated that it will no longer enforce federal drug laws where they are in conflict with state laws. Moreover, in an unusual showing of bipartisanship, several congressmen, led by Libertarian-leaning Republican Ron Paul and Socialist-leaning Democrat Barney Frank, recently proposed House Resolution 2306, which, if passed, would end federal prohibition of marijuana and instead leave the regulation up to the States.[14] If the tide keeps turning in the direction it has been, it may be possible that America's wrongful prohibition of marijuana will soon come to an end, and if this happens, other drugs could follow.

Conclusion

This country was founded on a few very simple principles, and one of them was that Americans should be left alone to do what they want with their bodies, so long as their actions are not hurting others. However, this principle has been and will continue to be neglected until Americans fight back and demand that their government repeal the regulations that have placed control of Americans' bodies in the hands of the government instead of the people where that power rightfully belongs. All of this started with Roosevelt and Wilson and the Protestant Progressives who just knew how we should all live.

They also knew how we should all die, as soldiers fighting savages. To their wars we march next.

Chapter 12

"The Supreme Triumphs of War"

Roosevelt and International Relations

All the great masterful races have been fighting races and the minute that a race loses its hard fighting virtues, then . . . it has lost its proud right to stand as the equal of the best . . . no triumph of peace is quite so great as the supreme triumphs of war . . . cowardice in race, as in an individual, is the unpardonable sin.

—THEODORE ROOSEVELT[1]

In 1899, after Rudyard Kipling returned to England from the United States, he wrote a poem characterizing the role America was to assume now that it had taken control of the Philippines following the Spanish-American War. This poem, "The White Man's Burden," set forth America's new imperialistic position:

> Take up the White Man's burden—
> Send forth the best ye breed—
> Go bind your sons to exile
> To serve your captives' need;
> To wait in heavy harness,
> On fluttered folk and wild—
> Your new-caught, sullen peoples,
> Half-devil and half-child.[2]

If the Founding Fathers were able to return to this country, they would not be able to recognize how it is today. They would not be able to fathom an America where someone could say the things Kipling, though an Englishman, had written.

President George Washington outlined the political philosophy of our country when he said that "the great rule of conduct for us in regard to foreign nations is . . . to have with them as little political connection as possible."[3] He believed that minimizing our foreign entanglements would keep us out of war, and staying out of war was important for our country because, in the words of James Madison, "of all the enemies to public liberty, war is, perhaps, the most to be dreaded, because it comprises and develops the germ of every other."[4] Thomas Jefferson echoed this sentiment in his first inaugural address in 1801, when he advocated for "peace, commerce, and honest friendship with all nations—entangling alliances with none."

For the next century, this remained the dominant philosophy in America. In 1821, John Quincy Adams declared:

> Wherever the standard of freedom and independence has been or shall be unfurled, there will be America's heart, her benedictions, and her prayers. But she does not go abroad *in search of monsters to destroy*. She is the well-wisher to the freedom and independence of all. She is the champion and vindicator of only her own.[5]

This non-interventionist policy wasn't just preached by the government; it was also practiced. When the Hungarians were fighting against the Hapsburg monarchy in 1848, many Americans supported their struggle. They applauded Louis Kossuth, one of the bravest Hungarian fighters, when he arrived in America. However, when Kossuth went before the American government, he was denied any help: "No public money, no arms, aid, or troops were forthcoming for the Hungarian cause."[6] Henry Clay, a Kentucky senator and notorious compromiser, explained to Kossuth that America could not break "our ancient policy of amity and non-intervention," and that

> [b]y our policy to which we have adhered to since the days of Washington . . . we have done more for the cause of liberty in the world than arms could

185

effect; we have shown to other nations the way to greatness and happiness. . . . Far better is it for ourselves, for Hungary, and the cause of liberty, that, adhering to our pacific system and avoiding the distant wars of Europe, we should keep our lamp burning brightly on this western shore, as a light to all nations.[7]

In 1863, even President Lincoln declined to join the French emperor in expressing outrage toward the Russian government, which had beaten back a Polish revolt.

So, how did we get so far from this policy of our Founding Fathers? The answer is Theodore Roosevelt.

Young Theodore Roosevelt

When Roosevelt was a mere four years old, he would dress up and play soldier. Wearing his uniform, he would run around asking, "[A]re me a soldier laddie too?"[8] He did this most frequently when he was having an asthma attack, to which he was prone as a young boy. Being a soldier meant being more of a man to Roosevelt.

In his teen years, his violent side became apparent. After Roosevelt had a lovers' quarrel with his future second wife, Edith Carrow, he "nearly rode his horse to death, and when a neighbor's dog barked at him, he took out a pistol and shot at it."[9] When Roosevelt was engaged to the woman who became his first wife, Alice Lee, he bought dueling pistols, which he planned to use if there were any rivals for her affection.

Roosevelt's violence was not limited to situations involving the women in his life. He also enjoyed "the rough sport of hunting, killing, and gutting his prey, at times openly exalting at gore."[10] In honor of his favorite sport, hunting, Roosevelt began the Boone and Crockett Club. Membership to this club was exclusively for men who had pursued and killed some type of large American game. Later on in his life, he would characterize killing other men as the most dangerous game of all.

In short, Roosevelt was a violent, war-loving man just waiting for the opportunity to see some real action. Sure enough, the opportunity presented itself, and Roosevelt stood ready to pounce on it.

The Love of War—Any War

By the end of the nineteenth century, Spain had only two colonies in the New World, Cuba and Puerto Rico, and only a couple of colonies in the Pacific, the most prized of which was the Philippines. Despite this limited presence, the United States felt threatened by the Spanish, and because the United States wanted to extend its own influence abroad, it felt that taking these colonies from Spain would be the best way to start increasing the strength of its navy and, through that, build a more powerful empire.

This belief in the connection between a strong navy and a powerful empire was popularized by Alfred Thayer Mahan's book, *The Influence of Sea Power Upon History, 1660-1783* (1890). As an avid reader of Mahan's writing, as well as having a personal acquaintance with him, Roosevelt was one of the many people who had been indoctrinated with the philosophy that a strong navy was necessary to exert global power. When civil unrest became apparent in Cuba, the American government saw an opportunity, and Roosevelt, along with Mahan's other disciples, began to anticipate eagerly the possibility of interfering with violence.

Though he was not president yet, Roosevelt took many steps to get us into this rising conflict as the assistant secretary of the navy. In general, Roosevelt thought, *"I should welcome almost any war, for this country needs one."*[11] With the circumstances being right in Cuba, Roosevelt simply could not resist. Though he craved more power to be able to influence America into going to war, at one point saying, "I'd give all that I'm worth to be just two days in supreme command. I'd be perfectly willing then to resign, for I'd have things going so that nobody could stop them,"[12] Roosevelt found a way to work with what powers he had.

After the USS *Maine* sank off the coast of Havana, Roosevelt strongly supported putting the blame on the Spanish, even though there had never been any official inquiry into Spanish responsibility. Roosevelt was very clear in his communications with others that he believed "[t]he Maine was sunk by an act of dirty treachery on the part of the Spaniards."[13]

Roosevelt, in his capacity as assistant secretary of the navy, also set about developing war plans should America go to war. He got into communication with Mahan's old base of operations, the Naval War College in Newport, Rhode Island, to consult with the military faculty on these plans.

More than just consulting, Roosevelt actually set about "moving ammunition to ships, authorizing the unlimited enlistment of seamen, and ordering guns from the Navy Yard to be shipped out for sea action."[14] He sent telegraphs halfway around the world with directions to start a siege of the Philippines should war in Cuba break out. It was said that "he had gone at things like a bull in a china shop."[15]

Roosevelt also pushed for war by offering to organize his own troop of men, whom he dubbed the Rough Riders, to join the fight. Roosevelt spoke with President McKinley himself on two occasions, asking him if he would permit Roosevelt to do this.

On April 25th 1898, the United States declared war against Spain, under the guise that we wanted to help Cuba win its independence. With the onset of war, Roosevelt's plans began to fall into place. Not only did America send troops to Cuba, battles were fought throughout the Caribbean and Pacific, just as he had envisioned. So, too, Roosevelt was allowed to go to war with his Rough Riders, and he resigned from his position as assistant secretary of the navy as a result. Having been granted this permission, Roosevelt was so concerned that the war would be over before he had a chance to get to the fight that he urged, "[D]o not make peace until we get to Puerto Rico."[16]

Arriving in Cuba, Roosevelt was able to find the glory he sought. While they were crossing the San Juan River, a hail of Spanish bullets rained down upon Roosevelt, his Rough Riders, and other American regiments. As the other American troops debated how to proceed against the Spanish, Roosevelt abandoned all thinking and demanded that his Rough Riders storm San Juan Hill and Kettle Hill, from which the Spanish were shooting down at the Americans.

Though his strategy worked, and the Americans quickly expelled the Spanish from the hills, this is not to say that Roosevelt hadn't been completely reckless with his troops' lives and at points even criminal toward them. While Roosevelt found the whole affair to be quite fun, rejoicing both times he was shot and abandoning himself to complete hysteria whenever he killed a Spaniard, not all of his men felt this way.

When Roosevelt saw his men's apprehension, he taunted them by calling them cowards. Roosevelt recounted in his book *The Rough Riders* an instance where he saw one of his men hiding from a spray of bullets and he was so disgusted by this man's behavior that he forced him to rise up into the oncoming bullets, whereby the man was instantly shot dead. Roosevelt was too callous to recount the name of this man whose death he had materially caused.

The war drew to a close with the signing of the Treaty of Paris. However, in an ironic twist not anticipated by the Cuban people, the United States did not allow Cuba to participate in the creation or signing of the Treaty. The United States acted as Cuba's parent and agent, only allowing Cuba to watch the proceedings and giving the Cuban government no say in the matter whatsoever. The Cubans were unable to make known any of their own wishes for their supposed independence.

To add insult to injury, immediately after Spain officially surrendered Cuba, an American military government was established there, prohibiting the Cuban revolutionary government from ever taking control.

What's more, the parade in Havana to celebrate the Cubans' victory was "completely American, and Cubans were denied the long-anticipated satisfaction of parading their troops through the capital."[17] At the end of the parade, the American flag, not the Cuban one, was raised over Havana.

So then, in what way had the United States allowed the Cuban people to be free from the control of a foreign power? Were we not just the next imperialist power to replace Spain in Cuba?

Feeling the unjustness of the situation that America had brought to Cuba, General Máximo Gómez, one of the Cuban revolutionary fighters, wrote in his diary on January 8th 1899 that

> Cuba cannot have true moral peace . . . which is what the people need for their happiness and good fortune—under the transitional government. This transitional government was imposed by force by a foreign power and, therefore, is illegitimate and incompatible with the principles that the entire country has been upholding for so long and in the defense of which half of its sons have given their lives and all of its wealth has been consumed.[18]

Fortunately for Cuba, it was able to free itself from the imperialistic United States three years after this war, when the Teller Amendment, which forbade the United States from annexing Cuba, passed through Congress. However, even this "freedom" came with certain restrictions that the Cubans were required to put into their constitution. For example, the United States maintained the right to intervene whenever it wanted to do so in Cuban affairs and to supervise Cuba's finances and foreign relations. This constitution, with all these restrictions, remained in place until it was repealed in 1930.

The end of the Spanish-American War also came with the United States' capture of the Philippines, Guam, and Puerto Rico from Spain. As for Guam and Puerto Rico, there was no reason given for the capture of either country. The truth is that the government figured it might as well acquire as much power and foreign territory as it could from this war. There was no compensation given to Spain for Puerto Rico, and the United States still holds it as a colony as a consequence of the Spanish-American War. The same holds true for Guam, which remains a colony of the United States more than one hundred years after the federal government stole it and claimed to liberate it.

The Philippines, like Cuba, were taken through force from Spain under the guise of helping them achieve independence. However, when the war ended, as part of the Treaty of Paris, America gave Spain $20 million so that the Philippines would become the property of the United States. So outraged by the hypocrisy of America, Andrew Carnegie "even went so far as to offer to purchase the independence of the Philippines with a check for $20 million—the amount the U.S. government had paid Spain for the islands."[19] Of course, the United States did not take him up on this offer. Eventually, the Filipinos had to fight another war, this time against their newest colonizer, the United States, in order to achieve independence.

These countries did not get their independence, and as it turned out, they would not even get full rights under their captor's Constitution. As we have seen in chapter 6, in a series of cases called the *Insular Cases*, the Supreme Court was asked to address the question of whether the Constitution follows the flag. In other words, would the people of the newly acquired territories have the same rights as any other American? In one of those cases, *Downes v. Bidwell* (1901), the Court ruled that only the incorporated territories would have full rights under the Constitution, while the unincorporated territories would not. Persons in Puerto Rico and Guam, which were not incorporated into the United States, but remained its colonies, would not be protected by the Constitution.

When the Jones Act was passed in 1917, Puerto Ricans were granted U.S. citizenship, and believing this meant they were now an "incorporated" territory, they rejoiced at the prospect of finally having full rights under the U.S. Constitution. The 1922 Insular Case, *Balzac v. People of Porto Rico*, dashed Puerto Rican hopes by declaring that this island remained unincorporated, thus they would not get full constitutional rights, even though they were American citizens.[20] Never mind that this ruling was a clear violation of our Constitution, which states that all persons must be treated equally. This is the status that still remains in Puerto Rico today. Likewise, the people of Guam were granted citizenship in 1950, yet they still do not have full constitutional rights either.

In reaction to America taking territories for itself at the end of the war and occupying them in a way that was indistinguishable from its Spanish predecessor, some Americans banded together to form the Anti-Imperialist League. This League defended the position of our Founding Fathers and was really "only another name for old-fashioned Americanism."[21] The League wanted to remind Americans of our roots and bring us back to them. To this end, William Jennings Bryan, an Anti-Imperialist, cried out:

> That the leaders of a great party should claim for any President or Congress the right to treat millions of people as mere "possessions" and deal with them unrestrained by the Constitution or Bill of Rights shows how far we have already departed from the ancient landmarks.[22]

Another Anti-Imperialist, an unidentified woman who wrote a letter to *Women's Journal*, characterized what America was doing as "an ineffaceable stain upon the flag four generations of Americans have held aloft as the emblem, not of conquest, but of liberty."[23] Still another Anti-Imperialist, William Graham Sumner, a professor at Yale University, begged for America to realize that "we have beaten Spain in a military conflict, but we are submitting to be conquered by her on the field of ideas and policies."[24] These men and women didn't stand a chance. Roosevelt's political career was on the rise, and with it their voices would be quashed by his larger-than-life persona.

The Roosevelt Corollary to the Monroe Doctrine

Roosevelt's influences during the Spanish-American War were only the beginning of his career in turning America into an imperialistic country. Once he became president in 1901, following the assassination of President William McKinley, Roosevelt was able to put his imperialistic plans in full swing.

To this end, Roosevelt added the Roosevelt Corollary to the Monroe Doctrine. Originally, the purpose of the Monroe Doctrine was to help countries in Latin America become independent by stopping any further European colonization in the Americas. While the United States threatened to take action against any European country that interfered in the Western Hemisphere, this did not mean that the United States would get involved in their affairs instead. Rather, the intention was that the Latin American countries would be left alone.

However, while Roosevelt was president, a situation was brewing in Venezuela that caught his attention. Under the current leader, Cipriano Castro, the country was frequently in revolt, and money was being spent that the government didn't have. Therefore, the Venezuelan government was defaulting on its debts to European countries, such as England, Germany, and Italy. Roosevelt feared that these conditions would encourage the European countries to invade Venezuela, thus establishing a presence in the Western Hemisphere. His concern escalated when the British, Germans, and Italians actually set up blockades of Venezuela's five major ports, demanding that Venezuela pay off the debts it owed them.

Roosevelt sent word to the European nations that were surrounding Venezuela that he was on the brink of enforcing the Monroe Doctrine to get them out. Even though the European countries eventually did back down, Roosevelt was unsettled by the implications of this event.

Then, in 1903, just a few short months after the close of the Venezuelan conflict, Roosevelt saw a similar situation on the rise in the Dominican Republic. This country, like Venezuela, owed a vast sum of money to some European countries, including Spain, Italy, and Germany. When these countries began closing in on the Dominican Republic, Roosevelt made a rare showing of restraint by declining to send U.S. forces to the Dominican

Republic. Nevertheless, Roosevelt was growing even warier of the possibility of European involvement in Latin America.

To end this concern, in 1904, Roosevelt added the Roosevelt Corollary to the Monroe Doctrine, subverting the original purpose of the Doctrine. The United States declared that it would intervene in Latin America in the case of "flagrant and chronic wrong doing by a Latin America neighbor," when originally nobody was supposed to be intervening at all.[25] Through this additional provision, Roosevelt believed that he could pre-empt any European desire to get involved. In this way, America became Latin America's police force.

Under this addition to the Monroe Doctrine, Roosevelt finally succumbed to mingling in Dominican affairs. In 1905, the United States took control of the Dominican Republic's finances. This marked the end of the days when America would only get involved in external affairs solely to protect its national security.

The Biggest Hole in the Earth

Roosevelt furthered America's descent into an imperialistic country when he pursued his dream to build and control a canal through Central America. In 1904 Roosevelt began to execute his plans for the canal. His chosen location for the project was Colombia. A French company owned the rights to the canal project there, so Roosevelt, authorized by Congress via the Spooner Act, paid forty million dollars to this company to buy out these rights. Simply having the rights to build the canal was not enough for Roosevelt; he also wanted to control the land on which the canal was built. To this end, Roosevelt offered to give ten million dollars to Colombia so that the United States would own the strip of land on which the canal was built. However, Colombia refused to accept this offer.

Roosevelt was unwilling to take no for an answer. "'We were dealing with a government of irresponsible bandits,' Roosevelt stormed. 'I was prepared to . . . at once occupy the Isthmus anyhow, and proceed to dig the canal.'"[26] The only reason Roosevelt stopped himself from taking the land from Colombia was that he knew there was a revolution brewing in

Panama, and this revolution could provide him with a pretext for grabbing up Colombia's land.

When the local revolt did finally occur, Roosevelt quickly sent the battleship *Nashville* to Panama as support for the rebels, knowing that his support would be decisive in determining the outcome of the war and that the rebels would be indebted to him for it. Sure enough, the rebels were successful in overthrowing the Colombians. Following this victory, Roosevelt offered ten million dollars *to the rebels* for the strip of land that he wanted for the canal, an offer they felt compelled to accept from their benefactor. Philippe Bunau-Varilla, Panama's ambassador to the United States, signed the Hay-Bunau-Varilla Treaty on November 6th 1903, accepting this offer. The ten million dollars that Roosevelt paid never made its way to the Colombian treasury.

Finally, Roosevelt had his strip of land for the canal. Never mind that he had contributed to the Panamanian struggle for independence solely to take advantage of that country and not because he actually cared at all about the Panama people's fight for freedom. It was not until 1921, under the Thomson-Urrutia Treaty, that the United States paid *to Colombia* a sum of ten million dollars for the land it had basically stolen by contributing to Panama's independence.

Even though Americans did not approve of Roosevelt's behavior, he did not care.

"There was much accusation about my having acted in an 'unconstitutional' manner," Teddy shrugged. "I took the isthmus, started the canal, and then left Congress—not to debate the canal, but to debate me. . . . While the debate goes on, the canal does too; and they are welcome to debate me as long as they wish, provided that we can go on with the canal."[27]

This statement epitomizes how little Roosevelt cared about abiding by the U.S. Constitution, following the will of the people, or respecting the separation of powers, and it is for all of these reasons that Roosevelt believed, "The canal was by far the most important action I took in foreign affairs during the time I was President. *When nobody could or would exercise efficient authority, I exercised it.*"[28]

The Great White Fleet

To display to the world that America was becoming a strong, imperialistic country, on December 16th 1907, Roosevelt ordered sixteen battleships to circumnavigate the globe, thereby showing off the power of the U.S. Navy. He called this the "Great White Fleet." This display of power was in reaction to the Japanese navy's decisive victory over Russia in 1905. Roosevelt suddenly felt compelled to make it clear that, while the Japanese navy might be strong, his was stronger. This trip, which lasted fourteen months, mainly focused on Latin America and the Pacific because those were the areas where Roosevelt cared most about establishing his dominance and increasing his power.

Roosevelt was so intent on sending this fleet out that he did not care how anyone else felt about it. "While some were concerned that the nation's Atlantic naval defenses would be weakened by the fleet's prolonged absence, others were concerned about the cost."[29] Maine Republican Senator Eugene Hale, the chairman of the Senate Naval Appropriations Committee, was so worried about the expense of this naval display that he threatened to diminish the fleet's funding. Roosevelt simply disregarded the senator's threats. Even when Congress tried to keep American tax dollars from being wasted on this voyage by only appropriating "funds for half the voyage," Roosevelt snidely said that he would still send the fleet out to the Pacific, and "the politicians would have to put up the money if they wanted to get it back."[30]

Ironically, many of the ships in the fleet were obsolete and in poor repair, but all that Roosevelt cared about was that America looked strong to the other countries, while American safety and fiscal prudence fell by the wayside.

Imperialism Since Roosevelt

Following Roosevelt's example, the United States has sent troops to fight or intervene in other countries on behalf of American interests almost every year since 1898. To this end, the United States, especially after World War II and under the guise of stopping the spread of communism, toppled foreign governments, implanted American puppets to run foreign lands, and kept many countries' powers limited, thus hoping to cause America to remain the strongest country in the world. The excuse every time is that the United States is helping people, not taking other lands as its colonies, much like what Roosevelt claimed during the Spanish-American War. This is only partly true. While the United States is not annexing any countries *per se*, by controlling who the government is and what that country can and cannot do, America has transformed those countries into *de facto* colonies.

Not only are these invasions a disgrace to what our Founding Fathers stood for, but many of these invasions have resulted in the deaths of countless Americans, as well as foreigners, and the costs, overall, are immeasurable. Shockingly, the media has ignored several of these invasions, and many more are done in secret, so that the American people, who remain unaware of what is really going on, aren't even given the opportunity to protest.

President Taft, who followed Roosevelt into the White House, enacted an imperialistic economic policy known as *dollar diplomacy*, which was originally postulated by Roosevelt after his experiences with the Venezuelan and Dominican Republic governments and their expansive European debts. The purpose of this policy was to create political stability abroad, and in order to do this, the United States, in essence, took control over many foreign countries' finances. In one instance, this led to Taft's unsuccessfully trying to take charge of Honduras by buying up all the debt it owed to the British.

In another instance, Taft provided military support to Nicaraguan rebels in order to overthrow the government there because he believed that was the only way he would be able to collect the money that Nicaragua owed to foreign investors. As a result of American support, the rebels were successful, and following the rebels' takeover, American banks took control of Nicaragua's customs collection. However, because America gained a great amount of financial leverage over this country during the two years after the rebels' takeover, the Nicaraguan people disliked this regime. This led to yet another rebellion in Nicaragua, whereby America supplied the troops necessary to suppress the revolt and maintain its regime, and except for a short period during 1925, the troops remained in Nicaragua for twenty-one years.

In 1953, CIA operative Kermit Roosevelt Jr., the grandson of Theodore Roosevelt, led a mission in Iran to overthrow a democratically elected government in favor of a dictator simply because the latter was an ally of the United States and the former had threatened to nationalize British oil interests. In

1954, the United States overthrew a democratically elected government in Guatemala. This was also the case in the Congo in 1960.

In 1963, the United States put Saddam Hussein in power by helping him overthrow the Iraqi government. In 1964, the United States overthrew yet another democratically elected government in Brazil. The United States helped overthrow the government in Ghana in 1966. We then backed a coup in Chile in 1973 that dispatched a dictator we hated—Salvador Allende—and helped another that we liked—General Augusto Pinochet—come to power.

Starting in 1978 and lasting through the 1980s, the United States helped train, arm, and finance the Afghan Mujahideen insurgents in Afghanistan to help them fight the Soviet Union. The Mujahideen were joined by Muslim volunteers from other countries, who were called Afghan Arabs, and so the United States helped train, arm, and finance them as well. Among these Afghan Arabs was Osama Bin Laden. But that's not all. Bin Laden transformed most, if not all, of these American-trained, American-armed, and American-financed Islamic militants into his Al Qaeda organization, thereby using U.S. training, weapons, and money to attack us, including 9/11.

Once again in 1980, the United States helped Saddam Hussein become the most powerful force in the Middle East. In 1981, the United States planted mines in civilian harbors and sank civilian ships in order to overthrow the government in Nicaragua.

Between 1982 and 1984, Congress enacted several pieces of legislation that made it illegal to provide arms to rebels in Honduras who were trying to overthrow the Honduran government. However, in 1985, President Reagan ignored the federal law that he had signed into existence, human rights groups, and the American public when he illegally sold arms to Iran and then used the money to finance the Honduran rebels. This became known as the Iran-Contra affair.

Once again, the United States helped overthrow Guatemala's government in 1993. In 2002, the United States helped fund an attempted coup of Venezuela's government. Then in 2003, the United States invaded Iraq to replace Saddam Hussein, the very leader we put in power in the 1960s, with a regime friendlier to the United States.

American involvement has not been limited to controlling foreign governments. Beginning in World War II, attention was put on acquiring land around the globe for U.S. military bases. Between 1939 and 1945, Franklin Delano Roosevelt focused on taking over British bases, and that ranged from the Caribbean to West Africa, offering wartime assistance in exchange. To this end, FDR signed the Destroyers for Bases Agreement with England on September 2nd 1940. Under this agreement, the United States offered to give fifty naval destroyers to Britain in exchange for the land rights of several British territories so that the United States could build naval and air bases there. The United States also gained land rights in places such as Newfoundland and Bermuda without giving the British any destroyers, thus taking advantage of the pressure that England felt to stay on good terms with the United States and thus getting these possessions for free.

This trend toward acquiring military bases has only grown since World War II. Today, military bases have become the equivalent of what it was to have a colony. However, "due to government secrecy, [U.S. citizens] are ignorant of the fact that our garrisons encircle the planet," and "this vast network of American bases on every continent except Antarctica actually constitutes a new form of empire—an empire of bases."[31]

According to the Stockholm Peace Research Institute, U.S. military spending accounts for 42.8 percent of the military spending of the entire world. China is second with 7.3 percent, followed by the U.K. at 3.7 percent and then France at 3.6 percent. This difference in size epitomizes how important having a powerful military and controlling the world are to the U.S. government. The sun never sets on the U.S. military nor on its nine hundred permanent installations throughout the world.

Conclusion

It is a sad truth to realize the extent of what Theodore Roosevelt set in motion and just how far we have come from the isolationist roots that our Founding Fathers bestowed upon us. At the heart of all the United States' unwanted meddling throughout the twentieth and twenty-first centuries lie the policies of Theodore Roosevelt, making us the most imperialistic country in the history of the world. It is Roosevelt who came in and destroyed our ideals; he is no hero as history would have us believe, but rather a menace to everything that our Founding Fathers stood for and everything that has made our country so great.

Can armies really make the world safe for democracy, or are they instruments of imperialism and oppression? Should we fight other people's wars for them? Woodrow Wilson thought we should. We look at his military follies and the catastrophic Great War next.

Chapter 13

A Reverberation of Horrors

Wilson and International Relations

We started, opened fire on them and as soon as we had got the range, we started sending shrapnel into them as fast as we could fire them. It was murder, as we could see the shells bursting from where we were and they were tearing holes into the ranks of the German infantry. The Germans started shelling . . . one team of black horses and the three drivers were smashed up into a pulp as a shell burst in right amongst them. And I shall never forget the sight when the smoke cleared away, you couldn't recognise anybody as the flesh of the man was mixed up with the horse. . . . That was our first real baptism of fire.

—Private Bert Camp[1]

As we read this story of a courageous soldier dealing with the horrors of World War I, we hope to ourselves that he did not go through this in vain, but that there was some noble purpose behind his suffering. The reality is that nothing during Woodrow Wilson's presidency had noble roots, even if he tried to dress it up as such. Rather, it seems that the theme of Wilson's entire presidency was promulgating horrors in order to meet nothing other than his self-aggrandizing goals of telling and compelling others how to live their lives, and it appears that Wilson's legacy only perpetuates the reverberation of those horrors that he put in motion.

What Happened in Nicaragua

At the end of 1909, while William Howard Taft was still president, American troops were sent to Nicaragua to support the rebels who were rising up against Jose Santos Zelaya, the president of Nicaragua. It took a few more years of fighting, but eventually the American-backed rebel, Adolfo Diaz, usurped the presidency.

By 1912, an insurrection rose up against Diaz, beginning a new wave of violence in Nicaragua. Diaz turned to America, asking for assistance in maintaining his power. Woodrow Wilson, who was now the president of the United States, offered Diaz a deal. He would provide Diaz with the requested assistance, so long as Diaz would make sure to keep American interests safe. Having made this agreement, Wilson sent about two thousand marines to assist Diaz, and with this help, Diaz was able to quash the rebellion.

Following this, elections were held in Nicaragua, and the American marines stayed to monitor the voting. Because of this, and because many rebels chose to boycott the election, Diaz was elected president. Otherwise, Diaz would have easily lost. In other words, the only reason Diaz was able to get elected to the presidency was that he was backed by the American military. With approximately 75 percent of the people in Nicaragua supporting the rebel cause instead of Diaz, he was clearly not the people's popular choice; he was the product of American meddling.

Nevertheless, America continued to put its support behind Diaz even after the election. The reason America continued to back this Nicaraguan dictator goes back to 1912, when America began facing a downturn in the profitability of the Panama Canal.

In 1912, Congress passed the Tolls Exemption Act, which allowed American ships to pass through the Panama Canal without paying tolls. The British protested this Act because they believed it was a violation of the Hay-Pouncefote Treaty signed in 1901. This Treaty had stipulated that the canal would be open to all nations on equal terms, which was clearly no longer the case since the U.S. government had effectively transferred the cost of paying for and maintaining the canal from consumers who bought the products transported in American ships to all other consumers.

Wilson had cared very little about the violation, recognizing the price advantage that it would give to American goods traveling through the canal in comparison to goods from other countries that also passed through the canal, since the American goods would no longer have to figure toll prices into their costs. Also, because the canal would become a relatively cheaper means to transport goods, this would lead railroads to reduce the costs of using train transportation, in order to compete better with the canals. Therefore, American goods traveling by train would pay smaller freight costs, resulting in lower costs and leading, once again, to lower prices and a better competitive advantage for American goods.

International pressure forced Wilson to abandon this plan and follow the Hay-Pouncefote Treaty instead. Having been forced to maintain equal terms for all nations passing through the Panama Canal, Wilson knew that the economic and military advantage of that canal was dead. He would only be able to get this advantage back by building yet another canal in South America that he would control absolutely, unlike the canal in Panama, which was weighed down by the Hay-Pouncefote Treaty.

It is curious that the former professor of constitutional law would abandon a treaty. (Sound familiar?) He certainly knew that under the Constitution, a treaty is, just like the Constitution, the supreme law of the land.

To this end, in 1914 Wilson pursued the Bryan-Chamorro Treaty with Nicaragua that not only solidified the unpopular Diaz's power, but also gave America the rights to build another canal, in addition to the Panama Canal, this time through Nicaragua. Specifically, this Treaty gave

> the US sole right to build a canal across the [Nicaragua] isthmus in exchange for $3,000,000. The US was also granted a renewable 99 year lease to build a naval base in the Gulf of Fonseca, on Nicaragua's Pacific Coast. Nicaragua also ceded a ninety-nine year lease to the Great and Little Corn Islands in the Caribbean.[2]

The three million dollars wasn't really a payment at all, since that was how much Nicaragua currently owed the United States; it was more like a canceling of debt, at best. In other words, America practically stole the land it wanted for the canal from Nicaragua. Never mind Nicaragua's loss, though; America was on its way toward reviving its old economic and military advantage.

Moreover, this Treaty gave the United States the right to interfere in the affairs of Nicaragua at any point should the United States deem it necessary in order to protect Nicaragua's independence.

Overall, Wilson had shamelessly used the American military to occupy Nicaragua, install a puppet government, and force the country into signing a treaty that promoted American interests, not Nicaraguan ones. If Wilson could have had his way entirely, he would have transformed Nicaragua into an American protectorate. However, the Senate rejected this idea and declined to ratify the Treaty that Wilson had negotiated. This was the first treaty signed by Wilson that the Senate rejected, but it would not be the last. Nevertheless, this was only the beginning of Wilson's pursuit to form protectorates in the Caribbean, "push[ing] the policy with far more vigor than his predecessors had."[3] So began Wilson's efforts to impose "democracy" forcefully in foreign nations. Never mind that nobody in Nicaragua or any of the other countries in which Wilson intervened actually got what *they* wanted, as one would expect of a democracy.

Who Should Govern Haiti?

Much like Nicaragua, Haiti was suffering from chronic insurrections by local rebels a hundred years ago. In 1915, when the rebellions came to a head, Wilson wrote to Robert Lansing, his secretary of state, "I fear we have not the legal authority to do what we apparently ought to do." Yet, Wilson continued, "I suppose there is nothing for it but to take the bull by the horns and restore order."[4] To this end, Wilson deployed U.S. troops to Haiti, forcing the Haitians to elect an American puppet government.

The American troops continued their stay in Haiti, in order to maintain the power of this puppet government, until 1934. In addition, Wilson forced a protectorate treaty on the Haitians, once the puppet government was in place, so that the United States could intervene in Haitian affairs as it pleased. In this way, America once again forced its ways on unwelcoming people under the guise of democracy though very little democracy remained to be seen. (Sound familiar?)

Who Should Govern the Dominican Republic?

In 1916, only a year after a protectorate had been set up in neighboring Haiti, the Wilson administration sent troops to intervene in the Dominican Republic, following a guerilla uprising there. Once the United States was in the Dominican Republic, it tried to set up a protectorate similar to the one in Haiti; however, the Dominican Republic authorities refused to cooperate with such an undertaking. Then the U.S. government went about setting up a different type of protectorate, one that relied on U.S. military rule.

After six years had passed, this military regime allowed a provisional Dominican government to take office. Two years later U.S. troops were withdrawn entirely, and an agreement was devised regarding the end of the military protectorate state in the Dominican Republic. Unfortunately, this agreement, made in 1924, provided that the United States would be in control of the Dominican Republic's international finances. It wasn't until 1941 that this control was finally lifted and the Dominican Republic was free of the United States' interference.

Who Should Govern Mexico?

Of all the interventions that took place prior to World War I, "Wilson's most egregious intervention occurred in Mexico."[5] Mexico was going through a bloody revolutionary war. Victoriano Huerta, a revolutionary, had seized power in a *coup d'état*. His main opposition was from Venustiano Carranza, who was the leader of another revolutionary group, the Constitutionalists; but other rebel parties, including those led by Pancho Villa and Emiliano Zapata, were giving Huerta difficulties.

Though this situation had nothing to do with Americans, Wilson felt the need to take sides. To this end, Wilson, who was a known racist, chose to support the much lighter-skinned, more Caucasian-looking Carranza over the darker Huerta. After all, "the idea of a dark colored leader in neighboring Mexico would be unsettling to a man like Wilson."[6]

In January 1914, Wilson's cabinet finally agreed with him on sending troops into Mexico. However, Wilson was looking for a good excuse to present to the American people about why we needed to get involved in this conflict, much the way the sinking of the USS *Maine* had functioned during the Spanish-American War.

On April 9th 1914, the right opportunity finally presented itself. "A group of American sailors from the U.S.S. *Dolphin* went into Tampico to go to a fuel warehouse, as they would usually do," and "a group of Huerta's soldiers, on alert for an attack and aware of the American tilt towards Carranza, confronted the sailors and eventually rounded them up."[7] Following this, the United States demanded that the Mexicans free the sailors and issue an apology for taking them captive. Though Mexico agreed to do this, its apology did not meet the public standards demanded by Wilson.

Wilson jumped on this breach and, on April 20th 1914, sent a message to Congress, asking for permission to "use the armed forces of the United States in such ways and to such an extent as may be necessary to obtain from General Huerta and adherents the fullest recognition of the rights and dignity of the United States."[8]

Wilson felt that he simply could not wait for congressional approval; he had received word that the Germans were heading toward Vera Cruz with a large shipment of arms intended for Huerta and his rebel followers. Therefore, before Congress even granted Wilson his request, Wilson decided to send troops, led by General John J. Pershing, into Mexico on April 21st 1914, without authorization, in order to occupy the port city of Vera Cruz.

The United States offered Carranza arms and more than two million pesos in exchange for his word that he would rule by terms favorable to the United States. Carranza accepted. By making this deal, he was able to defeat his bitter rival, Huerta. Because Wilson had known his support would be decisive in this conflict, he had, in essence, handpicked the future Mexican leader.

Even though Wilson had succeeded in getting his choice, Carranza, into the Mexican presidency, a resolution passed by Congress allowed Wilson to keep ten thousand American soldiers in Mexico in order to capture rebel leaders, such as Pancho Villa, that the United States still regarded as a threat.

Not for lack of trying, the troops were unable to capture Pancho Villa. However, all of the skirmishes that ensued during their pursuits, which included conflicts not only with the bandits but at times with the Mexican Army itself, led to a severe breakdown in Mexican and American relations.

Fortunately, Wilson withdrew the U.S. Army from Mexico, but he did that only because he decided that "Germany posed a greater threat to American security,"[9] and he needed the troops "in anticipation of entering World War I."[10] Nevertheless, "Latin America and Mexico have never forgotten Wilson's actions which have colored U.S. relations in the region ever since."[11]

Entering World War I

"The United States, traditionally a military power within its own region, had never been involved in a war in Europe before, nor had an official American army ever set foot on European soil."[12] Under Wilson, this was all about to change.

Wilson saw the war in Europe as an opportunity to promote his self-aggrandizing schemes abroad. Specifically, he wanted to promote a United States–style democracy in the rest of the world or, as he liked to say, "make the world safe for democracy." For example, under this scheme Wilson sought

> the destruction of the Austro-Hungarian monarchy. As a multi-ethnic state based not on 19th century nationalism but ancient dynastic loyalty cemented by a majority Catholic faith, it offended his modern notions of what should constitute a country; and as a good Princeton academic, who was in addition convinced that he personally embodied the Will of God, Wilson knew that he could do better.[13]

To this end, Wilson wanted to play a leading role in reshaping the world after the war, and he knew that "as head of a nation participating in the war, the president of the United States would have a seat at the peace table, but . . . if he remained the representative of a neutral country, he could at best only 'call through a crack in the door.'"[14] Desperate to fulfill his ego's wishes, Wilson made his greatest priority entering the European conflict. Never mind that this was a conflict among European princes that had nothing to do with America.

To Wilson's displeasure, when World War I, then called the Great War, broke out in Europe, he could not immediately send troops to Europe, even though he greatly wished to intervene in this conflict, because the American people overwhelmingly opposed the war. Wilson knew he would have to wait until the time was right. In the meantime, the president found other ways to give his support to the side that he favored, even as he continued to preach neutrality on the home front. Though permitting U.S. corporations to trade with all sides to ensure that America would garner the highest profits from this international conflict, Wilson favored trade with England and France. Additionally, so that England and France could continue to purchase war supplies and other necessities from the United States, the United States loaned money to these countries.

In ways other than supplying goods and funding trade, Wilson's acts were quite contrary to the neutral stance he took in public. These efforts were all part of his plan to get us into war. When England started a naval blockade, preventing the shipping of non-military goods into Germany with the intention of starving the Germans to death, Wilson supported the move, even though the British were acting directly contrary to international law. The secretary of state, William Jennings Bryan, pleaded with Wilson to stand up against this blockade, but Wilson adamantly refused.

Not only this, but Wilson also never issued any warnings to Americans about the risk that they would be taking if they traveled through war zones, even though the Germans had made it clear that they would be sinking any ships that crossed through. Wilson "assert[ed] a spurious right for citizens of neutrals to go wherever they pleased," even though "during the conflict with Mexico, he had issued a warning to Americans in Mexico that they remained there at their own risk."[15] This change in outlook had everything to do with the fact that Wilson wanted to provoke American outrage at the Germans, and he believed a few American casualties, resulting from Americans naïvely traveling through war zones, would do the trick.

Just as Wilson had hoped, on May 7th 1915 a German U-boat torpedoed the *Lusitania*, a British ship carrying American passengers. Just like that, Wilson had the American casualties—128, in fact—that he sought to outrage the American people.

Other government officials, such as Bryan, were appalled by what Wilson was doing. Wilson had given Americans a false sense of confidence in boarding British ships heading to war zones, even though the Germans themselves had made countless publications in American papers detailing the dangers of doing exactly this. In this way he had used *American* lives as pawns to bring himself one step closer to getting us into the war. (Sound familiar?)

Then, in 1916 the foreign secretary to the German Empire, Arthur Zimmerman, sent the Zimmerman Telegram to the German ambassador in Mexico, and the British intercepted and decoded it. In this telegram, Zimmerman told the German ambassador that if America declared war against Germany, he was to approach the Mexican government and offer to help the Mexicans regain territory that they had lost to America in 1848. Because of this telegram's implications, Wilson made sure to publicize it, thereby outraging the American people. Never mind that there was no real substance to the promise in the telegram, given that even if America and Germany went to war with one another, there was no serious way Germany would be able to attack the United States in the Southwest or assist the Mexicans in doing so.

Wilson officially cut diplomatic ties with Germany on February 3rd 1917, claiming the continued use of unrestricted submarine warfare as the reason. On February 26th, citing the possibility that German submarines might attack American ships, Wilson asked Congress to let him arm American merchant ships. When Congress did not give him such permission, "Wilson chose to ignore Congress, [and] decided to arm American merchant ships by executive order. He claimed that an old anti-piracy law gave him the authority to do so."[16]

Believing the time was finally right for him to reveal his war plans, Wilson went before Congress and announced his goal to make the world "safe for democracy." He asked Congress to declare America's entry into the war. However, Wilson "didn't explain how this was to be done by allying with the British Empire, which had colonies around the world [and was ruled by a king]; with France, which had colonies in Africa and Asia [and was ruled by Socialists]; and with Russia, which was ruled by a czar."[17]

It was profoundly ironic that Wilson believed he could pave the way to democracy by aligning himself with these oft very undemocratic countries; it seems that the irony may have been lost on him entirely, or rather that he simply didn't care about the hypocrisy of it all. So, "for the first time ever the United States would send a full army across the ocean. For the first time ever, the United States would directly involve itself in a European conflict on European soil. For the first time ever, American soldiers would march in Europe," and all because "Wilson longed to be a Christian statesman spreading morality . . . [and he] hoped to mediate the postwar peace."[18] And so the sad truth was confirmed that "no president has spoken more passionately and eloquently about the right of self-determination. Yet no president [has] intervened more often in foreign countries."[19]

Atrocities of World War I and Beyond

The operation opened promptly at 3:30 with the explosion of a battery of projectors with high explosives and another battery with chlorine gas. Shortly after, the Stokeses opened fire, while at 3:37 the artillery behind us began laying down a terrific barrage on the enemy's lines and the back areas. But the attack was not to prove a one sided affair. Our Stokeses had fired only 41 gas and 24 thermite bombs when the hostile machine guns, which had located our emplacements, covered the entire position with such an intense fire that further operation of the guns was not to be thought of. Moreover, the enemy's artillery replied to our own almost immediately, bombarding in a systematic fashion the entire ridge and particularly the road. The shells literally rained about, high explosives varying with gas and occasionally shrapnel. . . . [A]nd so we lay there, huddled together, nerves tense, weapons ready, determined, if the occasion should arrive, to sell our lives as dearly as possible, for I hardly believe there was one of us who expected to get away alive.

—WILLIAM L. LANGER[20]

This Great War that Wilson had promised would bring peace and democracy to the world, and in which he had been so quick to send American troops to fight, was one of the most inhumane and atrocious wars of all time.

During the war, soldiers used a wide array of chemical weapons against one another, including tear gas, mustard gas, chlorine, and phosgene. While the tear gas caused mild eye irritation, rather than death or any long-lasting disability, mustard gas caused soldiers' skin to blister, vomiting, internal and external bleeding, and the destruction of their bronchial tubes. When the injuries from mustard gas proved fatal, it would sometimes take an excruciating four or five weeks for the soldier to die. Because mustard gas could remain in the soil for months after it was originally released, infections were rampant.

Chlorine led to death by asphyxiation. If one did not die from the effects, he would spend the rest of his life suffering from lung damage. There were also many instances of blindness—temporary and permanent—caused by the gas. The sickly green color and awful stench of the gas made it easy to identify. Therefore, to prevent awareness of the gas once it was deployed and, thus, the opportunity to escape its gruesome effects, the British chemist John Davy eventually developed phosgene. It was the more deadly and completely undetectable upgrade from chlorine.

Outside of chemical warfare, there were other deadly developments. For example, soldiers used flamethrowers that spewed liquid fire at one another.

All of these brutal tactics took place with the soldiers inside trenches. These trenches were dugouts in the ground protected by barbed wire along the front. Directly opposite would be the enemy's trenches. The distance between the trenches was called no-man's-land. This system of trench warfare was the inevitable result of a deadly weapons revolution that was unmatched by advances in mobility.

Trench warfare proved to be a hell on earth. Soldiers were forced to live months, sometimes years, in trenches that were infested with rats, lice, frogs, slugs, horned beetles, and other pests. Living beside these disease-plagued creatures, soldiers caught trench fever, which was excruciatingly painful and took up to twelve weeks from which to recover, as well as trench foot, which caused gangrene to set in and led to eventual amputation of the foot.

Not only that, they were completely open to airplane bombing from above. Shellfire from the opposing side rained down into the trenches, killing men haphazardly. Additionally, if a soldier so much as peered over the edge of the trench, the opposing side tried to take him out with a sniper's bullet. Many new soldiers, who had just arrived at the trenches, lost their lives on their first day by doing this. In short, there were many ways a soldier could die before he even rose up from the trenches to launch an attack on the opposing side.

Those who survived were either horribly disfigured or permanently traumatized. The brutality of this war gave rise to the Lost Generation, which consisted of soldiers who had survived the war, but who were permanently disillusioned by their horrific experiences and had lost their will to live. The Lost Generation included writers such as Ernest Hemingway and F. Scott Fitzgerald, who wrote both bluntly and impassively about the horrors of war or other gruesome situations, which no longer fazed them.

In reality, the brutality during World War I was an extension of the brutality that arose in warfare during the time of Theodore Roosevelt. Since the United States began fighting in foreign wars, which was the consequence of Roosevelt's imperialistic policies, there have been thousands of cases of torture and abuse committed by or to U.S. soldiers.

The first use of waterboarding by American forces occurred during the Spanish-American War. Then, during the Philippine-American war, as Filipinos were fighting for their independence against the United States, American soldiers used the water cure on captured Philippine soldiers. It was so prevalent that *Life* magazine depicted this torture on its cover in 1902.

In another instance, the Omaha *World-Herald* published a letter written in May 1900 by A. F. Miller, of the Thirty-second Volunteer Infantry Regiment, that discussed how Miller's unit had uncovered hidden weapons by subjecting a prisoner to the water cure. In the letter, he described how to do it:

> Lay them on their backs, a man standing on each hand and each foot, then put a round stick in the mouth and pour a pail of water in the mouth and nose, and if they don't give up pour in another pail. They swell up like toads. I'll tell you it is a terrible torture.[21]

Then, of course, came World War I and the aforementioned brutality that the soldiers had to endure. Just as World War I seemed to confirm that America was permanently laying by the wayside the non-interventionist policies of the Founding Fathers, so, too, it seemed that World War I confirmed that American involvement in the use of brutal warfare tactics on an international scale was here to stay.

During the Vietnam War, violence was once again prevalent. In one instance, a twenty-year-old medic named Jamie Henry

[s]et his rifle down in a hut, unfastened his bandoliers and lighted a cigarette. Just then, the voice of a lieutenant crackled across the radio. He
reported that he had rounded up 19 civilians, and wanted to know what to
do with them. Henry later recalled the company commander's response:
Kill anything that moves. Henry stepped outside the hut and saw a small
crowd of women and children. Then the shooting began. Moments later,
the 19 villagers lay dead or dying.[22]

The most infamous incident of Vietnam was the My Lai Massacre, where
U.S. soldiers murdered more than five hundred unarmed civilians, most of
whom were women and children.

We know that we cannot consider this brutality a thing of the past. In
recent years in Iraq, there have been countless acts of brutality. For example,
there have been "numerous accounts of abuse and torture of prisoners held
in the Abu Ghraib Prison in Iraq . . . committed by personnel of the 372nd
Military Police Company, CIA officers, and contractors involved in the occupation of Iraq."[23] In fact, U.S. Army Major General Antonio Taguba was ordered
to investigate these incidents, and in a fifty-three-page report dated April 4th
2004, he found that "between October and December 2003 there were numerous instances of sadistic, blatant, and wanton criminal abuses of prisoners."[24]
The report also estimated that "60% of the prisoners at the site were not a
threat to society and that the screening process was so inadequate that innocent civilians were often detained indefinitely."[25]

General Taguba's report cited specific examples of torture and abuse,
including

[j]umping on prisoners' naked feet, videotaping and photographing naked
male and female detainees, forcibly arranging detainees in various sexually explicit positions for photographing, forcing detainees to remove their
clothing and keeping them naked for several days at a time, forcing groups
of male detainees to masturbate while being photographed and video-
taped, arranging naked male detainees in a pile and then jumping on them,
positioning a naked detainee on a MRE Box, with a sandbag on his head,
and attaching wires to his fingers, toes, and penis to simulate electric torture . . . placing a dog chain or strap around a naked detainee's neck and

having a female soldier pose for a picture, a male MP guard raping a female detainee, taking photographs of dead Iraqi detainees and MPs posing with cheerful looks, breaking chemical lights and pouring the phosphoric liquid on detainees . . . pouring cold water on naked detainees, beating detainees with a broom handle and a chair . . . sodomizing a detainee with a chemical light and perhaps a broom stick, and using military working dogs (without muzzles) to frighten and intimidate detainees with threats of attack, and in one instance actually biting and severely injuring a detainee.[26]

In another Iraq-related instance, President Bush himself spoke of his support for the use of waterboarding, like the water cure used by Roosevelt's military in the Philippines, against terrorism suspects. President Obama says he has banned this practice since he took office.

It is clear from these examples that American involvement in brutal international warfare, which was originally condoned during Roosevelt's time and established as a mainstay during Wilson's War, is a widespread problem even in our modern era. Whether our soldiers are the victims of foreign brutality and we senselessly allow them to endure it, or we ourselves are the ones inflicting the unspeakable horrors on other human beings, the time for this heinous trend to come to an end is now.

The League of Nations and Its Progeny

On November 11th 1918, the Germans surrendered, calling World War I to a close. Finally, Wilson had the opportunity to create a new world order, which he envisioned would be established via the creation of the League of Nations. When the Paris Peace Conference began on January 18th 1919, Wilson made sure that he personally headed the American delegation at the conference, so that he could play a hand in shaping the resulting treaty according to his vision.

Wilson didn't take any members of Congress along with him to this conference. The president saw no reason to get any of them involved, given that he believed that he could easily work around them. He believed that he could sidestep Congress by getting America involved in a preliminary treaty, which would grant American membership to the League of Nations via an executive agreement that did not require congressional approval. As a consequence of immediately placing the United States in the League, he reasoned, it would then be harder for the Senate to reject the premise of the League, since we would already be engaging in it.

The Senate's reaction to Wilson's League was far from positive. Idaho Senator William Borah, a Republican, declared on the Senate floor that "the mere reading of the constitution of the League will convince any reasonable mind, it seems to me, that the policies of [George) Washington . . . must depart if it is adopted." Borah was especially concerned because "already the United States had broken with the idea of staying out of Europe's affairs," and he was "hoping that this war would not create a new precedent," whereby "the United States and Europe open up the world to a forum where they can deal with one another's issues together."[27]

Not only Republicans attacked Wilson; fellow Democrats spoke out against what Wilson was trying to do. Missouri Senator James Reed railed against how far a departure the League would be from our Founding Fathers' principles. Specifically, he disliked Article X of the League's Covenant, which stipulated that the United States, like every other nation in the League, would be required to fight in any international conflicts that the League saw as an impediment to world peace, thus establishing itself as a world police force. This would only serve, he argued, to perpetuate American involvement in conflicts in which we had no interests.

Additionally, because the League would ultimately strip those countries it invaded of their sovereignty and make all of them *de facto* the League's colonies, the League seemed to advance an imperialistic ruling strategy contrary to the democratic principles of governing that America was claiming to represent.

Moreover, many members of Congress saw this article as usurping congressional power to declare war because we would now be at the mercy of the League's decisions. After all, Congress had been given this right, exclusively, by the Constitution itself. Members were certainly correct in thinking that this power should not suddenly be vested in the League of Nations, which was an international body.

Overall, because of huge opposition to the League of Nations by both the

American people and Congress, the United States never became a member, despite Wilson's best efforts.

It seems the American people and Congress were right not to want to join the League. In practice, the League proved to be an utter failure. From Italian nationalists seizing the Yugoslavian port of Fiume, to Polish troops seizing the Lithuanian city of Vilna, the League did nothing to prevent these events and did not come to the aid of the victims. Instead, it seemed that the League was playing favorites and condoning the actions of those countries that it liked, even when they were out of line.

In some ways, the League failed to such a degree that it paved the way for World War II. The League allowed Germany to start rearming itself even though this violated the peace treaty that concluded the Great War. When Germany stopped paying reparations, the League did nothing. Instead, it allowed France and Belgium to take aggressive action of their own against Germany. To this end, these countries invaded the Ruhr, which was Germany's most important industrial zone, causing much bitterness on the part of the Germans.

Fortunately, this disastrous brainchild of Wilson faced its demise during World War II. On a less fortunate note, the monumental failure of the League of Nations was not enough warning to posterity. Following World War II, a second-generation League of Nations, called the United Nations, was formed, and this time the United States was to be its biggest financial and military backer.

Since its inception, the failures of this international police power have been piling up. During the Cold War, the United Nations did nothing about the atrocities that Russia was committing against other countries, such as Hungary and Czechoslovakia, and even its own people. It also was useless in preventing the outbreak of the Vietnam War. The United Nations did nothing about the murderous dictator Pol Pot in Cambodia, even as he killed some two million of his own people, or about 21 percent of the country's total population. Talk about paving the way for world peace.

This is not to say the United Nations never gets involved. But when it does, it tends to be in those conflicts that are so far outside its control that it is merely expending lives fruitlessly. Nothing exemplifies this better than American involvement in Somalia during the 1990s. In December 1992, the

United Nations deployed peacekeeping and peace-building troops in Somalia, calling it Operation Restore Hope. By 1993 the United States withdrew all of its forces, following the deaths of eighteen American soldiers. Because of this, the United Nations operation, as a whole, quickly fell apart. To this day, the thugs running the government of Somalia remain a threat to everyone there, as well as to neighboring countries.

The United Nations' interference with Bosnia is another instance that embodies its failures. The United Nations declared certain areas in Bosnia safe for Muslims, but then it did nothing to secure the areas. Muslims, trusting in the United Nations, entered these "safe" areas, and thousands were slaughtered by the Serbs. So, too, the Serbs captured some of the United Nations' "blue helmets" and held them as hostages to deter any military response to the slaughter.

It seems that not only is the history of the United Nations fraught with blunders, but it is unlikely to improve. Those soldiers that make up the United Nations' peacekeeping operations are never chosen because they have military skills, but because their governments are willing to send them, so that the governments can get the financial benefits from doing so. These soldiers come together with incompatible training and equipment that is extremely difficult to reconcile. The soldiers are often disinterested in the purpose of their missions, at one point being described as "more interested in searching for sex than for cease-fire violations."[28]

Nevertheless, the United Nations lives on and continues to cost American taxpayers millions of dollars each year. The United States has provided the United Nations with 25 percent of its annual budget every year since 1945, to do virtually nothing or to intervene in the most helpless of causes in the most hapless ways.

Consequences of World War I for Russia

In 1917, while World War I was in full swing, the czarist government in Russia was overthrown, and it was replaced by what those who overthrew the czar called a democracy. However, there were Communist rebels bucking up against this fledgling democracy, and the Allied powers feared that a

Communist Russian Revolution might spread, thus preventing Russia from being able to help them fight against Germany and the other Central powers. The Allied powers devised a plan to impede the Communist movement in Russia. To this end, many of the Allied countries sent troops to support the anti-Communists. Wilson also contributed troops to this Russian intervention. This intervention, however, only prolonged the civil unrest.

Wilson also offered Russia a bribe to ensure that it would stay in the war, in case the efforts to stop the rebellion were unsuccessful. To this end, Wilson promised Russia a loan of $325 million, so long as Russia continued to fight. Never mind that the Constitution doesn't even give the president the power to lend money to foreign governments.

In order to lay hands on this desperately needed money, the Russian government launched one last offensive. It turned out to be a military catastrophe that "sowed the seeds of the destruction of the democratic government."[29] Because the Russian democracy lost much of its support by launching an unsuccessful military offensive when the people were barely in support of the war effort, this opened the way for Vladimir Lenin, who led the revolution, to garner the support he needed to usher in his Communist dictatorship.

Due to Wilson's meddling, both in sending troops that prolonged the domestic conflict and in bribing Russia to stay in the war, the seventy-year horror of Russian communism was allowed to germinate and spread throughout the country and the continent.

Consequences of World War I for Germany

Wilson's involvement in World War I also had toxic effects on Germany. The United States' entry into the war paved the way for the uprising of Nazism. Prior to the United States' entry into the war, the opposing factions in the war, which were largely stalemated at that point, had actually been heading toward negotiating peace, and if this had happened, only minor and very meaningless territorial adjustments would have been made, just as had been the case in all the previous European conflicts. However, the addition of the fresh and energized American forces enabled the Allies to have a decisive victory over the Germans, which in turn allowed for the harsh terms of the 1919 Treaty of Versailles.

The demoralizing terms of this Treaty, which, among other things, forced Germans to take full blame for the war, pay off all the war debt (a whopping $31 billion), fully disarm, have continued occupation by the Allied forces, and surrender all of their colonies and some of their motherland, "led to seething discontent in Germany and virtually guaranteed the rise of a demagogic leader. Adolf Hitler filled that role perfectly."[30] Even though Woodrow Wilson had long since passed, "we might well conclude that World War II was actually his war."[31]

Conclusion

Overall, "Woodrow Wilson dramatically expanded Theodore Roosevelt's expansionist policies."[32] Under Wilson, America no longer confined itself to intervening solely in Latin American skirmishes. Instead, he pushed the United States in the unprecedented direction of intervening in the affairs of European princes, and he began the movement toward a police power that would control the conflicts of the world over.

Because of this, soldiers have been subjected to the most brutal conditions, countries have been forced to endure the most humiliating treatment, and circumstances were made ripe for some of history's most brutal dictators. The truth is that "Wilson's foreign policy damaged America's image abroad and it never recovered."[33] Not only have we allowed his damaging legacy to stand; we have also allowed it to expand to the point where America itself might as well be considered the world's sole police force. So ask yourself, when are we finally going to stop our government from playing this role that it was never intended to have and that has bred horrors the likes of which we never should have known? The answer is *now*.

The Great War was also fought in the United States. It wasn't as violent or fatal as that on the Continent, but a war it was: On dissent and those who articulated it. Next we look at the government's assault on people who disagreed with it.

Chapter 14

Propaganda and Espionage

The Domestic Front During the Great War

Why, of course the people do not want war . . . but after all, it is the leaders of the country who determine the policy, and it is always a simple matter to drag the people along, whether it is a democracy or a fascist dictatorship or a Parliament or a Communist dictatorship . . . voice or no voice the people can always be brought to the bidding of the leaders. That is easy. All you have to do is to tell them they are being attacked and denounce the pacifists for lack of patriotism.

—HERMANN GOERING[1]

Can the Government Tell the Truth?

In August 1914, after Germany crossed into "neutral" Belgium, stories of military-perpetrated atrocities began to spread about how this imperialistic giant had crushed "poor little Belgium."[2] *Life* magazine published an article about how the German soldiers had speared tiny babies with their bayonets, cut off the hands of little boys, and amputated the breasts of women. Still other stories circulated about the savage way that German soldiers treated their dead, using the fat off their fallen brethren to make soap.

When American journalists were sent to Europe to follow the German troops through Belgium, they sent reports back to America saying that the atrocity stories were "groundless as far as [they were] able to observe."[3] So how did so many Americans come to believe directly the opposite?

Woodrow Wilson was reelected to the presidency in 1916. He had been the popular candidate because of his slogan "he kept us out of war." Americans, for the large part, wanted nothing to do with the conflict that was taking place overseas. Even though one-third of the U.S. population consisted of European immigrants, and many of these people were sympathetic to the governments in their homelands, Americans, as a whole, did not feel connected to the European conflict and were disinterested in America becoming involved.

In April 1917, only a few months after Wilson's election, however, America had declared its entry into the war. What had happened so that America's peace candidate and the people who elected him were suddenly mobilizing for war, in one of the greatest historical turnarounds of all time?

The truth is, Wilson was never the pacifist he had portrayed himself to be. Rather, his peace platform was a well-devised strategy to get himself elected president. In reality, he had goals on an international scale, which were his top priority, and he was willing to do anything to accomplish them, even if that meant lying about war and then conniving to enter it.

Specifically, Wilson wanted to play a part in creating the League of Nations. As we covered in the last chapter, that way he would be able to design the new world order, shaping it in America's "democratic" image. Sure enough, when it became patently obvious to Wilson that he would have to enter the war in order to take part in his pet project, he began to mislead the American people. To do this, he built a clever propaganda apparatus, which manipulated the people into supporting the very same war they had elected him to keep them out of.

Wilson began this propaganda movement by capitalizing on the tragic sinking of the RMS *Lusitania* in May 1915. Because Germans had torpedoed the ship and 128 Americans had died, Wilson used this event to create American outrage that led to support of the Triple Entente, including England, France, and Russia. Newspapers across the country printed bold headlines and impassioned editorials. Former president Theodore Roosevelt summed up the sentiment when he said,

The sinking of the *Lusitania* was not only an act of simple piracy, but . . . it represented *piracy* accompanied by murder on a vaster scale than any old-time pirate had ever practiced before being *hung for his misdeeds.* . . . This was merely the application on the *high seas* . . . of the principles which when applied on land had produced the innumerable *hideous tragedies* that have occurred in Belgium and in Northern France. The use of the phrase, *"strict accountability,"* of course, must mean . . . that action will be taken by us without an hour's *unnecessary delay.*[4]

What nobody seemed to know was that this was a British ship, flying a British flag, carrying 4 million rifle cartridges and 1,250 cases of shrapnel shells, intended to be used against the Germans. Moreover, the Germans had actually placed publications in the *New York Times*, warning Americans that they would be placing themselves at risk if they were aboard British ships traveling through war zones. There had even been specific warnings against boarding the *Lusitania*.

William Jennings Bryan, Wilson's secretary of state, tried to encourage Americans to realize that "a ship carrying contraband should not rely on passengers to protect her from attack."[5] However, this perspective was largely covered up, eventually causing Bryan to resign because he wanted no part of willfully misleading the American people into war. In his resignation letter, Bryan wrote to Wilson, "I cannot join without violating what I deem to be an obligation to my country and the issue involved is of such moment that to remain a member of the Cabinet would be as unfair to you as it would to the cause nearest my heart, namely, the prevention of war."[6]

In April 1917, Wilson created the Committee on Public Information (CPI) through an executive order. The purpose of the CPI was to create support for the war domestically. Wilson appointed George Creel, a journalist famous for his sensational writing techniques, to be the head of this agency. Under Creel, the CPI persuaded businesses, the media, academia, and the art world to come together and present the American people with a unified message.

The approach of the CPI was sophisticated for its time. It relied on the techniques of modern psychology to persuade people. This approach was so subtle that people often thought their change in opinion had come from within themselves and not from some external force. Specifically, the CPI made emotional appeals and demonized the enemy. The CPI also used repetition and focused on indoctrination rather than logical arguments.

Because "any emotion may be 'drained off' into any activity by skill-ful manipulation," American propaganda relied on scare tactics, targeting the public's fears.[7] For example, a propaganda poster pictured a grimacing German soldier with bloody hands and a bloody bayonet above the words "beat back the Hun with liberty bonds." In another play on the American people's fear, propagandists quickly spread the idea that anyone who did not support the war was a traitor and would be treated as such by his fellow countrymen.

Americans were also told that they needed to fear for their national secu-rity, even though, in reality, there was no serious threat that Germany would attack America. The British navy had the German navy confined to its ports, and all of the Germans' armed forces were tied up in battles across Europe. Even if our national security was linked to that of England, as the govern-ment wanted us to believe, there was no real chance of a German victory in Europe, given that the war had already been stalemated for three years.

Additionally, even if Germany had conquered France or Belgium, it wouldn't have been able to hold onto its conquered territories for long because there would have been too many insurrections, and it would have been too costly for the Germans to manage. American propaganda would have none of this logic.

American propaganda used bold, patriotic colors to foster a sense of nationalism. It created slogans such as "the world needs us . . . enlist" to play on the sense of duty and slogans such as "together we win" and "get in the game with Uncle Sam" to appeal to the sense of camaraderie. According to Harold Lasswell, a political scientist and communications theorist at Yale University, "every war must appear to be a war of defense against a menac-ing, murderous aggressor. There must be no ambiguity about who the public is to hate."[8] (Sound familiar?) To this end, the CPI used atrocity stories to demonize the Germans. This is how the stories about the German soldiers spearing babies and slicing off the hands of boys and the breasts of women became known. The Wilson administration circulated them. It didn't matter to the CPI that many of the atrocity stories they were spreading never actu-ally happened or were the tales of wars long since passed. The CPI was not concerned with disseminating the truth; it wanted to spread hate and fear among the American people.

The CPI was so effective that, according to Dr. Michael F. Connors, author of the book *Dealing in Hate: The Development of Anti-German Propaganda* (1966), these "incredible tales of German barbarism in Belgium and France gave rise to a myth of unique German savagery that continues to color the thinking of many persons to this day."[9]

This American propaganda led to intolerant behaviors on the home front. Americans were encouraged to reject German culture, and under this encouragement, sauerkraut was renamed liberty cabbage, hamburger was renamed Salisbury steak, "dashounds were renamed liberty dogs, German measles were renamed liberty measles, and the City University of New York reduced by one credit every course in German. Fourteen states banned the speaking of German in public schools."[10] (Sound familiar?) Of course, the intolerance went too far in some instances.

In Van Houten, New Mexico, an angry mob forced a German American miner to his knees, made him kiss the American flag, and made him denounce the German government.

In Delphos, Ohio, five German Americans were hunted down by more than 450 townsmen and forced to salute and kiss the flag, threatened that they would otherwise be hung from nearby telephone poles. In the same town, an American flag was nailed to the door of a store owned by Barney Lindermann. He was told that if he removed it, he would be drowned in a canal. Local people did this because he refused to buy liberty bonds.

In Collinsville, Illinois, an angry mob actually hung a German American miner, Robert Prager, accusing him of hoarding explosives, despite his declarations of loyalty to the very end. In West Frankfort, Illinois, Frances Bergen, a woman of German origin, was ridden on a rail through town, the procession pausing at times so she could wave the American flag and shout out praise for Wilson.

Nothing was done to punish this behavior. Apparently there was no line that could be crossed if you were acting in support of the war.

If you think about it, this lying, this manipulation, this brainwashing, is not a thing confined to the past. Other presidents since Wilson have followed his example of conning the American people. Former president George W. Bush was one of them.

Although President Bush had promised during his campaign in 2000 that he would not send troops abroad for nation building, the truth was that he wanted a war, and after the events of September 11th 2001, he knew just how to get one. Bush delivered a speech to the American people, telling us that it was necessary "to disarm Iraq of weapons of mass destruction, to end Saddam Hussein's support for terrorism, and to free the Iraqi people."[11] He used provocative language, playing on the people's emotions just like Wilson did nearly a century earlier.

Bush stated that "our cause is just" and that "the future of peace and the hopes of the Iraqi people now depend on our fighting forces in the Middle East."[12] Bush also vilified the enemy, telling us that "American and coalition forces face enemies who have no regard for the conventions of war or rules of morality. Iraqi officials have placed troops and equipment in civilian areas, attempting to use innocent men, women and children as shields for the dictator's army."[13]

The reality of the situation was that the Pentagon had used false reports, which claimed Saddam Hussein had weapons of mass destruction, because Bush needed a pretext to get us into war. Like Wilson, who wanted to father the League of Nations, Bush had ulterior motives for war. He was interested in enhancing his power by expanding his control over the world's supply of oil and wanted to reward certain oil companies in the process with increased profits.

Bush knew that a war, in general, would have the effect of giving him more power. Furthermore, Bush, after his years as an alcoholic, became a very self-righteous man who wanted to impose his ideology on the rest of the world. Moreover, the Republican Party wanted to validate Bush as president, believing this was necessary because the election of 2000 had been so close, and Republican leaders thought that making him out to be a war hero was the way to do it.

Last, Bush wanted to seek a harsh revenge, without seeming too vindictive, for the devastating events of 9/11 and for Saddam's attempts to kill his father, former president George H. W. Bush. At one point Bush even admitted his personal stake in pursuing Saddam, saying, "[A]fter all, this is the guy who tried to kill my dad."[14]

Like Wilson, Bush went to the media to help him manipulate the American people. By the second week in November 2001, Bush had already sent Karl Rove, his special advisor, to meet with more than forty Hollywood executives. The purpose was to make sure they were on board with sending messages to the people that would line up with the government's war efforts. Heart-wrenching war movies such as *Black Hawk Down*, *We Were Soldiers*, *Behind Enemy Lines*, and *Hurt Locker* soon followed.

Bush was not above making outlandish accusations, such as "anyone who is not with us, is with the terrorists"; much like when Wilson accused war dissenters of being traitors.[15]

Just as the propaganda of World War I bred intolerance on the home front, so did the propaganda of the post–9/11 era, and Congress made sure to capitalize on it. When the French expressed opposition at the United Nations about the Bush administration's decision to invade Iraq, anti-French sentiment quickly spread though America. Starting with Congress, French fries were called freedom fries and French toast was called freedom toast. Soon many American people began to follow this lead. This intolerance became so widespread that French's mustard company felt the need to hold a press conference to clarify that its name was a family one, having nothing to do with the country, so that angry Americans would not boycott it.

As it turns out, President Obama falls within Wilson's ranks as well. Most Americans thought that the election of President Obama would usher in a new, less bellicose foreign policy. During his 2008 campaign, Obama scorned the war as "Bush's War" and promised that he would get our troops out of Iraq. Yet once again we were manipulated by the lies of another would-be president, who was willing to say whatever he thought we wanted to hear just to get elected.

While we no longer have troops fighting in Iraq, as of the writing of this book, Obama has actually escalated the number of troops in Afghanistan and has made statements that he is willing to deploy troops to Pakistan as well. He says this is necessary to ensure our national security, but the real reason we are still fighting wars is that Obama knows war is an exceptionally good way to expand government control (never mind that this is at the expense of the American people's personal freedoms) and to serve the interests of the financial elite.

Obama has intensified Bush's military operations in other ways. In 2001, Bush began the use of drones, or unmanned aerial vehicles against members of Al Qaeda he believed to be hiding out in Afghanistan. He started a minor campaign in Yemen in 2002. In 2004, he extended this practice to Pakistan.

After Obama took office, he reinstated the use of drones in Yemen in 2011, this time planning a widespread campaign like that in Afghanistan and Pakistan. Not only that, Obama is escalating the use of drones in Afghanistan and Pakistan. The German magazine *Der Spiegel* did some research and found that

> in the 21 months since his inauguration, President Obama has ordered or approved 120 drone attacks on Pakistan. There were 22 such attacks in September 2010 alone, reportedly killing more than 100 people. In contrast, Obama's predecessor Bush ordered just 60 attacks in eight years.[16]

While it has been argued that the use of drones prevents us from sacrificing American lives, and it is a more financially sound policy, this argument does not justify what we are doing. The truth is that by using these drones, we are mostly killing innocent civilians. According to a recent Gallup poll, the people in Pakistan fear America more than their longtime enemy, India, and more than the Taliban. However, the U.S. government does not want us to know this. In fact, "civilian casualties were deliberately overlooked to avert the public reaction."[17]

In well-publicized drone attacks, President Obama killed an American cleric, Anwar al-Awlaki, and his sixteen-year-old son while father and son were riding in a car in Yemen.[18]

President Obama has forced us into additional conflicts besides those with which we were involved during Bush's presidency. Because of Obama, we fought a war in Libya. To garner support, Obama made public appeals to the conscience of the American people, claiming, for instance, that there would be brutal massacres in Benghazi if we did not send troops to stop the now dead Libyan dictator, Colonel Muammar Gaddafi, and that allowing these massacres would be an insult to our democratic ideals. Never mind that Gaddafi "did not massacre civilians in any of the other big cities he captured—Zawiya, Misrata, Ajdabiya."[19]

In reality, the reason President Obama engaged us in this war is that he did not like the threat to his authority that the once cooperative Gaddafi posed. To Obama, it's not the massacre of thousands of people or the slap in democracy's face that was of any concern. The real concern to him was, quite simply, his ego, and American lives were put at risk for that reason alone.

Silencing Opposition

According to historian Bertrand Russell regarding wartime propaganda, "the greatest difficulty was the purely psychological one of resisting mass suggestion, of which the force becomes terrific when the whole nation is in a state of violent collective excitement."[20] Still, Wilson felt the need to do more than simply lie to the people and manipulate them. To this end, Wilson brought about a movement to censor and suppress what the people were saying and writing.

The Espionage Act, which was passed in 1917, was meant to criminalize interfering—even if the "interference" consisted of mere words—with military operations or recruitment, encouraging military insubordination, and giving support to America's enemies. Under the Act, the postmaster general was given the authority to refuse to mail any material that was in violation of the Act. Federal agents had lawful authority to look through people's mail so that they could determine which writings were permissible and which ones were unlawful. So much for the freedom of speech and the right to privacy.

As if this wasn't crossing the line enough, Wilson extended the Act when he signed into law the Sedition Act in 1918. The Sedition Act criminalized any speech that was "disloyal, profane, scurrilous, or abusive" about the U.S. government or any language that caused people to feel this way about the government.[21] The punishments for violating these Acts could be very severe, ranging from steep fines to long prison sentences and even the death penalty.

Approximately two thousand people were charged under the Espionage and Sedition Acts. Specifically, the government used these Acts to target its political enemies, in particular the left-wing Socialists or, as the government liked to call them, *anarchists* (much like our modern label, *terrorists*). The price Americans paid so that the government could suppress the voices of its opponents was, of course, a terrible infringement on their right to free speech.

In *Abrams v. United States* (1919), five Russian Socialists were sentenced to jail for twenty years each simply because they had spoken out against sending American troops to Russia and against American interference with the Russian Revolution.[22]

In another instance, on the night of August 4th 1917, Philip Randolph, a Socialist and the founder of a black civil rights magazine, *The Messenger*, delivered a speech in Cleveland encouraging blacks to "resist conscription and fight at home to 'make America unsafe for hypocrisy.'"[23] The clever phrase was a play on the words of Wilson's battle cry of making "the world safe for democracy." As Randolph spoke, copies of *The Messenger* were being sold to spectators. A federal agent was attracted to the scene by the large crowd and bought a copy of *The Messenger*. Not liking what he saw, he pulled Randolph off the stage where he was addressing the crowd and took him to the police for further investigation. There he was charged with violating the Espionage Act.

The indictment against Randolph and his colleagues was dismissed by a white federal judge because, as Randolph said, "[H]e couldn't believe we were old enough, or, being black, smart enough to write that red-hot stuff in *The Messenger*."[24] It's sad when the sting and stench of racism are the only things that stop a judge from violating his sworn duty to uphold the Constitution.

Masses Publishing Company of New York City published a magazine called *The Masses* that ran anti-war and anti-draft cartoons, poems, and articles. In July 1917, Masses Publishing Company tried to send out its August issue of the magazine, but Thomas Gedney Patten, the postmaster general of New York, refused to mail the materials, claiming that they violated the Espionage Act. When notified of this, Masses offered to take out any of the material that the postmaster general found offensive, but he declined to tell Masses what exactly was inappropriate about its publication. Masses brought suit against Patten to enjoin him from refusing to mail *The Masses*. Fortunately, Judge Learned Hand, who presided over the case, had the wisdom to grant Masses its injunction rather than perpetuate the cycle of injustice. In his opinion, Hand wrote that potentially incendiary speech must be permitted unless it proximately or directly leads to civil unrest or a violation of the law, and he did not believe Masses had gone beyond this boundary line.

Victor Burger was the publisher of several German newspapers in

Wisconsin. Because of the anti-war editorials featured in these newspapers, Burger was convicted in 1918 under the Espionage Act and sentenced to twenty years in federal prison. Even so, the people of Wisconsin elected him to the House of Representatives that same year. However, the Congress refused to seat him. Once again the people elected him in the special election held to fill his vacant seat, but Congress would not have him. It would seem that voters' opinions mattered very little in this Progressive "democracy" of ours. The Supreme Court overturned his sentence in 1921, and Burger went on to be elected to another three terms in Congress, where he sat with those whose blindness had rejected him.

In 1917, when the Y.M.C.A. asked Louis Nagler, the assistant secretary of state in the State of Wisconsin, to contribute, he refused, saying,

> I am through contributing to your private grafts. There is too much graft in these subscriptions. No, I do not believe in the work of the Y.M.C.A. or the American Red Cross, for I think they are nothing but a bunch of graft-ers. . . . Not over ten or fifteen percent of the money goes to the soldiers or is used for the purpose it was collected.[25]

In response, the authorities charged him under the Espionage Act. He was convicted and sentenced to twenty years in prison. Fortunately for Nagler, the Supreme Court eventually reversed his conviction in 1920.

Emma Goldman began the monthly publication of *Mother Earth*, an anarchist journal, and was the founder of the No Conscription League. Directly after the passing of the Espionage Act, federal agents raided her *Mother Earth* offices. Following this, she was arrested under the Espionage Act. During her trial, she urged,

> We say that if America has entered the war to make the world safe for democracy, she must first make democracy safe in America. How else is the world to take America seriously, when democracy at home is daily being outraged, free speech suppressed, peaceable assemblies broken up by overbearing and brutal gangsters in uniform; when free press is curtailed and every independent opinion gagged? Verily, poor as we are in democ-racy, how can we give of it to the world?[26]

The court turned its back on this argument and sentenced her to two years in prison. In 1919, she faced a deportation hearing and was eventually shipped out of America and sent to Russia.

In still another instance, presidential candidate and leader of the Socialist Party Eugene V. Debs was charged under the Espionage Act after he delivered a speech, which was directed toward working-class Americans, telling them that they were the principal fighting force behind the war; therefore, they alone should be the ones to decide matters of war and peace. He was convicted and sentenced to ten years in prison and was barred from public speaking and voting for life.[27] In 1921, President Warren G. Harding pardoned Debs for committing the "crime" of free speech.

Robert Goldstein, a German immigrant to America, wrote and produced *The Spirit of '76*, a film celebrating America's victory in the American Revolution. It depicted many of the crucial moments in that struggle, including the signing of the Declaration of Independence and Paul Revere's ride, as well as battles that the colonial soldiers bravely fought against the British army. This included the Wyoming Valley Massacre, where British soldiers impaled the babies, shot the women, and took the young girls captive.

Even though the movie portrayed a 140-year-old historical event, the government refused to allow this movie to be seen by the public because it showed an American ally, the British government, in too negative a light. Apparently, the American government can even erase history if it gets in the way of the message the government is trying to send out.

In the case *United States v. Motion Picture Film "The Spirit of '76"* (1917), Goldstein received a ten-year prison sentence because he retold history in a truthful way, yet one that displeased Woodrow Wilson.[28] When even certain universally accepted historical facts are prohibited speech, it seems there is no limit to what the government can stop you from saying when it conflicts with its goals. It is dangerous to be right when the government is wrong.

At this point you must be asking yourself, where did all of these judges find the constitutional authority to make these rulings? Doesn't the First Amendment protect the right to free speech, absolutely, or did the amendment leave room for limitations to be imposed? The answer to the questions lies squarely within the text of the amendment, which reads, "Congress shall make no law respecting an establishment of religion, or prohibiting the free exercise thereof; or abridging the freedom of speech, or of the press; or the right of the people peaceably to assemble, and to petition the Government for a redress of grievances." By reading these words exactly as they are written, we can see only one interpretation, which is that there can be no lawful governmental limits, whatsoever, on the freedom of speech. Any Act that Congress passes contrary to the plain language of the Constitution is unconstitutional, and any judge who upholds such a law has no authority to do so. In the words of Justice Hugo Black, the famous "no law" language in the First Amendment simply means "no law."[29]

Even though the Sedition Act was repealed in 1921, the Espionage Act was still law in 1973. In *United States v. Anthony Joseph Russo and Daniel Ellsberg* (1973), Daniel Ellsberg, a U.S. military civilian intelligence analyst, released the Pentagon Papers, which was a top-secret government document regarding the United States' decision making in relation to the Vietnam War, to the *New York Times*. For these actions, the Nixon administration argued that Ellsberg was guilty under the Espionage Act. The case was dismissed because of the government's misconduct and illegal evidence gatherings, having burglarized the office of Ellsberg's psychiatrist in order to read confidential files on him and illegally wiretapping his phone, among other things. In so doing, the Supreme Court articulated a version of First Amendment jurisprudence that arguably invalidated the Espionage Act.

Dianne Feinstein, the former mayor of San Francisco and current senior U.S. senator from California, made statements in 2010 that she would like to see Julian Assange prosecuted under the Espionage Act. Assange is the editor in chief of WikiLeaks, a website that aims to bring governments around the world to transparency by publishing their classified documents. Particularly offensive to Senator Feinstein was Assange's publication of Iraq and Afghan war documents pertaining to the United States' involvement in those wars. Because of Feinstein's and others' crusade against him, Assange acknowledges that it is not safe for him to come to America, the country that boasts that it gives the maximum protection to people's rights, including free speech.

In another recent instance, former government employee Thomas Drake faced charges under the Espionage Act simply for being "a public-interested whistle-blower who struggled to bring attention to what he saw as multi-billion-dollar mismanagement."[30] Government bureaucrats and prosecutors sought to use the Espionage Act as a way to get back at Drake for airing their dirty laundry. On the eve of the trial, the prosecution struck a deal with Drake. They would drop the ten felony charges against him, which carried with them a thirty-five-year prison sentence, if he would plead to the lesser charge of "exceeding authorized use of a computer." Drake accepted the plea deal. He was no doubt innocent of even that, but the government needs its pound of flesh. Thomas Drake is living proof that it is dangerous to be right when the government is wrong.

In response to this change in events, the federal district court judge on the case "said that Mr. Drake had been through 'four years of hell' and that the dragging out of the investigation—and then the dropping of the major charges on the eve of trial—was 'unconscionable.' . . . 'It doesn't pass the smell test.'"[31] At least one branch of government was smart enough not to be deceived by what the Obama administration was up to.

The fear remains that if one calls into question what the government is doing, the government will find a way to turn you into a traitor. Even though President Obama claimed to be a strong supporter of whistle-blowers during his campaign, he is clearly on the hunt for anyone who shares damaging information about his administration.

In a similar vein, following the attacks on 9/11, Bush signed into law the Patriot Act. This Act radically altered the requirements for search warrants, allowing them to be self-written by the cops who serve them, effectively allowing searches without a warrant. The Act also approved "sneak and peek" searches, which allowed officers to search someone's home without the person even knowing about it. It gave more latitude for wiretaps and self-written warrants for Internet monitoring and granted permission to the government to check on our library records and purchases from bookstores. In short, this Act has done to the Fourth Amendment what the Espionage and Sedition Acts did to the First. It seems that Wilson set us down the ever widening path of encroachments on our civil liberties in the name of war, from which we still suffer today.

Conclusion

We call ourselves a democracy. But think about this: The governments that have used the same manipulation tactics and suppression of speech popularized by Wilson during World War I are some of the worst dictatorships this world has ever seen.

For example, in the Soviet Union, leaders such as Lenin and Stalin built a huge propaganda apparatus that targeted the Russian people in much the same way as Wilson targeted Americans. Specifically, during Stalin's reign, propaganda was put forth that characterized Stalin, as well as the Soviet government as a whole, as perfect. Posters, radio broadcasts, and books portrayed Stalin as a fatherly figure and someone who was kind, generous, and only wanted to help Russia.

When Stalin decided he wanted to go to war, the Soviet propagandists evoked raw emotions in support of the war and constantly drilled the party line. Many of these posters instilled Russians with the sense that it was their duty to fight for Mother Russia and that the enemy was a heinous criminal that needed to be stopped. One propaganda piece, the film *Girl No. 217*, told the fictitious story of a young Russian girl who was enslaved to a cruel German family and was brutally mistreated.[32] Now think about it: Isn't this exactly what Wilson did through the CPI?

In reality, Stalin did not care about Russia's honor or the Russian people who were suffering. His only concern was that he control Eastern Europe, and to this end, he sent millions of Russian soldiers on a suicidal march toward the front lines, without adequate food, clothing, or bullets. Of course, this reminds us of our own presidents' self-aggrandizing goals, such as spreading the gospel of democracy, which was at the root of World War I and the present American wars in the Middle East. When Stalin signed the Molotov–Ribbentrop Pact, an alliance between Russia and Germany, he proclaimed that the alliance was necessary to protect Russia, sounding more than vaguely familiar to the pre-textual "national security" concerns raised by Wilson, Bush, and Obama.

Moreover, Stalin crushed even the smallest whisper of dissent. Freedom of speech was replaced by extreme censorship of all materials published in the Soviet Union. So great was the censorship power of Russia's Censorship Agency, no movie, poster, book, school lesson, or drawing could be published or publicly seen without the agency's approval. The government only allowed the publication of materials that put the Soviet Union and its leaders in a positive light. In many instances, images were even altered to fit the current party policies, and any images that were distributed without official approval were suppressed.[33] Under this policy, thousands of people were sent to prison and labor camps because they questioned the policies of Stalin. How is this any different from what Wilson was doing under the Espionage and Sedition Acts?

It is a very sad truth that the manipulation and speech suppression that Wilson resorted to during World War I, and that Bush and Obama have continued using in more recent times, are in the same vein as have been in all the worst governments throughout the twentieth century, including Nazi Germany, the USSR, North Korea, the Republic of China, Iraq, Iran, and the Taliban in Afghanistan. Truth and freedom are sacrificed for power.

Not only must we recognize that we fit within the ranks of these oppressive governments; we must also come to terms with the fact that we are hypocrites to the utmost degree. Many of these countries and governments were and currently are enemies of the United States, and while we denounce them for their undemocratic principles and crusade to remake them in our "superior" image, we continue to do the very same things as they do within our very own country.

While the United States boasts of the rights enjoyed in America, according to the Press Freedom Index, the United States is actually twentieth in the world for preserving freedom of the press and was fifty-sixth in 2006.[34]

All this, of course, is the impact of Wilson's legacy, which our modern leaders continue to follow. It makes no difference whether the president is a Republican or a Democrat. Presidents from Wilson to Obama have resorted to manipulating and downright lying to the American people, as well as suppressing our most basic rights, so that they can shape us into the unquestioning soldiers of their self-aggrandizing schemes.

All these wars and all this government needed cash. How could the Progressives get their hands on everyone's cash? Next, the income tax.

Chapter 15

The Government's Grand Larceny

The Birth of the Federal Income Tax

When there is an income tax, the just man will pay more and the unjust less on the same amount of income.

—Plato, *The Republic*

The American Revolution was fought in the name of Americans' right to life, liberty, and the pursuit of happiness. However, according to Frank Chodorov, "The freedoms won by Americans in 1776 were lost in the revolution of 1913."[1] The passage of the Sixteenth Amendment, which enabled a federal income tax, signified Americans handing over the freedoms earned by the blood of their forefathers and entrenching themselves into a slavery contrary to the very essence of our nation's beginning. How is it that the American people allowed such a travesty to befall them?

Changing the Constitution So the Rich Could Fund the Government

Like other Progressives, Theodore Roosevelt wanted an income tax to siphon off some of the earnings of the rich. Since the Constitution of the United States forbad such a tax, to the Progressives that simply meant that the Constitution should be changed.

—Thomas Sowell[2]

Ironically, the idea for an income tax came from the British system, from which the American people gained freedom by fighting the Revolutionary War. The British income tax was derived from the time when the king owned all the real estate. Because one's land was actually the king's possession, he could tax any income derived from it, even if he couldn't tax the property itself.

Of course, when the Founding Fathers wrote the Constitution, they rejected this premise. Instead, Congress's power to tax was laid out in Article I, Section 8, of the Constitution as follows: "To lay and collect Taxes, Duties, Imposts and Excises, to pay the Debts and provide for the common Defence and general Welfare of the United States; but all Duties, Imposts and Excises shall be uniform throughout the United States."

Article I, Section 2, required that if Congress wished to enact direct taxes, those "direct Taxes shall be apportioned among the several States which may be included within this Union, according to their respective Numbers." In other words, unlike the British system, the original Constitution never contemplated that the federal government would have a financial relationship with individual persons. Rather, the federal government could only tax the states as a whole, not the people living within those states.

As quickly as 1812, America began to see the first perversions of the Founding Fathers' intentions. Because America was then engaged in the War of 1812 against the British, it had amassed what was at that time a staggering debt of $100 million. The government had already doubled the rate at which it was taxing customs duties on imports, its most significant source of revenue. The result was that the taxes dampened trade, thus leading to less tax revenue than before the imposition of the higher rates. The government began looking for other options, and among these was the proposal for an income tax. Though the income tax did not come to fruition at that time, the idea was put out there, waiting to take hold.

The idea for an income tax once again came out into the open during the Civil War, as a means to finance the Union army, which was costing on average $1,750,000 per day. Unfortunately, this time the idea became action, and on August 5th 1861, Congress enacted a flat tax of 3 percent on income over $600. Congress soon realized that this tax was insufficient to meet its ever increasing budget demands, so a year later, before this first tax went into effect, Congress passed the Revenue Act of 1862, which revised the tax rate such that there would be a 3 percent tax on income between $600 and $10,000 and a 5 percent tax on income over $10,000. Revisions were made yet again in 1864, establishing

- a 5 percent tax rate on income between $600 and $5,000,
- a 7.5 percent tax rate on income between $5,000 and $10,000, and
- a 10 percent tax rate for income over $10,000. Subsequently, Congress raised the income tax for earnings over $5,000 to 10 percent.

Even after the war ended in 1865, the government continued to tax income as a means to pay off its debt. By 1866 the federal government was receiving a total of $73 million annually from income taxes, or about 30 percent of its total revenues. However, the government did make some changes to the tax rates in 1867, whereby all income above $1,000 would be taxed at 5 percent.

Then, when this income tax expired in 1870, Congress enacted a new one, which taxed incomes above $2,000 at 2.5 percent. It wasn't until this income tax law expired in 1872 that the United States finally went without an income tax again for some time.

Though people challenged the income tax in its aftermath, the Supreme Court's beliefs, at that time, were aligned with those of Congress. In the 1881 case *Springer v. United States*, the Supreme Court, in a unanimous opinion, upheld the constitutionality of the income tax, mysteriously and mischievously characterizing it as an indirect tax and thus rendering it unnecessary to be apportioned among the states.[3]

Having gained popularity with the government, in the years between 1874 and 1894, forms of an income tax were offered in sixty-eight different bills in Congress in the hopes of reinstating the income tax. It wasn't until the Panic of 1893 that the environment became ripe for the government to succeed in pushing through its agenda. Following this crisis, the Wilson-Gorman Tariff Act of 1894 was passed, placing a 2 percent tax on all incomes above $4,000. Interestingly, this was done without President Cleveland's signing off on it because he resolutely believed that it was unconstitutional.

It seemed that Cleveland was not alone in his belief. In the 1895 case *Pollock v. Farmers' Loan & Trust Co.*, the Supreme Court finally rallied to defend the integrity of the Constitution. In his decision for that case, Chief

Justice Fuller explained that just like a tax on property itself, a tax on income from that property was also a direct tax, given that the tax on the income from the property, just like a tax on the property itself, had a direct impact on the value of the property. As such, the unapportioned income tax imposed by the Wilson-Gorman Tariff Act of 1894 was ruled unconstitutional.[4]

Unfortunately, after the Supreme Court effectively struck down a direct federal income tax as unconstitutional, the movement for one did not die. In the years 1896 and 1908, the Democratic Party endorsed amending the Constitution to enable a federal income tax, thus circumventing the decision in *Pollock*. The main reason why Democrats supported the income tax was to embarrass the Republican Party, which, by opposing it, would look like the party of big business. The Democrats never expected that the income tax would return.

The Republicans, also believing the income tax would never pass, thought it would be better in terms of preserving the party's reputation to overcome the Democrats' agenda via the people rather than directly. Therefore, on June 16th 1909, Republican president William Howard Taft addressed the Congress, endorsing an amendment to the Constitution to allow for an unapportioned income tax.

Following this, Republican senator Norris Brown from Nebraska submitted two proposals, which, if passed, would facilitate such an amendment. These were passed through the Senate, and on July 12th 1909, the House of Representatives passed the resolution as well, enabling it to be submitted to the state legislatures.

In conjunction with this movement for an income tax, many promises were made. To begin, Senator Brown had said that the income tax amendment "lays no tax, promises to lay none, but simply and solely restores to the people a power many times sustained but finally denied by the courts."[5] This led people to believe that the income tax authorized by the amendment would be used only during emergency situations.

In addition, the government assured Americans that the federal income tax would not hit wage-earning workers. Rather, it would only tax the super-wealthy and people investing money and not actually performing manual labor to acquire it. In support of this proposition, Theodore Roosevelt gave a speech in 1910, stating,

No man should receive a dollar unless that dollar has been fairly earned. Every dollar received should represent a dollar's worth of service rendered—not gambling in stocks, but service rendered. The really big fortune, the swollen fortune, by the mere fact of its size, acquires qualities which differentiate it in kind as well as in degree from what is possessed by men of relatively small means. Therefore, I believe in a graduated income tax on big fortunes, and in another tax which is far more easily collected and far more effective—a graduated inheritance tax on big fortunes, properly safeguarded against evasion, and increasing rapidly in amount with the size of the estate.[6]

This from a man who inherited great wealth and never worked a non-government job. With such promises abounding, the state legislatures immediately began ratifying the amendment.

During this time, the election of 1912 was in full swing. All three presidential candidates—William Howard Taft, Theodore Roosevelt, and Woodrow Wilson—supported the unapportioned direct income tax. Nobody dared to challenge the force of the Progressive movement. By February 3rd 1913, the necessary passage by three-fourths of the states had been garnered, and ratification was completed. The Sixteenth Amendment became a part of the U.S. Constitution, stating in its official capacity: "The Congress shall have power to lay and collect taxes on incomes, from whatever source derived, without apportionment among the several States, and without regard to any census or enumeration."

Shortly after the ratification of the Sixteenth Amendment, President Woodrow Wilson signed the Revenue Act of 1913. It imposed a system of income tax that was the direct precursor to what we have in place today. It allowed for a personal exemption of $3,000 for individuals and $4,000 for married couples, and it contained a graduated tax rate. The lowest tax rate was 1 percent on income below $20,000, and the highest tax rate was 7 percent on income above $500,000. In 1913, $500,000 was the modern equivalent of $11,400,000.[7] The resulting revenue raised, however, amounted to a mere $28 million. In the next year, the income tax brought in $41 million, and because the government increased the upper tax rate from 7 to 15 percent, this led to $68 million in tax revenue the year after that.

Then, seeing the profitability of rate increases and needing to cover the burgeoning costs of World War I, Congress raised the upper, called the *marginal*, tax rate to 67 percent in 1917 and 77 percent in 1918. In other words, what had started out as a minimal tax seemed to be spiraling out of control. Though the marginal tax rate fell following the end of the war, from 73 percent throughout most of the 1920s to 24 percent in 1929, it never became as low as the pre-war rates again. This was especially the case because, after the passage of the Eighteenth Amendment, which prohibited alcohol and thus prevented the government from collecting excise taxes from its sale, the income tax became the predominant source of revenue for the government.

The marginal tax rate began to increase again in the 1930s; in 1931 it was increased to 25 percent, followed by 63 percent in 1932 and 79 percent in 1936. These increases were in response to the ever-increasing costs of implementing all the social programs of the New Deal.

The 1940s saw more change; the marginal tax rate was raised to 81 percent in 1941 and reached an astonishing height of 94 percent during 1944 and 1945 to pay for the costs of World War II. This 94 percent tax rate applied to any income over $200,000, the equivalent of $2.4 million in today's dollars.[8] In other words, any income earned over $200,000 would be done so almost exclusively for the government and, in essence, would transform the effort made to obtain this portion of one's income into slave labor.

Despite this, the Supreme Court has repeatedly upheld the direct unapportioned income tax since the ratification of the Sixteenth Amendment. For example, in the first major case challenging the income tax, *Brushaber v. Union Pacific Railroad Co.* (1916), Frank Brushaber, a stockholder in Union Pacific Railroad Company, argued that it was fiscally improper for the Union Pacific Railroad Company to comply with the new tax law.[9] More specifically, he felt that the Revenue Act of 1913 violated the Due Process Clause of the Fifth Amendment to the U.S. Constitution, given that under this law the government was taking the corporation's property without due process of law. He sought an injunction to prevent the government from collecting income taxes from the company. The Supreme Court unanimously rejected his argument, holding, in a morally disingenuous fashion, that the Due Process Clause of the Fifth Amendment is not a limitation on the taxing power of Congress, given that Congress has always had the constitutional power to tax Americans and the only thing the Sixteenth Amendment did was remove the apportionment requirement, such that all taxes would now be treated as indirect taxes had been treated prior to the amendment.

Fortunately, it seems that 1945 was the high-water mark for American taxation. The last time the marginal tax bracket was taxed at more than 90 percent was in 1963 (91 percent), and since that time, the top tax bracket's tax rate has been in constant decline. From 1988 to 1990 it hit a low of 28 percent. Currently it sits at 35 percent. Yet its vast scale-backs have done nothing to eradicate significant waste and inefficiencies, as well as the countless inequalities and unjust provisions of the tax code that have led to governmental regulation of our behavior.

Stealing and Wasting Your Money

The cabinet position of commissioner of Internal Revenue, which was created by President Abraham Lincoln in 1862 as a means of enforcing the taxes enacted to fund the Civil War, was transformed into the Bureau of Internal Revenue in 1918. Ever since its inception, the Bureau, re-named the Internal Revenue Service (IRS) in 1953, has been continuously growing. After the first year alone, the size of the Bureau doubled. The growth was spurred onward when the Bureau realized that doubling the size of its staff was still not enough to handle all the yearly returns within the year they were received. In 1919, the Bureau was still processing many 1917 tax returns.[10]

The advent of Prohibition also led to increases in the size of the Bureau of Internal Revenue, given that for the first seven years of Prohibition the federal police enforcing Prohibition were a part of the Bureau of Internal Revenue and maintaining its previous size would not have provided enough staff to serve this function as well.

Today, the IRS employs more than 100,000 persons. These employees are largely members of the National Treasury Employees Union and are generously compensated. In fact, compensation has been particularly generous in recent years: Although the use of electronic filing and computer processing of returns has greatly cut down the human IRS workload, employees who are part of the union are not simply let go, even if their services are no longer necessary. They continue to receive a paycheck from the government despite their virtually pointless role at the IRS. It is no wonder then that due to the IRS's bloated size, coupled with its unfathomable compensation policy, the IRS is running a budget as high as $12.2 billion per year. It goes without saying that much of this spending merely amounts to a colossal waste of taxpayers' dollars.

The income tax leads to waste and inefficiency in other contexts. Because the income tax denies Americans the fruits of their labor, it breeds bitterness, which, in turn, transforms itself into dishonesty, whereby people evade their income taxes. This is such a pervasive problem that, according to Frank Chodorov, "no other single measure in the history of our country has caused a comparable disregard of principle in public affairs, or has had such a deteriorating effect on morals."[11]

Not only that, but today the majority of federal income tax returns go completely unchecked by a human eye. They are run through a computer that flags amounts that seem irregular and then gives them to a human for investigation and possible audit. Because of this procedure, there is widespread non-enforcement, thus allowing people to get away with the tax abuse that the system is encouraging. "[W]hat people owe but don't pay amounted to more than $350 billion last year [ ]—a shortfall that, to make up, increased the average taxpayer's bill by more than a third."[12] There is clearly a problem with a system that cannot meet the goals for which it was designed and therefore must cast an ever-wider net to compensate.

Taxation Is Theft

It is indisputable that humans have a right to life and, therefore, a right to the fruits of life's labor: "[T]he means of life must be identified with life itself."[13] As such, it is logical for humans to object to the government's taking these fruits just as much as they would object to a common thief's doing so. We may try to convince ourselves that when the government takes these fruits it is merely the price we pay for law and order, but when we get right down to it, robbery is robbery no matter who perpetrates it. Period.

This robbery largely affects the pockets of the poorest Americans, the very class of Americans who were promised they would be unaffected by the income tax. While income tax was the product of "soak the rich propaganda, [garnering] support in the envy of the incompetent, the bitterness of poverty, the sense of injustice which our monopoly economy engenders,"[14] in reality, because there are more people in the lower brackets than in the higher ones, it is actually the poor who are bearing the brunt of income taxes. The fact that the income tax system is graduated does nothing to mitigate this, given that even a small tax on an income of $15,000 a year will cause the payer some hardship, while a 35 percent tax on $400,000 leaves something to live on comfortably, but still a great deal taken.

This problem is further compounded because the poor primarily draw their incomes from wages, for which there is a record, while the wealthy also make money from sources such as investments and numerous forms of gambling, for which there exists no concrete record, thus leading to underreporting. The consequence is that the entirety of a poor person's income is being taxed, while portions of a wealthy person's are not.

Taxation has proved to be theft in other, more universal, ways as well. The initial direct unapportioned federal income tax was collected in a far different manner from what Americans are used to today. Instead of payroll taxes being withheld from each paycheck that an American received, Americans were required to pay the full amount of income tax on its due date. Then, in 1942, the government decided to switch to a withholding system, believing, in a very paternalistic fashion, that the people could not be trusted to hold onto enough of their income to pay off all their taxes at the end of the year. Therefore, the government should, in essence, be in charge of monitoring Americans' funds, rationing how much of his paycheck each American receives.

By switching to the withholding system, income tax has taken theft to a whole new dimension. The withholding system leads to many Americans receiving a tax refund each year after filing taxes, and while Americans do regain possession of property the government extracted from them, there is something they can never recover. Had the money been in Americans' possession all along, they would have earned interest on it or invested it. The government does not account for this when it writes refund checks.

Overall, the consequence of this governmental theft, which is permissible under the income tax, is that it discourages productivity. No matter how much one makes, "workers [get] to figuring their "take home" pay, and to laying off when this net, after taxes, show[s] no increase comparable to the extra work it would cost."[15] Not only this but the production level of a nation is determined by the purchasing power of the people and, thus, is reduced by the extent to which the income tax diminishes the people's purchasing power. "It is a silly sophism, and thoroughly indecent, to maintain that what the state collects it spends, and that therefore there is no lowering of total purchasing power."[16]

The government tries to offset the fact that taxation is, in reality, theft by postulating that the necessary *quid pro quo* exists, such that this is an equitable trade, given that it provides certain essential services in exchange for the funds it takes. "But, the essential condition of trade, that it be carried on willingly, is absent from taxation. . . . If we get anything for the taxes we pay it is not because we want it; it is forced on us."[17] Therefore, no equitable trade exists as the government would have us believe.

Moreover, it is not entirely true that the government spends the money it takes from Americans on essential services. In one instance, "funding the 'common good' with our tax dollars include[d] buying a new fleet of luxury jets for Congress because military transports [were] not good enough for sensitive Congressional aristocrats."[18] In another instance, dubbed MuffinGate, the government was caught spending sixteen dollars per muffin at its conferences, amounting to a cost of four thousand dollars in muffins at one conference alone! This is hardly one of the essential services on which we envision our tax dollars being spent.

Do What We Say, and We'll Lower Your Taxes

Today, countless provisions of the Internal Revenue Code favor one action over another. The most glaring of these provisions in the current tax code are rewards for having larger families, giving to charities, owning a home, investing, and pursuing higher education.

In the first instance, the Internal Revenue Code allows individuals a one-thousand-dollar tax exemption for each child that he or she claims as a dependent; the more children one has, the less taxes he pays compared to someone with a comparable job. Additionally, the Earned Income Tax Credit provision of the Code, which is directed at helping low-income families, determines the maximum level of credit that one can receive based on one's income and the number of children one has up to a maximum of three. Even though two families may be equally poor, the one with more children will get a bigger tax credit (a reduction in taxes owed) from the government. In other words, the government is using the tax code to make a value judgment on the desirability of people having children.

The Internal Revenue Code gives a tax deduction to people who have made charitable contributions. Although these non-profit organizations are beneficial to society, and contributions are their primary source of funding, the government uses the tax code to enforce this particular value judgment on Americans.

Of all the tax deductions given to people who make charitable donations, the least appropriate are tax exemptions given to people who donate to religious organizations. The First Amendment to the U.S. Constitution guarantees the freedom of religion and the absence of its involvement with the government. Inherent in this is the constitutional principle that the government cannot prevent any person from practicing his religion, nor can it enact legislation favoring a certain religion over another or simply favoring religion over non-religion. However, by giving tax breaks to people who make religious donations, the government is in fact making a value judgment on the desirability of being pious. Not only that, but instead of a complete separation of church and state, the government is indirectly funding officially recognized religious organizations via this tax break.

The Internal Revenue Code favors individuals who own homes over individuals who do not. This favoritism is directly expressed through the mortgage interest deduction as it allows homeowners to reduce their taxable income by the amount of interest paid on their home loans. It also awards tax credits for first-time homeowners. No similar provisions exist for those who rent; thus the government is once again using the tax code to make a value judgment that the Constitution reserves for individuals—this time on the desirability of homeownership.

Even individuals who are not wealthy enough to own homes are enticed by these provisions into taking on mortgages that they cannot pay off. This is what led directly to the sub-prime mortgage crises that caused the current economic recession.

In the Obama years, the federal government has begun to use the tax code as a means of spreading its "green" initiatives. Homeowners can receive a tax credit for 30 percent of the cost of specific products, such as solar panels, energy-efficient windows, insulation, doors, roofs, and heating and cooling equipment.[19]

Additionally, from 2005 through 2010, Americans were able to receive tax credits based on fuel economy for hybrid vehicles that they purchased. Today, the government offers tax credits of $2,500 to $7,500, depending on battery capacity, for plug-in electric vehicles. Not only is the government making value judgments, this provision merely serves as a means for the rich to get richer, considering that only the well-to-do can afford these green products and therefore benefit from the tax breaks associated with them.

The government has used the Internal Revenue Code as a means of encouraging people to pursue higher education. For example, the Lifetime Learning Credit and the Hope Credit are given to people who show that they spend over a certain amount on tuition and other education-related expenses. The tax code allows people who took out loans in order to attend school to deduct the amount of student loan interest that they pay each year from their adjusted incomes. The government is making a value judgment not only on the superiority of pursuing school-based forms of higher education, but also on the superiority of pursuing higher education as opposed to directly entering the workforce.

The IRS Code has been used to tell Americans how they should be earning their money because of the different tax rates the Code places on earned compared to unearned income. Earned income is simply the income that is earned from actually working. Wages are the most common form of earned income. On the other hand, unearned income comes from dividends, profits, and capital gains.

While taxes on earned income currently range from 10 percent for income under $8,375 to 35 percent for income over $373,650 for individual returns, taxes on unearned income are subject to a much lower graduated tax rate table.[20] The sad truth is that the majority of Americans receiving earned income are poor, while the majority of Americans receiving unearned income are wealthy. This dichotomy is just an elaborate scheme to benefit the Americans who do not need it over those who do.

Conclusion

While the Sixteenth Amendment is a legitimate amendment and, as such, is an official part of the Constitution, the reality is that, because of what this amendment enables the government to do, it is unconstitutional. In reality, it profoundly upsets the structural framework of the federal government, which was contingent upon the delegation of power by the states to the federal government. Even though the iconic first three words of the Constitution are "We the people," in fact and in history, the Constitution was ratified by the states, not the people, received delegated powers from the states, not the people, and was never intended to regulate individual human beings.

The Sixteenth Amendment utterly bypasses the states and permits direct federal regulation of persons, a lamentable state of affairs directly prohibited by the Framers. Not only that, but "it is by this fiscal policy, rather than by violent revolution, or by an appeal to reason, or by popular education, or by way of any ineluctable historic forces, that the substance of socialism is realized."[21] The vision of the Founding Fathers has been rejected because we have sold away the democracy they fought so hard to establish for us. The personal income tax, more than any other policy of the government, shattered the Jeffersonian ideal of inalienable rights of every person and accepted the Marxist view of state supremacy. Who owns your income? You or the federal government?

All this has been made possible through the chicanery of Woodrow Wilson and his disingenuous promises to use the federal income tax in a stingy way. Or was it the naiveté of those who believed his promises? The Wilsonian tax system has enabled the government to bribe some Americans. And the government will never return to the confines of the Constitution until we can all keep what we have earned.

Chapter 16

What Have We Learned from All This?

Napoleon once famously remarked that history is not the record of events that have *actually* preceded us; it is the record of what people like to *believe* has preceded us. Americans, educated in state schools and taught the state's version of history, have for the most part falsely believed that Theodore Roosevelt and Woodrow Wilson saved the American Republic. In reality, they helped to destroy it.

The modern-day equivalent of Napoleon's observation is George Santayana's iconic lesson that those who are ignorant of the past are doomed to repeat it. If history has taught us anything, it is that we need to understand how we got here in order to appreciate how to get away from here. Government is essentially the negation of freedom. Thus, a keen appreciation of the numerous and insidious ways that government in a free society has accumulated wealth and power will help us to understand, challenge, and diminish that government and thus to enhance our freedom.

Jefferson believed that in the long arc of history, we can see repeated over and over again the struggle for individual freedom against a monopoly of force. The monopoly of force has killed, stolen, lied, and cheated its way into power and wealth. The first two decades of twentieth-century America—an era arguably dominated by Theodore Roosevelt and Woodrow Wilson— are not an exception to Jefferson's conclusion; rather, they are a heightened paradigm of it. In those twenty or so years, the role of the federal government changed so radically that it would never be the same again. One could make the same argument about the Civil War era, but the changes it brought about were produced by guns and blood. The changes generated by the Progressive Era were produced by persuasion and distortion and fear.

Theodore Roosevelt and Woodrow Wilson and their colleagues literally persuaded and lied and frightened Americans into believing that personal freedom and big business were greater threats to their temporal happiness than permanent Big Government. I am being a bit cute here, since the term *Big Government*, now used derisively to characterize what the Progressives have brought us, was an unknown term in the time of Theodore and Woodrow. That was so simply because the federal government in 1900 was not big. No American government was. In those days, state and local governments addressed the day-to-day business of government, and that day-to-day business was a tiny fraction of what government does today. The federal government was not the behemoth it is today. For the most part, it remained within the confines of the Constitution.

As we have seen, Theodore Roosevelt and Thomas Woodrow Wilson, each a child of privilege and an Ivy League education and family wealth, changed the arc of history by dramatically moving it away from the realm of "that government is best which governs least" and toward the realm of "the government exists to do for people what they cannot do for themselves." This was a dramatic and largely peaceful departure from the constitutional structure established by the Founders.

Roosevelt, a bully, and Wilson, a constitutional scholar, each pushed aside the traditionally accepted and constitutionally mandated restrictions on the federal government and used it as an instrument to redistribute wealth, regulate personal behavior, enrich the government, and enhance the government's health with wars.

From compulsory state-prescribed education to the rise of the regulatory state, from the destruction of state sovereignty to the rise of Jim Crow, from federal regulation of selected businesses to federal generation of selected labor unions, from Prohibition to war to the draft to the income tax to punishing the exercise of free speech, this era witnessed the most dramatic peaceful shift of power from persons and from the states to a new and permanent federal bureaucracy in all of American history. All this came about because the men—and the one happy change that came from the Progressive Era was the recognition of the legal equality of women—in whose hands the Constitution was reposed for safekeeping largely failed at the job they were hired to perform. Each one swore to preserve the Constitution; instead, they assaulted it. They failed to restrain themselves and to restrain the government. They failed to preserve the liberties that the Constitution was enacted to guarantee.

They demonstrated for us the sad truism that the Constitution is only as valid as the fidelity to it of the human beings in whose hands it is reposed for safekeeping. The Founders wrote the Constitution largely to keep the government off the people's backs. Theodore Roosevelt and Woodrow Wilson rejected that idea. They believed that the Constitution was written to enable those in power to bend society and government and popular attitudes to their wills. History has taught us the mortal danger of that belief. Either the Constitution means what it says, or it doesn't. If it does, then those in government who fail to abide by it have brought us all our woe, and we must reject them and their successors. If it doesn't mean what it says, then it is meaningless.

As one of the great Supreme Court dissents has rationally argued, if the Constitution is not upheld when it pinches those in power as well as when it comforts them, it may as well be abandoned.

Postscript

As I was concluding the final edits on this book, the Supreme Court of the United States released its long-awaited decision on the constitutionality of Obamacare. The opinion, which was written by Chief Justice John Roberts, is a tortured and twisted analysis of federal power that would have delighted Theodore Roosevelt and Woodrow Wilson. It held that the federal government can write any law and regulate any behavior—whether the subject of the law or regulation is encompassed by a power granted to the federal government in the Constitution or not—so long as the consequence of violating the law or rejecting the regulation is the imposition of a tax.

This decision is a lesson for all of us who fear the continued abuse of the Constitution. But this abuse began long ago.

Of the 17 lawyers who have served as Chief Justice of the United States, John Marshall—the fourth Chief Justice—has come to be known as the "Great Chief Justice." The folks who have given him that title are the progressives who have largely written the history we are taught in government schools. They revere him because he is the intellectual progenitor of federal power. Marshall's opinions over a thirty-four-year period during the nation's infancy—expanding federal power at the expense of personal freedom and the sovereignty of the states—set a pattern for federal control of our lives and actually invited Congress to regulate areas of human behavior nowhere mentioned in the Constitution. He was Thomas Jefferson's cousin, but they rarely spoke. No Chief Justice in history has so directly and creatively offered the feds power on a platter as he.

Now he has a rival.

The true motivations for the idiosyncratic rationale in the health care decision written by Marshall's current successor are likely known only to him. Often five-member majorities on the court are fragile, and bizarre compromises are necessary in order to keep a five-member majority from becoming a four-member minority. Perhaps Chief Justice Roberts really means what he wrote—that congressional power to tax is without constitutional limit—and his opinion is a faithful reflection of that view, without a political or legal or intra-court agenda. But that view finds no support in the Constitution or our history. It even ignores one of the most famous of John Marshall's aphorisms: The power to tax is the power to destroy.

The reasoning underlying the 5 to 4 majority opinion is the court's unprecedented pronouncement that Congress' power to tax is unlimited. The majority held that the extraction of thousands of dollars per year by the IRS from individuals who do not have health insurance is not a fine, not a punishment, not a payment for government-provided health insurance, not a shared responsibility—all of which the statute says it is—but rather is an inducement in the form of a tax. The majority likened this tax to the federal taxes on tobacco and gasoline, which, it held, are imposed not only to generate revenue but also to discourage smoking and driving. The statute is more than 2,700 pages in length, and it establishes the federal micromanagement of about 16 percent of the national economy. And the court justified it constitutionally by calling it a tax.

A different 5 to 4 majority, which consisted of the chief and the four dissenting justices who would have invalidated the entire statute as beyond the constitutional power of Congress, held that while Congress can regulate commerce, it cannot compel one to engage in commerce. The same majority ruled that Congress cannot force the states to expand Medicaid by establishing state insurance exchanges. It held that the congressional command to establish the exchanges combined with the congressional threat to withhold all Medicaid funds—not just those involved with the exchanges— for failure to establish them would be so harmful to the financial stability of state governments as to be tantamount to an assault on state sovereignty. This leaves the exchanges in limbo, and it is the first judicial recognition that state sovereignty is apparently at the tender mercies of the financial largesse of Congress.

The logic in the majority opinion is the jurisprudential equivalent of passing a camel through the eye of a needle. The logic is so tortured, unexpected, and unprecedented that even the law's most fervent supporters did not offer or anticipate the court's rationale in its support. Under the Constitution, a tax must originate in the House of Representatives (which this law did not), and it must be applied for doing something (like earning income or purchasing tobacco or fuel), not for doing nothing. Under the Constitution, if the government wants your wealth, as opposed to your income, it must sue you for it. In all the history of the court, it never has held that a penalty imposed for violating a federal law was really a tax. And it never has converted linguistically the legislative imposition of a penalty into the judicial construction of a tax, absent finding subterfuge on the part of congressional draftsmanship.

I wonder whether the Chief Justice realizes what he and the progressive wing of the court have done to our freedom. If the feds can tax us for not doing as they have commanded, and if that which is commanded need not be grounded in the Constitution, then there is no constitutional limit to their power, and the ruling that the power to regulate commerce does not encompass the power to compel commerce is mere sophistry.

Notes

Introduction

1. Cited in John Milton Cooper Jr., *The Warrior and the Priest: Woodrow Wilson and Theodore Roosevelt* (Cambridge, MA: Belknap Press of Harvard University, 1983), 1.
2. Ibid., 20.
3. Theodore Roosevelt Diaries, http://lcweb2.loc.gov/ammem/trhtml/trdiary3.html.
4. Woodrow Wilson's Administration: Personal Loss, Firstworldwar.com, http://www.firstworldwar.com/features/wilsonadministration.htm.
5. http://www.corsinet.com/braincandy/dying.html.
6. Ibid.

Chapter 1: The Bull Moose: Roosevelt's New Party in His Own Image and Likeness

1. Kenneth Jackson, ed., *The Encyclopedia of New York City* (New Haven, CT: Yale University Press, 1995), 1019.
2. Jon Stewart, *The Daily Show*, 18 August 2010, interview with Roosevelt biographer Edward Kohn, http://www.thedailyshow.com/watch/wed-august-18-2010/edward-kohn.
3. "The Heat Wave of 1896 and the Rise of Roosevelt," NPR Books, 11 August 2010, http://www.npr.org/templates/story/story.php?storyId=129127924.
4. "Happy Anniversary to the First Scheduled Presidential Press Conference," American Chronicle.com, 15 March 2006, http://www.americanchronicle.com/articles/view/6883.
5. Lewis Gould, "1912 Republican Convention," *Smithsonian*, August 2008, http://www.smithsonianmag.com/history-archaeology/1912-republican-convention.html.
6. An Irish-American humorist by the name of Finley Peter Dunne described the encounter as "a combynation iv th' Chicago fire, Saint Bartholomew's massacree, the battle iv th' Boyne, th' life iv Jesse James, an' th' night iv th' big wind." Cited in ibid.
7. 198 U.S. 45 (1906).
8. Gould, "1912 Republican Convention."

9. Ibid.

10. "Honeyfuggle," World Wide Words, http://www.worldwidewords.org/weirdwords/ww-hon2.htm.

11. Anthony Gregory, "In a Relationship, and It's Complicated," Mises Daily, 1 June 2011, http://mises.org/daily/5345.

12. John Gable, "The Bull Moose Years," Theodore Roosevelt Association, http://www.theodoreroosevelt.org/life/bullmoose.htm.

13. Ibid.

14. Ibid. Theodore Roosevelt beat Taft by 47,477 votes, or 16 percent of the popular vote. The official vote totals were 15,570 for La Follette, 118,362 for Taft, and 165,809 for Roosevelt.

15. Ibid.

16. Gould, "1912 Republican Convention."

17. Ibid.

18. Biography, "William Howard Taft," Miller Center, http://millercenter.org/President/taft/essays/biography/1.

19. Mark Brandly, "How Big Is Bush's Big Government?" Ludwig von Mises Institute, 18 April 2006, http://www.lewrockwell.com/orig7/bush-big-govt.html.

20. "Teddy Roosevelt: 'No Room in This Country for Hyphenated Americans,'" Reaganite Republican (blog), 20 May 2010, http://reaganiterepublicanresistance.blogspot.com/2010/05/teddy-roosevelt-no-room-in-this-country.html.

21. Timeline for Theodore Roosevelt, Theodore Roosevelt Association, http://www.theodoreroosevelt.org/life/timeline.htm.

22. Jon Stewart, *The Daily Show*, 9 December 2010, interview with Roosevelt biographer Edmund Morris, http://www.thedailyshow.com/watch/thu-december-9-2010/edmund-morris.

23. "It Takes More Than That to Kill a Bull Moose," The Leader and the Cause, Theodore Roosevelt Association, http://wwwtheodoreroosevelt.org/research/speech%20kill%20moose.htm.

Chapter 2: Reeducation Camps: Compulsory Education

1. Quoted in James Ostrowski, "How Did We Get into This Mess?" LewRockwell.com, 20 November 2009, http://www.lewrockwell.com/ostrowski/ostrowski93.1.html.

2. Murray N. Rothbard, "The Progressive Era and the Family," LewRockwell.com, 2003; first printed in *The American Family and the State*, ed. Joseph R. Peden and Fred R. Glahe (San Francisco: Pacific, 1986), http://www.lewrockwell.com/rothbard/rothbard28.html.

3. Theodore Roosevelt, speech on religion in public schools, http://www.theodore-roosevelt.com/images/research/txtspeeches/784.pdf.

4. Ibid.

5. Woodrow Wilson, address to the Association of Colleges and Preparatory Schools of the Middle States and Maryland, 29 November 1907, Woodrow Wilson Presidential Library and Museum, http://woodrowwilson.org/library-a-archives/wilson-elibrary.

6. Arthur Wallace Calhoun, *A Social History of the American Family*, originally published in 1917–19.

7. Quoted in Rothbard, "The Progressive Era and the Family."

8. Quoted in Murray N. Rothbard, "Education: Free and Compulsory," Mises Daily, 9 September 2006, http://mises.org/daily/2226. Isabel Paterson was a journalist, author, political philosopher, literary critic, and one of the founders of American Libertarianism.

9. Jonah Goldberg, *Liberal Fascism: The Secret History of the American Left* (New York: Doubleday, 2008), 88.

10. Theodore W. Grippo, *With Malice Aforethought: The Execution of Nicola Sacco and Bartolomeo Vanzetti* (Bloomington, IN: iUniverse, 2011), 11–12.

11. John Taylor Gatto, "An Angry Look at Modern Schooling: Extending Childhood," Odysseus Group, http://johntaylorgatto.com/chapters/2b.htm.

12. Ibid.

13. Rothbard, "Education: Free and Compulsory."

14. *South Dakota v. Dole*, 483 U.S. 203 (1987).

15. Gatto, "An Angry Look at Modern Schooling: Extending Childhood."

16. David B. Tyack, *The One Best System: A History of American Urban Education* (Cambridge: Harvard University Press, 1974), 73.

17. Rothbard, "The Progressive Era and the Family."

18. Warren Throckmorton, "The Cincinnati Bible Wars: When the KJV Was Removed from Public Schools," *Christian Post*, 4 May 2011, http://www.christianpost.com/news/the-cincinnati-bible-wars-when-the-kjv-was-removed-from-public-schools-50096/.

19. Deborah Rieselman, "The Cincinnati Bible War: Stories of Segregation, Slander and Secularization," UC Magazine, http://magazine.uc.edu/issues/0404/bible.html.

20. Quotes by Theodore Roosevelt, http://www.goodreads.com/quotes/show/213140.

21. Woodrow Wilson, "Importance of Bible Study," 30 December 1912, Woodrow Wilson Presidential Library and Museum, http://woodrowwilson.org/library-a-archives/wilson-elibrary.

22. *Pierce v. Society of the Sisters of the Holy Names of Jesus and Mary*, 268 U.S. 510 (1925).

23. Ibid.

24. National Conference of State Legislatures, http://ncsl.org.

25. *Meyer v. Nebraska*, 262 U.S. 390 (1923).

26. *Wisconsin v. Yoder*, 406 U.S. 205 (1972).

27. Ibid.

28. Ibid.

29. Ibid.

30. *Combs v. Homer-Ctr. Sch. Dist.*, 540 F.3d 231, 249 (3d Cir. 2008).

31. Rothbard, "Education: Free and Compulsory."

32. See *Combs v. Homer-Ctr. Sch. Dist.*, 540 F.3d 231, 249 (3d Cir. 2008).

33. For example, a student at West Hoke Elementary School in North Carolina had her homemade lunch taken away from her. The school forced her to eat chicken nuggets instead of her sandwich, banana, potato chips, and apple juice. Laura Willard, "Healthy School Lunch: Chicken Nuggets Trump Turkey Sandwich," She Knows Food and Recipes, 15 February 2012, http://www.sheknows.com/food-and-recipes/articles/949863/healthy-school-lunch-chicken-nuggets-trump-turkey-sandwich.

34. Healthy, Hunger-Free Kids Act of 2010, PL 111-296, 13 December 2010, 124 Stat 318.

35. *Tinker v. Des Moines Independent Community School District*, 393 U.S. 503 (1969).

36. *New Jersey v. T.L.O.*, 469 U.S. 325 (1985).

37. *Vernonia School Dist. 47J v. Acton*, 515 U.S. 646 (1995).

38. *Ingraham v. Wright*, 430 U.S. 651 (1977).

39. *Bethel School Dist. No. 403 v. Fraser*, 478 U.S. 675 (1986).

40. *Hazelwood School Dist. v. Kuhlmeier*, 484 U.S. 260 (1988).

41. *Morse v. Frederick*, 127 S. Ct. 2618 (2007).

42. *Layshock ex rel. Layshock v. Hermitage School District*, 593 F.3d 249 (2010).

43. Public School Student, Staff, and Graduate Counts by State, National Center for Education Statistics, http://nces.ed.gov/pubs2003/snf_report03/.

44. Murray N. Rothbard, "The Business of Government," LewRockwell.com; first published in *The Freeman*, September 1956, http://www.lewrockwell.com/rothbard/rothbard131.html.

Chapter 3: Quiet Men with White Collars: The Rise of the Regulatory State

1. C. S. Lewis, *The Screwtape Letters*, rev. ed. (San Francisco: Harper, 1982), introduction, x.

2. "FDA Steps Up Enforcement against Raw Milk," Farm-to-Consumer Defense Fund, 26 April 2010, http://www.farmtoconsumer.org/aa/aa-26april2010.htm.

3. Ron Paul, "The Milk Police," Congressman Paul's website, http://paul.house.gov/index.php?option=com_content&task=view&id=1867&Itemid=69.

4. Wendy Cole, "Got Raw Milk? Be Very Quiet," *Time*, 13 March 2007, http://www.time.com/time/health/article/0,8599,1598525,00.html.

5. Paul, "The Milk Police."

6. U.S. Food and Drug Administration, http://www.fda.gov/.

7. Jim Powell: *Bully Boy: The Truth about Theodore Roosevelt's Legacy* (New York: Crown Forum, 2006), 169–76.

8. Ibid.

9. Ibid.

10. Michael Chapman, "TR: No Friend of the Constitution," *CATO Policy Report* 24, no. 6 (November/December 2002): 14.

11. F. Jay Murray, "Don't Lose Sleep Over Borates and Mattresses," Murray and Associates, http://www.natbat.com/news/Don't%20Lose%20Sleep%20 Over%20Borates%20and%20Mattresses.htm.

12. *United States v. Two Hundred Cases of Adulterated Tomato Catsup*, 211 F. 780 (1914).

13. Ibid.

14. Powell, *Bully Boy*, 179.

15. *U.S. v. Forty Barrels and Twenty Kegs of Coca-Cola*, 241 U.S. 265 (1916).

16. Ibid., 574.

17. Gail Jarvis, "The Rise and Fall of Cocaine Coca-Cola," LewRockwell.com, 21 May 2002, http://www.lewrockwell.com/jarvis/jarvis17.html.

18. Oscar E. Anderson Jr., "The Pure Food Issue: A Republican Dilemma, 1906-1912," *American Historical Review* 161 (April 1956).

19. Harvey W. Wiley, *An Autobiography* (Indianapolis, 1930).

20. Anthony Gaughan, "Harvey Wiley, Theodore Roosevelt, and the Federal Regulation of Food and Drugs," Harvard Law School, 2004, http://leda.law .harvard.edu/leda/data/654/Gaughan.pdf.

21. Jon Blackwell, "1906: Rumble over 'The Jungle,'" *The Trentonian*, http:// www.capitalcentury.com/1906.html.

22. Ibid.

23. Powell, *Bully Boy*, 163.

24. Upton Sinclair biography, *Spartacus Educational*, http://www.spartacus .schoolnet.co.uk/Jupton.htm.

25. Powell, *Bully Boy*, 166.

26. William Anderson, "The Free Market: Bully in the Pulpit," Mises Institute, February 1998, http://mises.org/freemarket_detail.aspx?control=96.

27. Powell, *Bully Boy*, 157.

28. Robert L. Rabin, "Federal Regulation in Historical Perspective," *Stanford Law Review* 38 (May 1986): 1189.

29. Powell, *Bully Boy*, 166.

30. David Dieteman, "The Living Constitution," LewRockwell.com, 7 December 2000, http://www.lewrockwell.com/orig/dieteman5.html.

31. Woodrow Wilson, *The New Freedom* (Garden City, NY: Doubleday, Page, & Co., 1921), 48.

32. Chapman, "TR: No Friend of the Constitution," 14.

33. Rabin, "Federal Regulation in Historical Perspective," 1189.

34. Woodrow Wilson, speech, Joint Session of Congress, 5 December 1916, Woodrow Wilson Presidential Library and Museum, http://woodrowwilson .org/library-a-archives/wilson-elibrary.

35. William L. Anderson, "The Progressive Era: The Myth and the Reality," LewRockwell.com, 14 June 2006, http://www.lewrockwell.com/anderson/ anderson132.html.

36. Ron Shirtz, "US Polycracy," LewRockwell.com, 29 December 2008, http:// www.lewrockwell.com/shirtz/shirtz11.html.

37. Rabin, "Federal Regulation in Historical Perspective," 1189.

38. Shirtz, "US Polycracy."

39. Llewellyn H. Rockwell Jr., "FBI Meltdown: The Root Cause," LewRockwell .com, 20 July 2001, http://www.lewrockwell.com/rockwell/fbi.html.

40. John Fox, "Birth of the FBI," FBI website, July 2003, http://www.fbi.gov/ about-us/history/highlights-of-history/articles/birth.

41. Anthony Gregory, "How the Left Learned to Stop Worrying and Love the FBI," Lewrockwell.com, 30 March 2010, http://www.lewrockwell.com/ gregory/gregory197.html.

42. Tom Burghardt, "Big Brother FBI: Data-Mining Programs Resurrect 'Total Information Awareness,'" LewRockwell.com, 12 October 2009, http:// www.lewrockwell.com/orig10/burghardt2.1.1.html.

43. John W. Whitehead, "The FBI: Going Rogue," 14 February 2011, https://www .rutherford.org/publications_resources/john_whiteheads_commentary/ the_fbi_going_rogue.

44. Ibid.

45. Judson Berger, "FBI's New Rules to Give Agents More Leeway on Surveillance," Foxnews.com, 13 June 2011, http://www.foxnews.com/politics/2011/06/13/ fbis-new-rules-to-give-agents-more-leeway-on-surveillance/#ixzz1TQcvyX00.

46. Burghardt, "Big Brother FBI."

47. Whitehead, "The FBI: Going Rogue."

48. The United States Constitution, Article 1, Section 1, emphasis added, U.S. House of Representatives website, http://www.house.gov/house/Constitution/Constitution. html. Other citations of the Constitution within this book rely on this site.

49. *J. W. Hampton, Jr. & Co. v. United States*, 276 U.S. 394 (1928).

50. *Panama Refining Co. v. Ryan*, 293 U.S. 388 (1935).

51. Ibid., 432.

52. *Mistretta v. United States*, 488 U.S. 361 (1989).

53. *Mistretta* at page 413, Scalia, J. dissenting.

54. *Mistretta* at page 415, Scalia, J. dissenting.

55. *Mistretta* at page 426, Scalia, J. dissenting.

56. "PA DEP Secretary Responds to White House Decision on Ozone Standard," Harrisburg, Pennsylvania, PRNewswire, 9 September 2011.

Chapter 4: The Government's Printing Press: The Federal Reserve

1. Woodrow Wilson, State of the Union Address, 2 December 1913, Woodrow Wilson Presidential Library, http://wwl2.dataformat.com/Search.aspx.

2. Theodore Roosevelt, *Social Justice and Popular Rule: Essays, Addresses, and Public Statements* (Salem, NH: Ayer Company Publishers, 1910), 403–4.

3. Woodrow Wilson, speech, Joint Session of Congress, 23 June 1913, Woodrow Wilson Presidential Library, http://wwl2.dataformat.com/Search.aspx.

4. Cigarettes were used as currency during World War II because the German mark had become utterly useless. G. Edward Griffin, *The Creature from Jekyll Island* (Westlake Village, CA: American Media, 2010), 144.

5. Murray N. Rothbard, "The Origin of the Federal Reserve," *Quarterly Journal of Austrian Economics* 2, no. 3 (Fall 2009).

6. Wilson, speech to Congress, 23 June 1913.

7. Griffin, *The Creature from Jekyll Island*, 12.

8. Rothbard, "The Origins of the Federal Reserve."

9. Griffin, *The Creature from Jekyll Island*, 12–13.

10. Ibid., 14.

11. Ibid.

12. Ibid., 434.

13. Ibid., 161.

14. Ibid.

15. U.S. Const., art. 1, sec. 8.

16. *Legal Tender Cases*, 79 U.S. 457 (1870).

17. *Hepburn v. Griswold*, 75 U.S. 603 (1869).

18. *McCulloch v. Maryland*, 17 U.S. 316 (1819).

19. *Knox v. Lee*, 79 US 457 (1871); *Parker v. Davis*, 79 U.S. 457 (1871).

20. *Legal Tender Cases*, 79 U.S. 457 (1870).

21. *Julliard v. Greenman*, 110 U.S. 421 (1884).

22. Woodrow Wilson to Ralph Pulitzer, 9 October 1913, Woodrow Wilson Presidential Library, http://ww12.dataformat.com/Document.aspx?doc=34490.

23. Griffin, *The Creature from Jekyll Island*, 20.

24. Ibid., 148, emphasis added.

25. Murray N. Rothbard, *A History of Money and Banking in the United States* (Auburn, AL: Ludwig von Mises Institute, 2002).

26. Ellen Hodgson Brown, *Web of Debt: The Shocking Truth About Our Money System and How We Can Break Free*, 3rd ed. (Baton Rouge, LA: Third Millennium Press, 2008), 123.

Chapter 5: Destruction of Federalism: The Seventeenth Amendment

1. Paul Rosenberg, "We Do Not Have a Federal Government," LewRockwell.com, 24 August 2011, http://www.lewrockwell.com/orig11/rosenberg-p3.1.1.html.
2. Theodore Roosevelt, *Social Justice and Popular Rule: Essays, Addresses, and Public Statements* (Salem, NH: Ayer Company Publishers, 1910), 88–89.
3. Woodrow Wilson, campaign speech, Hartford Connecticut, 25 September 1912, Woodrow Wilson House, http://www.woodrowwilsonhouse.org/index.asp?section=timeline&file=timelinesearch_day&id=1274.
4. Ralph A. Rossum, *Federalism, the Supreme Court, and the Seventeenth Amendment: The Irony of Constitutional Democracy* (Lanham, MD: Lexington Books, 2001), 182.
5. Jonah Goldberg, *Liberal Fascism* (New York: Doubleday, 2008), 88.
6. Ibid., 89.
7. Ibid.
8. Ibid., 92, emphasis added.
9. 39 Cong. Ch. 246; 14 Stat. 244 (1866).
10. Rossum, *Federalism, the Supreme Court, and the Seventeenth Amendment*.
11. Ibid.
12. C. H. Hoebeke, "Democratizing the Constitution: The Failure of the 17th Amendment," *Humanitas* 9, no. 2 (1996), http://www.nhinet.org/hoebecke.htm.
13. *Federalist* No. 51.
14. Quoted in Robert A. Goldwin and William A. Schambra, eds., *How Federal Is the Constitution?* (Washington, D.C.: American Enterprise Institute, 1986), xiii. See "What Is Federalism?" ThisNation.com, http://www.thisnation.com/textbook/federalism-what.html.
15. U.S. Const. art I, § 7.
16. U.S. Const. art II, § 2.
17. U.S. Const. art I, § 3.
18. Jonathan Marshall, "William Graham Sumner: Critic of Progressive Liberalism," *Journal of Libertarian Studies* (1979).
19. Thomas J. DiLorenzo, "Repeal the Seventeenth Amendment," LewRockwell.com, 17 May 2005, http://www.lewrockwell.com/dilorenzo/dilorenzo93.html.
20. U.S. Const. art I, § 8.
21. *South Dakota v. Dole*, 483 U.S. 203 (1987).
22. Ibid.
23. Ibid.

24. Rossum, *Federalism, the Supreme Court, and the Seventeenth Amendment*, emphasis added.

25. Ibid.

26. Ibid.

27. Ibid.

Chapter 6: The "Lesser Races": Racism and Eugenics

1. As quoted by Glenn Beck, "Progressives' Writings Reveal Closeted Racism," Foxnews.com, 4 August 2010, http://www.foxnews.com/story/0,2933,598609,00.html.

2. As quoted in Charles Burris, "The Key to Understanding the State," LewRockwell.com, 7 August 2009, emphasis added, http://www.lewrockwell.com/blog/lewrw/archives/32254.html.

3. Theodore Roosevelt, "National Life and Character," TeachingAmericanHistory, http://teachingamericanhistory.org/library/index.asp?document=1138.

4. Ibid.

5. Ibid.

6. Declaration of Independence, emphasis added.

7. Ibid., emphasis added.

8. *Skinner v. State of Okl. ex. rel. Williamson*, 316 U.S. 535 (1942).

9. *Balzac v. Porto Rico*, 258 U.S. 298 (1922).

10. *Downes v. Bidwell*, 182 U.S. 244 (1901).

11. John A. Garraty, "Holmes's Appointment to the U.S. Supreme Court," *New England Quarterly* 22, no. 3 (September 1949): 294.

12. Ibid., 295.

13. Hon. Gustavo A. Gelpi, "The Insular Cases: A Comparative Historical Study of Puerto Rico, Hawai'i, and the Philippines," 58 APR Fed. Law. 22 (2011).

14. Theodore Roosevelt, "The Administration of the Island Possessions," Coliseum, Hartford, Connecticut, 22 August 1902, http://www.theodore-roosevelt.com/images/research/speeches/tradminisland.pdf.

15. Theodore Roosevelt, "The Expansion of the White Races," celebration of the African Diamond Jubilee of the Methodist Episcopal Church, Washington, D.C., 18 January 1909, http://www.theodore-roosevelt.com/images/research/speeches/trwhiteraces.pdf.

16. *Downes v. Bidwell*, 182 U.S. 244 (1901).

17. Robert Stinnett, *Day of Deceit: The Truth about FDR and Pearl Harbor* (New York: Simon & Schuster, 2000), 173.

18. Theodore Roosevelt, "On American Motherhood," National Congress of Mothers, Washington, D.C., 13 March 1905.

19. Ibid.

20. Roosevelt, "National Life and Character."

21. *Buck v. Bell*, 274 U.S. 200 (1927).

22. Ibid.

23. Ibid.

24. Theodore Roosevelt, letter to Charles Davenport, 3 January 1913, DNA Learning Center, http://www.dnalc.org/view/11219-T-Roosevelt-letter-to -C-Davenport-about-degenerates-reproducing-.html.

25. Elvira Nieto, "Woodrow Wilson and White Supremacy: An Examination of Wilson's Racist and Antidemocratic Policies," Suite101, 20 June 2009, http:// www.suite101.com/content/woodrow-wilson-and-white-supremacy-a126787.

26. "Lies and Racism of Woodrow Wilson," Worldfuturefund, http://www .worldfuturefund.org/wffmaster/Reading/war.crimes/US/Wilson.htm.

27. Nieto, "Woodrow Wilson and White Supremacy."

28. Ibid.

29. Damon W. Root, "When Bigots Become Reformers: The Progressive Era's Shameful Record on Race," *Reason*, May 2006, http://reason.com/ archives/2006/05/05/when-bigots-become-reformers/print.

30. Annual abortion statistics, http://www.abort73.com/abortion_facts/us _abortion_statistics/, site last updated 15 November 2011.

31. "Abortion Statistics," Abortiontv.com, http://www.abortiontv.com/Misc/ AbortionStatistics.htm#United States.

32. Jonah Goldberg, *Liberal Fascism* (New York: Doubleday, 2008), 273.

33. Ibid.

34. Steven Levitt, *Freakonomics* (New York: William Morrow, 2009), 140.

Chapter 7: Service or Slavery?: Conscription

1. "Young Man, You Owe Milton Friedman a Thank You," Trying Liberty.com, 28 July 2011, http://tryingliberty.com/2011/07/28/ young-man-you-owe-milton-friedman-a-thank-you/.

2. An Act for enrolling and calling out the national Forces, and for other Purposes, 37 Cong. Ch. 74, Match 3, 1863, 12 Stat, 731.

3. "Conscription in the United States," Wikipedia, 2 June 2011, http:// en.wikipedia.org/wiki/Conscription_in_the_United_States.

4. *Holmes v. United States*, 391 U.S. 936 (1968).

5. "The Confederate Conscription Law," *Encyclopedia Virginia*, http:// encyclopediavirginia.org/Twenty-Slave_Law; see also "The Men in the Union and Confederate Armies," Civilwarhome.com, http://www.civilwarhome .com/themen.htm.

6. *Arver v. U.S.*, 245 U.S. 366 (1918).

7. Ron Paul, "The Crime of Conscription," LewRockwell.com, 26 November 2003, http://www.lewrockwell.com/paul/paul144.html.

8. *Schenck v. United States*, 249 U.S. 47 (1919).

9. William Norman Grigg, "Conscription = Communism," LewRockwell.com, 31 May 2005, http://www.lewrockwell.com/orig5/grigg-w5.html.

10. Ibid., emphasis added.

11. Ibid.

12. *Qualls v. Rumsfeld*, 357 F.Supp.2d 274 (2005).

13. Ibid.

14. Paul, "The Crime of Conscription."

Chapter 8: The Government Tries to Pick Winners: Labor Law and the Regulation of the Workplace

1. Robert Higgs, *Crisis and Leviathan: Critical Episodes in the Growth of American Government* (New York: Oxford University Press, 1987), 120.

2. Patrick J. Wright and Michael D. Jahr, "Michigan Forces Business Owners into Public Sector Unions," *Wall Street Journal*, 25 December 2009, http://online.wsj.com/article/SB10001424052748703478704574612341241120838.html.

3. Ibid.

4. As quoted in Morgan Reynolds, "A History of Labor Unions from Colonial Times to 2009," Mises Daily, 17 July 2009, http://mises.org/daily/3553.

5. Ibid.

6. *Loewe v. Lawlor*, 208 U.S. 274 (1908).

7. Jonathan Grossman, "Origin of the U.S. Department of Labor," U.S. Department of Labor website, www.dol.gov. Article originally appeared in the *Monthly Labor Review*, March 1973.

8. Reynolds, "A History of Labor Unions from Colonial Times to 2009."

9. Jonathan Grossman, "The Coal Strike of 1902—Turning Point in U.S. Policy." U.S. Department of Labor website, *http://www.dol.gov/oasam/programs/history/coalstrike.htm*.

10. "Theodore Roosevelt's Labor Record: Does Labor Get a Square Deal? It Has from Theodore Roosevelt!" Published by National Progressive Party (New York City: Mail and Express Job Print, Stoddard-Sutherland Press, 1912), http://debs.indstate.edu/p9646t5_1912.pdf.

11. Grossman, "The Coal Strike of 1902."

12. *Youngstown Sheet & Tube Co. v. Sawyer*, 343 U.S. 579 (1952).

13. William L. Anderson, "The Courts and the New Deal," LewRockwell.com, 25 October 2005, emphasis in original, http://www.lewrockwell.com/anderson/anderson123.html.

14. *Lochner v. New York*, 198 U.S. 45 (1905).

15. *The Slaughterhouse Cases*, 83 U.S. 36 (1873). Dissent by Field, J.

16. *Allgeyer v. Louisiana*, 165 U.S. 578 (1897).

17. Ibid.

18. David E. Bernstein, *Rehabilitating Lochner: Defending Individual Rights against Progressive Reform* (Chicago: University of Chicago Press, 2011), 17.

19. Ibid., 26.

20. Ibid.

21. Brief for Defendants, *Lochner v. New York*, 198 U.S. 45 (1905).

22. Bernstein, *Rehabilitating Lochner*, 29.

23. Ibid.

24. *Lochner v. New York*, 198 U.S. 45 at page 53 (1905).

25. *Hammer v. Dagenhart*, 247 U.S. 251 (1918).

26. Ibid., 273–74.

27. Lew Rockwell, "In Defense of Child Labor," LewRockwell.com, reprinted from *The Free Market*, published by the Ludwig von Mises Institute, May 1990, http://www.lewrockwell.com/archives/fm/05-90.html.

28. Gregory Bresiger, "Employers Are Saying, Sorry, Kid, No Job Here," *New York Post*, 17 July 2011.

29. "Theodore Roosevelt's Labor Record," Ibid.

30. Ibid.

31. Associated Press, "California's Recall History Dates Far Back," Foxnews.com, 16 June 2003, http://www.foxnews.com/story/0,2933,89538,00.html.

32. See *In re Marriage Cases*, 43 Cal.4th 757 (2008).

33. Reynolds, "A History of Labor Unions from Colonial Times to 2009."

34. Ibid.

35. *West Coast Hotel Co. v. Parrish*, 300 U.S. 379 (1937).

36. *NLRB v. Jones & Laughlin Steel Corp.*, 301 U.S. 1 (1937).

37. National Labor Relations Act (Wagner Act), *Pub.L.* 74-198, 49 Stat. 449.

38. *Wickard v. Filburn*, 317 U.S. 111 (1942).

39. *Gonzales v. Raich*, 545 U.S. 1 (2005).

Chapter 9: The Government's New Straw Man: Anti-trust

1. Thomas Sowell, "The 'Progressive' Legacy," LewRockwell.com, 16 February 2012, http://lewrockwell.com/sowell/sowell73.1html.

2. Robert Higgs, *Crisis and Leviathan: Critical Episodes in the Growth of American Government* (New York: Oxford University Press, 1987), 110.

3. Thomas J. DiLorenzo, "The Truth about the 'Robber Barons,'" Mises Daily, 23 September 2006, http:/mises.org/daily/2317.

4. Ibid.

5. Ibid.

6. Ibid.

7. *Charles River Bridge v. Warren Bridge*, 36 U.S. 420 (1837).

8. D. T. Armentano, *The Myths of Antitrust: Economic Theory and the Legal Cases* (New Rochelle, NY: Arlington House, 1972).

9. *Munn v. Illinois*, 94 U.S. 113 (1877).

10. Ibid.

11. Llewellyn H. Rockwell Jr., "Antitrust: A Political Weapon," LewRockwell .com, 6 April 2000, http://www.lewrockwell.com/Rockwell/antitrust.htm.

12. Sherman Antitrust Act, 2 July 1890, ch. 647, 26 Stat. 209.

13. Quote on business, from 23 August 1902, *Presidential Addresses and State Papers* (1910), 103.

14. Robert L. Rabin, "Federal Regulation in Historical Perspective," *Stanford Law Review* 38 (May 1986).

15. *United States v. E. C. Knight Company*, 156 U.S. 1 (1895).

16. Ibid.

17. Armentano, *The Myths of Antitrust: Economic Theory and the Legal Cases*, 57.

18. Ibid.

19. Ibid.

20. Ibid.

21. *Northern Securities Co. v. United States*, 193 U.S. 197 (1904). Dissent by Holmes, J.

22. DiLorenzo, "The Truth about the 'Robber Barons.'"

23. William L. Anderson, "The Progressive Era: The Myth and the Reality," Future of Freedom Foundation, 9 June 2006, http://www.fff.org/freedom/ fd0602d.asp.

24. Ibid.

25. *United States v. American Tobacco Co.*, 221 U.S. 106 (1911).

26. *United States v. American Tobacco Company*, Circuit Court 164 *Federal Reporter 700* (S.D.N.Y. 1908).

27. Armentano, *The Myths of Antitrust: Economic Theory and the Legal Cases*, 91–96.

28. Ibid.

29. Ibid., 94.

30. William Anderson, "The Free Market: Bully in the Pulpit," Ludwig von Mises Institute, February 1998, http://mises.org/freemarket_detail .aspx?control=96.

31. Clayton Antitrust Act of 1914 (*Pub.L.* 63-212, 38 Stat. 730, enacted 15 October 1914).

32. Federal Trade Commission Act of 1914 (15 U.S.C §§ 41–58.)

33. Ehud Kamar, "Beyond Competition for Incorporations," *Georgetown Law Journal* 94 (August 2006): 1725, 1769.

34. Christopher Grandy, "New Jersey Corporate Chartermongering, 1875-1929," *Journal of Economic History* 49 (September 1989).

35. Kamar, "Beyond Competition for Incorporations," 1769.

36. Grandy, "New Jersey Corporate Chartermongering, 1875-1929."

37. Ibid.

38. Murray N. Rothbard, "War Collectivism in World War I," Ludwig von Mises Institute, 20 April 2010, http://mises.org/document/2024. First published in *A New History of Leviathan*, ed. Ronald Radosh and Murray N. Rothbard (New York: Dutton, 1972), 1.

39. Ibid., 4.

40. Ibid.

41. Robert Higgs, *Crisis and Leviathan: Critical Episodes in the Growth of American Government* (New York: Oxford University Press, 1989).

42. Rothbard, "War Collectivism in World War I."

43. Ibid.

44. Thomas J. DiLorenzo, "Should Wal-Mart Be Broken Up?" Mises Daily, 19 July 2006, http://mises.org/daily/2248.

45. Barry C. Lynn, "Breaking the Chain: The Antitrust Case Against Walmart," *Harper's Magazine*, July 2006, http://harpers.org/archive/2006/07/0081115.

46. Ibid.

47. Ibid.

48. Llewellyn H. Rockwell, Jr. "The Incredible Stuff Machine," LewRockwell .com, 14 January 2006, http://www.lewrockwell.com/rockwell/ incredible-stuff.html.

49. Daniel A. Crane, "Obama's Antitrust Agenda," *Regulation* (Fall 2009); see also Stephen Labaton, "Obama Takes Tougher Antitrust Line," *New York Times*, 12 May 2009; Tamara Lytle, "Obama's New Antitrust Rules Have Big, Powerful Companies Sweating," *U.S. News & World Report*, 20 May 2009.

50. Murray Rothbard, *Man, Economy and State with Power and Market, 2nd ed.* (Auburn, AL: Mises Institute, 2004), 1255.

Chapter 10: Mismanagement, Waste, and Hypocrisy: Conservation

1. As quoted in Thomas J. DiLorenzo, "Bully Boy: The Neocons' Favorite President," 1 September 2006, LewRockwell.com, http://www.lewrockwell .com/dilorenzo/dilorenzo106.html.

2. David Boaz, "Private Property Saved Jamestown and, with it, America," Georgia Public Policy Foundation, 25 May 2007, http://www.gppf.org/ article.asp?RT=7&p=pub/General/property070525.htm.

3. Jim Powell, *Bully Boy: The Truth About Teddy Roosevelt's Legacy* (New York: Crown Forum, 2006).

4. American Antiquities Act of 1906, National Park Service, http://www.nps .gov/history/local-law/anti1906.htm.

5. Hal Rothman, "The Antiquities Act and National Monuments," *Cultural Resource Management* 22, no. 4 (1999), http://crm.cr.nps.gov/archive/22-4/22-04-5.pdf.

6. Ibid.

7. *The Irrigation Age* 12 (December 1897): 76.

8. Jane Morgan, "'Have Faith in God and U.S.': Failure on the Boise Project, 1905-1924," *Idaho Yesterdays* 50, no. 1 (Spring 2009).

9. Ibid.

10. Ibid.

11. *Hyde v. United States*, 225 U. S. 347 (1912).

12. Powell, *Bully Boy*.

13. Katie Pavlich, "Catastrophic Wildfires? Thank the Greenies and the Forest Service," Townhall.com, 11 June 2011, http:// townhall.com/columnists/katiepavlich/2011/06/11/ catastrophic_wildfires_thank_the_greenies_and_forest_service/page/2.

14. Ibid.

15. *Tennessee Valley Authority v. Hill*, 437 U.S. 153 (1978), emphasis added.

16. Jonathan H. Adler, "The Endangered Species Act after 30 Years—Bad for Your Land, Bad for the Critters," *Wall Street Journal*, 31 December 2003.

17. Ibid.

18. Michael S. Coffman, "The Problem with the Endangered Species Act," Newswithviews.com, 2 August 2003, http://www.newswithviews.com/ Coffman/mike2.htm.

Chapter 11: A Fierce Attack on Personal Freedom: Prohibition

1. Global Commission on Drug Policy, PDF available at http://www .globalcommissionondrugs.org/Report.

2. Interview with Daniel Okrent, Review, 5 May 2010, http://bnreview .barnesandnoble.com/t5/Interview/Daniel-Okrent/ba-p/2564.

3. "Prohibition," Digital History, http://www.digitalhistory.uh.edu/database/ article_display.cfm?HHID=441.

4. Woodrow Wilson, Veto of Prohibition Bill, 27 October 1919, Woodrow Wilson Presidential Library, http://ww2.dataformat.com/Document. aspx?doc=29525.

5. "'No Temperance in It . . .': Woodrow Wilson & Prohibition," Rustycans.com, http://www.rustycans.com/HISTORY/prohibition.html, citing *Gavit to Wilson, 22 November 1916, Papers of Woodrow Wilson 40:42.*

6. "Organized Crime and Prohibition," University at Albany website, http:// www.albany.edu/~wm731882/organized_crime1_final.html.

7. "Prohibition," Digital History.

8. "Treaty of Versailles," Wikisource, http://en.wikisource.org/wiki/
Treaty_of_Versailles/Part_X#Article_295.

9. David Solomon, "The Marihuana Tax Act of 1937," Schaffer Library of Drug
Policy, http://www.druglibrary.org/Schaffer/hemp/taxact/mjtaxact.htm.

10. Laurence French and Magdaleno Manzanárez, *NAFTA & Neocolonialism*
(Lanham, MD: University Press of America, 2004), 129, http://books.google
.com/books?id=4ozF1Yg-c4MC&pg=PA129&hl=en#v=onepage&q&f=false.

11. 532 U.S. 483 (2001).

12. 541 U.S. 1 (2005).

13. Office of National Drug Control Policy, http://ofsubstance.gov/blogs/
pushing_back/archive/2011/06/02/51896.aspx.

14. "Marijuana Bill Officially Introduced to Congress by Ron Paul, Barney
Frank," *Los Angeles Times*, 23 June 2011, http://latimesblogs.latimes.com/
washington/2011/06/marijuana-bill-officially-introduced-to-congress-by
-ron-paul-barney-frank.html.

Chapter 12: "The Supreme Triumphs of War": Roosevelt and International Relations

1. Callie Oettinger, "Commander in Chief: President Theodore
Roosevelt on Washington's Forgotten Maxim," Command Posts,
27 October 2011, http://www.commandposts.com/2011/10/
president-theodore-roosevelt-on-washingtons-forgotten-maxim/.

2. Rudyard Kipling, "The White Man's Burden," 1899, Modern History
Sourcebook, Fordham University, http://www.fordham.edu/halsall/mod/
kipling.asp.

3. Ralph Raico, "America's Will to War: The Turning Point," LewRockwell.com,
28 April 2011, http://www.lewrockwell.com/raico/raico42.1.html.

4. Ibid.

5. Ibid., emphasis added.

6. Ibid.

7. Ibid.

8. Evan Thomas, *The War Lovers* (New York: Back Bay Books, 2010), 20.

9. Ibid., 28.

10. Ibid., 39.

11. "Roosevelt Appointed Assistant Secretary of the Navy," Timeline for *Crucible
of Empire: The Spanish-American War*, PBS website, http://www.pbs.org/
crucible/tl7.html.

12. Theodore Roosevelt, *Letters from Theodore Roosevelt to Anna Roosevelt Cowles,
1870–1918* (New York: Charles Scribner's Sons, 1924), 212.

13. Thomas, *The War Lovers*, 213.

14. Ibid., 217.

15. Ibid., 209.

16. Ibid.

17. Jerry A. Sierra, "The War for Cuban Independence: After the War," Historyofcuba.com, http://www.historyofcuba.com/history/scaw/scaw3.htm.

18. Ibid.

19. Murray Polner and Thomas E. Woods Jr., eds., *We Who Dared to Say No to War: American Antiwar Writing from 1812 to Now* (New York: Basic Books, 2008), 89.

20. *Balzac v. People of Porto Rico*, 258 U.S. 298 (1922).

21. Polner and Woods, *We Who Dared to Say No to War*, 99.

22. Ibid., 104.

23. Ibid., 97.

24. Ibid., 93.

25. "Monroe Doctrine," Academic Dictionaries and Encyclopedias, http://universalium.academic.ru/151304/Monroe_Doctrine.

26. "The Panama Canal," Small Planet Communications, http://www.smplanet.com/imperialism/joining.html.

27. Ibid.

28. Ibid., emphasis added.

29. Kennedy Hickman, "Circling the Globe: The Voyage of the Great White Fleet," About.com, http://militaryhistory.about.com/od/battleswars1900s/p/greatwhitefleet.htm.

30. Carl Nolte, "Great White Fleet Visited S.F. 100 Years Ago," *San Francisco Chronicle*, 6 May 2008, http://articles.sfgate.com/2008-05-06/bay-area/17154899_1_great-white-fleet-golden-gate-atlantic-fleet.

31. Chalmers Johnson, "America's Empire of Bases," Common Dreams, 14 January 2004, http://www.commondreams.org/views04/0115-08.htm.

Chapter 13: A Reverberation of Horrors: Wilson and International Relations

1. John Coles, "The Flesh of the Men and Horses Was Mixed Up," *The Sun*, 22 October 2010, http://www.thesun.co.uk/sol/homepage/news/campaigns/our_boys/3191390/Diary-of-WWI-soldier-emerges-to-shed-light-on-horror-of-conflict.html.

2. J. R. Bolling, "The US and Nicaragua Sign the Bryan-Chamorro Treaty," Woodrow Wilson House, http://www.woodrowwilsonhouse.org/index.asp?section=timeline&file=timelinesearch_day&id=895.

3. "Protectorates and Spheres of Influence: U.S. Protectorates Prior to World

War II," *Encyclopedia of the New American Nation*, http://www
.americanforeignrelations.com/O-W/Protectorates-and-Spheres-of-Influence
-U-s-protectorates-prior-to-world-war-ii.html.

4. Ibid.

5. Don Keko, "Woodrow Wilson: A Flip Flop on Foreign Policy," *American History Examiner*, 13 April 2011.

6. Gabriel Homa, "The Actions Behind the Rhetoric: The Foreign Policy Practices of Woodrow Wilson" (thesis, Rutgers, May 2009), http:/history
.rutgers.edu/index.php?option=com_docman&task=doc_details&gid=150
&ltemid=99999999.

7. Ibid.

8. Ibid.

9. Keko, "Woodrow Wilson: A Flip Flop on Foreign Policy."

10. Ibid.

11. Ibid.

12. Homa, "The Actions Behind the Rhetoric."

13. Joshua Snyder, "The Emperor and the Peasant," LewRockwell.com, 19 March 2008, http://www.lewrockwell.com/snyder-joshua/snyder-joshua12.html.

14. John Dwyer, "The United States and World War I," LewRockwell.com, 26 January 2004, http://www.lewrockwell.com/orig3/dwyer3.html.

15. George C. Leef, "Wilson's War," Future Freedom Foundation, 5 May 2006, http://www.fff.org/freedom/fd0601g.pdf.

16. Homa, "The Actions Behind the Rhetoric."

17. Jim Powell, *Wilson's War: How Woodrow Wilson's Great Blunder Led to Hitler, Lenin, Stalin & World War II* (New York: Crown Forum, 2005), 98.

18. Homa, "The Actions Behind the Rhetoric."

19. David Foglesong, *America's Secret War Against Bolshevism* (Chapel Hill: University of North Carolina Press, 2001), 11.

20. William L. Langer, *Gas and Flame in World War I* (New York: Knopf/Borzoi, 1965), 73–83. William L. Langer was an engineer in Company E, 1st Gas Regiment Chemical Warfare Service, U.S. Army. http://historymatters.gmu
.edu/d/5327/.

21. Paul Kramer, "The Water Cure: Debating Torture and Counterinsurgency—a Century Ago," *Annals of American History*, 25 February 2008.

22. Nick Turse and Deborah Nelson, "Vietnam Horrors: Darker Yet," *Los Angeles Times*, 6 August 2006, http://articles.latimes.com/2006/aug/06/nation/
na-vietnam6.

23. Martin Frost, "Abu Ghraib," http://www.martinfrost.ws/htmlfiles/abu
_ghraib2.html.

24. Ibid.

25. Ibid.

26. Ibid.

27. "Borah Demands a Vote on League: Declares Wisdom of the People Alone Can Guide the Nation on Such an Enterprise," *New York Times*, 22 February 1919.

28. Max Boot, "Paving the Road to Hell: The Failure of U.N. Peacekeeping," *Foreign Affairs*, March/April 2000, http://www.foreignaffairs.com/articles/55875/max-boot/paving-the-road-to-hell-the-failure-of-u-n-peacekeeping.

29. Leef, "Wilson's War."

30. Ibid.

31. Ibid.

32. Keko, "Woodrow Wilson: A Flip Flop on Foreign Policy."

33. Ibid.

Chapter 14: Propaganda and Espionage: The Domestic Front During the Great War

1. Gustave Gilbert, "Interview with Hermann Goering at Nuremberg, 18 April 1946," *Thom Hartmann Program*, http://www.thomhartmann.com/forum/2011/01/interview-hermann-goering-nuremberg-april-18-1946-gustave-gilbert.

2. "Voices of the Great War," *The Great War*, PBS website, http://www.pbs.org/greatwar/chapters/ch2_voices1.html.

3. H. C. Peterson, *Propaganda for War: The Campaign Against American Neutrality* (Port Washington, NY: Kennikat Press, 1968), 55, cited in Thomas Fleming, *Illusion of Victory* (New York: Basic Books, 2004), 52.

4. "United States Must Act at Once on *Lusitania*, Says Colonel Roosevelt," *New York Times*, 10 May 1915.

5. John Dwyer, "The United States and World War I," LewRockwell.com, 26 January 2004, http://www.lewrockwell.com/orig3/dwyer3.html.

6. "Bryan Hands in Resignation, The President Accepts It," *The Twice-A-Week Dispatch* (Alamance County, NC), 11 June 1915, http://www.alamance-nc.com/ACPL/THE%20TWICE-A-WEEK%20DISPATCH/1915-06-11.pdf.

7. Wartime Propaganda, World War I, "The War to End All Wars," http://www.100megspop3.com/bark/Propaganda.html.

8. Ibid.

9. Ibid.

10. Ibid.

11. George W. Bush, "President Discusses Beginning of Operation Iraqi Freedom," White House website, http://georgewbush-whitehouse.archives.gov/news/releases/2003/03/20030322.html.

12. Ibid.

13. Ibid.

14. "Bush Calls Saddam 'the Guy who Tried to Kill My Dad," CNN, 27 September 2002, http://articles.cnn.com/2002-09-27/politics/bush.war .talk_1_homeland-security-senators-from-both-parties-republican-phil -gramm?_s=PM:ALLPOLITICS.

15. Bill Sardi, "Hollywood's New War Flicks," LewRockwell.com, 20 February 2002, http://www.lewrockwell.com/orig/sardi12.html.

16. Klaus Brinkbaumer and John Goetz, "Taking Out the Terrorists by Remote Control," Spiegel Online, 12 October 2010, http://www.spiegel.de/ international/world/0,1518,722583,00.html.

17. "Bush-Obama Drones Have Killed 2,043 People (Mostly Civilians) in Pak during Last Five Years," Hive Daily, 3 January 2011, http://thehivedaily.com/ blog/2011/01/03/bush-obama-drones-have-killed-2043-people-mostly -civilians-in-pak-during-last-five-years/.

18. Tom Finn and Noah Browning / Sana'a, "An American Teenager in Yemen: Paying for the Sins of His Father?" Time, 27 October 2011.

19. Anthony Gregory, "From Waco to Libya: 18 Years of Humanitarian Mass Murder," LewRockwell.com, 19 April 2011, http://www.lewrockwell.com/ gregory/gregory210.html.

20. Wartime Propaganda, World War I, "The War to End All Wars."

21. "Acts, Bills, and Laws, May 16, 1918," U.S. History, http://www.u-s-history .com/pages/h1345.html.

22. Abrams v. United States, 250 U.S. 616 (1919).

23. Jervis Anderson, A. Philip Randolph: A Biographical Portrait (Berkeley: University of California Press, 1986).

24. Ibid.

25. United States v. Nagler, 252 F.R. 217, 218 (District Court, W.D. Wisconsin, 25 July 1918).

26. Emma Goldman, "Address to the Jury," American Rhetoric: Top 100 Speeches, http://www.americanrhetoric.com/speeches/emmagoldmanjuryaddress.htm.

27. Debs v. United States, 249 U.S. 211 (1919).

28. United States v. Motion Picture Film, 252 F. 946 (1917).

29. David L. Hudson Jr., "Overview of Libel and Defamation," First Amendment Center, http://www.firstamendmentcenter.com/press/topic .aspx?topic=libel_defamation.

30. Jane Mayer, "The Secret Sharer," New Yorker, 23 May 2011, http://www .newyorker.com/reporting/2011/05/23/110523fa_fact_mayer.

31. Scott Shane, "No Jail Time in Trial Over N.S.A Leak," New York Times, 16 July 2011.

32. *Girl No. 217*, Film Affinity, http://www.filmaffinity.com/en/film633871.html.

33. "Falsification of History," University of Minnesota, http://www.tc.umn
.edu/~hick0088/classes/csci_2101/false.html.

34. "Press Freedom Index 2006," Reporters without Borders, http://en.rsf.org/
spip.php?page=classement&id_rubrique=35.

Chapter 15: The Government's Grand Larceny: The Birth of the Federal Income Tax

1. As quoted in Adam Young, "The Origin of the Income Tax," Mises Daily, 7
September 2004, http://mises.org/daily/1597.

2. Thomas Sowell, "The 'Progressive' Legacy," LewRockwell.com, 16 February
2012, http://lewrockwell.com/sowell/sowell73.1.html.

3. *Springer v. United States*, 102 U.S. 586 (1881).

4. *Pollock v. Farmers' Loan & Trust Company*, 158 U.S. 601 (1895).

5. Charlotte Twight, "Evolution of Federal Income Tax Withholding: The
Machinery of Institutional Change," *Cato Journal* 14, no. 3 (Winter 1995),
http://www.cato.org/pubs/journal/cj14n3-1.html.

6. Theodore Roosevelt, "The New Nationalism," 31 August 1910, http://www
.presidentialrhetoric.com/historicspeeches/roosevelt_theodore/
newnationalism.html.

7. CPI Inflation Calculator, Bureau of Labor Statistics, http://www.bls.gov/
data/inflation_calculator.htm.

8. Inflation Calculator, Westegg.com, http://www.westegg.com/inflation/infl.cgi.

9. *Brushaber v. Union Pacific R. Co.*, 240 U.S. 1 (1916).

10. "The Income Tax Arrives," Tax Analysts, http://www.taxhistory.org/www/
website.nsf/Web/THM1901?OpenDocument.

11. Frank Chodorov, "Taxation Is Robbery," Ludwig von Mises Institute, from
Frank Chodorov, *Out of Step: The Autobiography of an Individualist* (New York:
Devin-Adair Company, 1962), 216–39, http://mises.org/etexts/taxrob.asp.

12. Brian Kelly—Taxes, Op-ed, "Tax System Isn't Fair," Political Guide, http://
www.thepoliticalguide.com/Profiles/Senate/Pennsylvania/Brian_Kelly/
Views/Taxes/.

13. Chodorov, "Taxation Is Robbery."

14. Ibid.

15. Ibid.

16. Ibid.

17. Ibid.

18. Ibid.

19. Tax Credits, Rebates & Savings, U.S. Department of Energy, http://www
.energy.gov/taxbreaks.htm.

20. 2011 Tax Table, Internal Revenue Service, http://www.irs.gov/pub/irs-pdf/
    i1040tt.pdf; Ten Things to Know about Capital Gains and Losses, Internal
    Revenue Service, http://www.irs.gov/newsroom/article/0,,id=106799,00
    .html.
21. Chodorov, "Taxation Is Robbery."

Acknowledgments

This book is based on many years of study and frustration, and one year of intensive work.

The study was my own formal education, during the opening process of which it became apparent to me that the past 100 years of American history, with exceptions in the areas of civil rights for minorities and equal rights for women, have been good for the growth of government and bad for the freedom of individuals. The frustration that I recall was as a high school and college student discovering that at nearly every turn, starting with the Progressive era, natural rights, constitutional fidelity, small government values, and maximum liberty virtues were regularly, consistently, systematically, and inexorably diminished by the federal government. As a student, I tried to look for bright spots in the history of American government in the 20th century, but found only a few. The trend has been decidedly against human freedom. The trend has vindicated Jefferson's dire warning that in the long run, government will grow and liberty will shrink.

The year of intensive research which produced this book was no happier. History is what it is. We can reinterpret it, but obviously, we cannot alter it. But for me this time around, I had some wonderful companions on my intellectual travels. My research assistants, Alyssa Bongiovanni, Todd Henderson, Patrick Sweeney, and Leigh Wilson, all law students then and lawyers now, worked diligently and with much passion in performing the raw research that was the skeleton for this book.

My producers for my short-lived show on the Fox Business Network, *FreedomWatch*, were and are some of the finest professionals with whom I have worked. Gary Schreier, Christopher Wallace, Gena Binkley, Patrick McMenamin, Austin Petersen, Edward Krayewski, Todd Seavey, Jordan Chariton, Nate Chaffetz, Lainie Frost, Kate Preziosi, Nicholas Monte, and Anne Hartmayer, and my personal assistant, Mary Kate Cribbin, and my personal producer, George Szucs, Jr., all contributed to this work. Many wrote paragraphs for me to use on air that have found their way here. Most were with me when, as the work on this book was just about completed, our beloved *FreedomWatch* was taken to pasture.

My close Fox colleagues, Bill Shine, Dianne Brandi, Suzanne Scott, Charles Gasparino, David Asman, John Stossel, Stuart Varney, and Bill Hemmer have always encouraged my work; this book and my on-air work, as well. My friend James Conley Sheil edited this book with skill and diligence, as he has all its predecessors. My Boss, Roger Ailes, gave me the platform from which to advance the ideas ultimately articulated in this book and is largely responsible for all my post-judicial public work. He has trusted me and I have trusted him. Our personal loyalty is bi-lateral and unquestioned. Roger is the greatest person in all the media today; a visionary and a genius who created Fox News Channel out of nothing, and found a place for me.

All of these friends and colleagues have tugged and pulled my thoughts and energies in various directions. Each has made me a harder worker and a better communicator, and, I like to think, a more thoughtful person. Whatever virtues, if any, this book may be deemed to have, is because of their collaborative efforts and influence upon me. Whatever faults lie in the pages that precede this, are mine and mine alone.

About the Author

ANDREW P. NAPOLITANO is the Senior Judicial Analyst for Fox News Channel where he provides on-air legal, political, and economic analysis throughout the day on weekdays. He is the youngest life-tenured Superior Court judge in New Jersey history. He is a former trial and appellate lawyer and law school professor. The present book is the seventh Judge Napolitano has written on the U.S. Constitution. He also writes a weekly column that is seen and read by millions of persons. He is a nationally recognized expert on the U.S. Constitution and human freedom.

Judge Napolitano received his A.B. from Princeton University and his J.D from the University of Notre Dame.

Index

ALSO FROM
JUDGE ANDREW P. NAPOLITANO

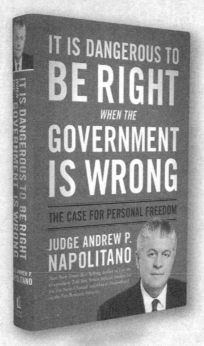

If the government exists to serve us, and if freedom is part of our humanity, how can the government take freedom from us? Is human freedom in America a myth, or is it reality? The United States of America was born out of a bloody revolt against tyranny. Yet almost from its inception, the government here has suppressed liberty. Within the pages of *It Is Dangerous To Be Right When The Government Is Wrong*, *New York Times* best-selling author Judge Andrew P. Napolitano lays out the case that the U.S. government, whose first obligation is to protect and preserve individual freedoms, actually does neither.

Available wherever books and ebooks are sold.

THOMAS NELSON
Since 1798

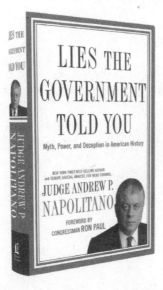

9781595553515-B